ISLAM AND IDENTITY IN EASTERN INDONESIA

Michael Hitchcock

THE UNIVERSITY OF HULL PRESS

THE
UNIVERSITY
OF HULL
PRESS

Cover: An illustration showing part of a tapestry-woven sash (Bimanese, *salampé*; Sumbawanese, *pebasa*) which was published in *De Weefkunst* (J.E. Jasper & Mas Pirngadie, vol. 2, *De Inlandsche Kunstnijverheid in Nederlandsch Indië*, The Hague 1912).

ISLAM AND IDENTITY IN EASTERN INDONESIA

British Library Cataloguing in Publication Data

A catalogue record for this book is available from the British Library.

ISBN 0 85958 646 4
Published 1996

Phototypeset in 11 on 12pt Palatino by Gem DTP, 37 Hunter Road, Elloughton, Brough and printed by the Central Print Unit, the University of Hull.

Contents

List of Maps and Illustrations   vi

Acknowledgements   viii

I	Introduction	1
II	Geographical and Historical Background	21
III	Trade and Islam	38
IV	Islam and Ethnicity	57
V	Court Society	73
VI	Handicrafts and Gender	89
VII	The Sacred Kris	105
VIII	Symbolic Cloth	120
IX	Houses and Palaces	136
X	Tourism and Identity	156
XI	Conclusions	167

Appendix   180

Bibliography   193

Index   205

List of Maps and Illustrations

The Sultan and his retinue   Frontispiece
Map 1 Indonesia and Sumbawa   Frontispiece
Map 2 Bima and Raba   Frontispiece

Opposite page

1.	Villagers in Ntobo	16
2.	Wooden house in Salama village	17
3.	Wild pig hunting	24
4.	Ploughs drawn by water buffalo	25
5.	Rice harvest in Salama	28
6.	Locked rice granaries	29
7.	Mosque in Sumbawa Besar	44
8.	A Bugis sailing ship in Bima Bay	45
9.	Sultanate tomb	50
10.	Sultanate tombstone	51
11.	Sulawesi style houses	60
12.	Ship building	61
13.	Women wearing the sarong veil to market	68
14.	Local version of the Malay martial art *silat*	69
15.	The original wooden palace	74
16.	Entrance to the prime minister's residence	75
17.	Pillars in the prime minister's residence	80
18.	Carved naga head	81
19.	The bride and groom dressed as a prince and princess	98
20.	The groom's costume, based on court dress	99
21.	Basket makers	102
22.	Potter at work	103
23.	Piston bellows	108
24.	Blacksmith's forge	109
25.	Sultan Ibrahim (c. 1905) wearing the Bimanese royal kris	116
26.	Iron and silver belt buckle	117
27.	Body tension loom	124
28.	A weaver in Ntobo	125
29.	Nineteenth century royal sarong	132
30.	Nineteenth century royal sarong - detail	133
31.	Temporary field shelter	138
32.	Drawing of an A-frame house	139

33.	Carpentry tools	144
34.	Carpentry tools	145
35.	Drawing of a lowland house	150
36.	Raised floor of a lowland house	151
37.	The Sultan's Palace	164
38.	Wooden house painted to resemble an aircraft fuselage	165

Acknowledgements

The research on which this book is based was made possible with grants from the Economic and Social Research Council and the British Academy. Permits were granted by Lembaga Ilmu Pengetahuan Indonesia and Prof Dr I. Gusti Ngurah Bagus of Universitas Udayana, Denpasar, kindly agreed to be my sponsor.

For their generosity and professional help I am deeply indebted to Abdul Karim Sahidu, Abdulmuis Rahim Nggampo, A Dieng Talu, Jonathan Agranoff, Prof Dr AJ Bernet Kempers, Rita Bolland, Dorothy Burnham, Dr Ian Caldwell, Dr Peter Carey, Dr Henri Chambert-Loir, Dr Chua Soo-Pong, Prof John Clammer, Janet Cochrane, Prof Dr De Casparis, Haji Djafar Amyn, Haji Djafar AR, Dr Brian Durrans, Dr John Edmondson, Ir Fachrurrozie Sjarkowi, Jean Fawcett, Anton Fernhout, Prof Dr A Gerbrands, Lewis Hill, Idrus Yahya, Dr Sian Jay, the late Princess Kalisom, Prof VT King, the late Dr Peter Lienhardt, Massir Q Abdullah, Robyn Maxwell, Peter Narracott, Prof Rodney Needham, Keith Nicklin, Dr Max Nihom, H Oemarharoen, Rodric Owen, Stella Rhind, Ny H Siti Maryam Rachmat Salahuddin, Dr Deborah Swallow, Dr Ken Teague, Itie van Hout, Zoë Wakelin-King, Susan Walker, Helen Wolf.

During the course of my research I made use of the facilities of a wide range of institutions and organisations, and I am especially grateful to the Australian Museum, Sydney; Australian National Gallery, Canberra; Balfour Library, Oxford; Bodleian Library, Oxford; Brynmor Jones Library, Hull; Business School, University of North London; Canadian International Development Association; Centre for South-East Asian Studies, Hull; Horniman Museum and Library, London; Kantor Pendidikan dan Kebudayaan, Bima; Kantor Perindustrian, Bima; Koninklijk Instituut voor Taal-, Land- en Volkenkunde, Leiden; Linacre College, Oxford; Museum Ethnographers Group; Musium Negeri Nusa Tenggara Barat, Mataram; Museum of Mankind, London; Pitt Rivers Museum, Oxford; Rijksmuseum voor Volkenkunde, Leiden; Royal Anthropological Institute Library, London; Het Technische Hogeschool, Delft; Tropenmuseum, Amsterdam; Tylor Library, Oxford; Universitas Mataram, Mataram.

This book is partly based on my D. Phil thesis in the Department of Ethnology and Prehistory, Oxford University, which was supervised by the late BAL Cranstone and Dr RH Barnes. I am indebted to both supervisors for their kindness and intellectual guidance. I am especially grateful to the following journals for allowing me to publish extracts from my articles: *Bijdragen tot de Taal-, Land- en Volkenkunde, Indonesia Circle, Journal of the Anthropological Society of Oxford, Journal of Social Issues in Southeast Asia.*

My warmest thanks go to my host in Leiderdorp - Jacqueline Palsma; my hosts in Salama - Abubakar M Sidik and Jawariah; the members of La Mbila; my two 'highlanders by adoption' - Peter and Anne Just; my great friend and companion - Daina Griva; and finally my many friends in Indonesia.

A portrait of the Sultan and his retinue taken shortly after the annexation of Bima by the Netherlands East Indies. The back row comprises *dari* heads and the Sultan's bodyguard (with blowpipe) and two turbaned soldiers. Sultan Ibrahim, Prince Salahuddin, the Dutch representative, Prime Minister and two other ministers are seated in the middle row. The three commoners in the front bear the royal betel set.

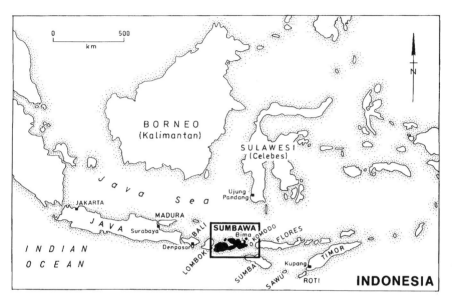

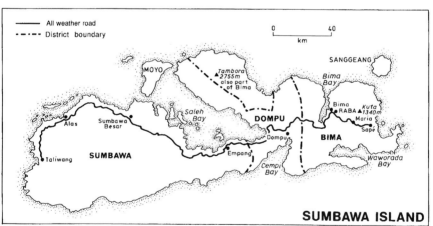

Indonesia and Sumbawa.

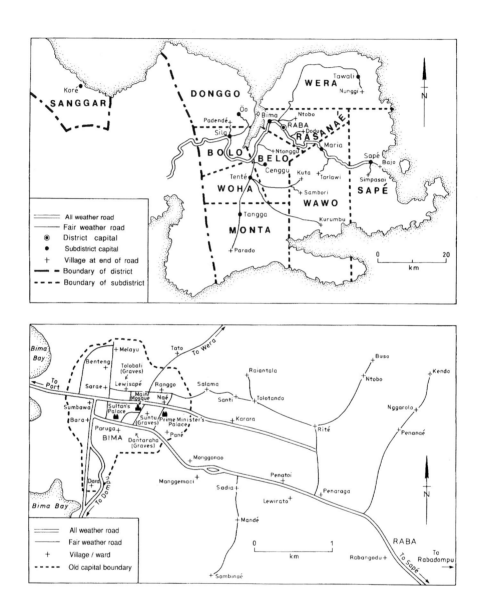

Bima and Raba.

I

Introduction

The former kingdom of Bima lies on the eastern peninsula of the Indonesian island of Sumbawa. Before its conversion to Islam, the kingdom was ruled by a succession of Hindu rajahs whose names are recorded in the annals of the court. According to dynastic myths, the kings of Bima have Javanese origins and are the descendants of a prince and naga princess. Like rulers elsewhere in maritime South-East Asia, the royal household of Bima were believed to have ancestors who were heavenly born. The name Bima has Hindu-Javanese origins and appears to be derived from Bhima, one of the heroes of the Mahabharata, the great shadow theatre epic. Despite its Indic name, Bima is best known as a Muslim Sultanate that rose to prominence in eastern Indonesia after the accession of Sultan Abdul Kahir in the early 17th century. The kingdom eventually became the foremost Sultanate on Sumbawa, dominating its neighbours while ruling western Flores and laying claim to the island of Sumba. At its height the Sultanate of Bima held sway over a territory that was roughly comparable in size to the modern state of Hawaii.

Located midway down the archipelago, Bima, with its good natural harbour, has long been a port-of-call. The court's power and wealth was closely associated with trade, and thus the capital is located close to Bima Bay. The majority of the population refer to themselves as Dou Mbojo, though the coastal society is ethnically diverse. Distinct highland peoples are encountered in the island's rugged interior. The kingdom is thus named after a prince and not a people and, though the Dou Mbojo are often referred to in the literature as the 'Bimanese', this is not strictly correct. In accordance with Muslim tradition, the Sultans of Bima tried to establish a haven of peace, in which the traders and seafarers of different ethnic origin could conduct their business in safety under the green banner of Islam. The Sultanate also attempted to reconcile differences based on locality and ethnicity by absorbing these disparate elements into the Sultanate system. Court ceremonials were not only used to re-affirm the supremacy of the ruling elites, but to draw attention to the contribution made by the different cultures to the common good.

The Sultanate's identity was defined with the aid of court ceremonials and invented traditions, but Bima was not strictly a 'theatre state' (cf. Geertz 1980). Bima's legitimacy was not ultimately dependent on an elaborate and self-fulfilling ritual cycle, but on the control of trade and the exercise of real military strength. The court's prestige was, however, regularly re-affirmed in public with the aid of music, theatre and dance, and above all with the use of an awesome material culture. In Bima one encounters the hallmarks of a Muslim kingdom: sacred kris, brocaded fabrics, gilded jewellery, jewel encrusted regalia and tombs emblazoned with Muslim calligraphy. By its material culture alone, Bima can readily be distinguished from its neighbours in eastern Indonesia, who are justly famed in the literature for their ikat fabrics and richly carved statuary. Sharply attired in gold, scarlet and vermilion, the Bimanese nobility contrast markedly with counterparts dressed in the more subdued hues of the islands to the east.

Bima is a Muslim outpost in a largely non-Muslim Indonesian region and thus its identity is closely associated with that of Islam. Unlike their eastern neighbours the Bimanese were drawn into the Malay world through their trading links and conversion to Islam. Thus their material culture resembles that of their trading partners and political allies, especially the Malays and Makasars. Although Muslim societies are encountered further east in Nusa Tenggara, none match the Sultanate of Bima in terms of size, complexity and political influence. Despite the adoption of a Malay style culture, the Sultanate of Bima was not completely absorbed into the Malay political order and retained a distinctive local identity. The Bimanese kingdom came into existence long before the era of Islamization, and thus Muslim missionaries had to contend with well-established local allegiances when they arrived in eastern Indonesia. Bima is doubly interesting because it also lies on the fringes of Indic influence in eastern Indonesia and thus shares elements of a common heritage with Java. Furthermore, despite its Islamic affiliation, the kingdom of Bima did not entirely forget its eastern Indonesian roots, and elements of a non-Muslim past can be detected in its material culture.

Like the Malay courts, Bima was basically a trade emporium which was dominated by local people who exchanged indigenous products for imported goods. These courts facilitated the entry of world religions, especially Islam, and provided the means by which foreign artistic ideas were introduced; but they were never entirely cut off from the upriver and hinterland peoples with whom they traded (Taylor & Aragon 1991: 19). The arts of the Malay courts, though enriched through foreign contact, often express local Indonesian themes. Their artistic products helped to affirm political and social relations, and to link the ruler and his people to divine powers and spiritual forces.

Perspectives on Indonesian Islam

Indonesia is the world's largest Muslim nation, but is not an Islamic state. The country is neither governed according to Islamic law, *Shari'ah*, nor is strictly secular. Instead the regime promotes a national philosophy, known as *Pancasila* (five principles), which emphasizes religious tolerance. The first principle of this state code is represented by a star on the Indonesian coat-of-arms; it symbolizes the belief in God, though the religion is not specified. The important point is that the citizen must believe and in theory Indonesians can belong to any religion; but in practice the state emphasizes world religions such as Islam and Christianity, often at the expense of indigenous belief systems. There are small-scale religions in Indonesia, but their adherents have long been under pressure to assimilate and join one of the world religions. Despite their religious diversity, however, the overwhelming majority profess Islam and, given Indonesia's status as the world's fourth most populous nation, their numbers are considerable. Approximately 85% of Indonesia's population, which reached 186 million in 1992, subscribe to Islam; there are more Muslims here than anywhere else on Earth.

Despite their numerical significance, Indonesia's Muslims remain poorly understood by the outside world. There are many received opinions concerning Islam in Indonesia, not least because the strength of the oral tradition in South-East Asia has made it difficult to apply the kinds of analyses that are usually reserved for written texts. Because Islam was introduced to South-East Asia from two of the world's great literary centres, the Middle East and India, the donors are often accorded higher status than the receivers. Scholars steeped in the values of the Arab and Indian worlds have also found it difficult to contend with the vernacularization of the Islamic tradition in South-East Asia. No matter how strong the sense of belonging to the world of Islam, there is an extraordinary patriotism to local identities in South-East Asia. South-East Asian identities are not necessarily stronger than those found elsewhere, but they are often more readily identifiable within the Islamic context. These identities are often expressed in ways that are unfamiliar to scholars grounded in the Middle Eastern tradition, and this has led many to conclude that Islam in Indonesia is somehow qualitatively different. As Snouck Hurgronje has emphasized repeatedly, popular religions live alongside the official faith in all Muslim countries, without the Muslim community being any less pure in sentiment and deed (de Josselin de Jong 1977: 178-9).

Indonesian forms of Islam have not been extensively researched by social and cultural anthropologists and this has prolonged the shelf life of seminal, though outdated, studies such as Geertz's *The Religion of Java* (1960). The finds of social scientists also appear to be at variance with one another and South-East Asian specialists have questioned their general applicability; but in the absence of sustained research it is difficult to reconcile different points of view, fill gaps and clarify perspectives (Hitchcock 1991: 582). Islam is also a universalistic faith that transcends ethnic and national boundaries and therefore poses special problems for the researcher interested in culture and identity. While external observances, such as the five pillars of Islam, may be tangible and thus open to analysis, internally held values are less accessible. Central to being a Muslim is entry into an imaginary world perceived by all believers that shapes the perceptions of Muslims everywhere. Although this shared vision influences the Muslim sense of identity throughout the world, it is open to different kinds of interpretation. It is partly because of this complexity that scholars have held diametrically opposed views regarding the nature of Islam in different cultural contexts. As the following passages illustrate, this is particularly the case in Indonesia where much of the debate has concerned the Javanese, the largest Muslim society in South-East Asia.

> The inhabitants of Java, with the exception of a few scattered mountaineers retaining the superstition of their forefathers, and unworthy of notice in general consideration, are orthodox Mohamedans, following like all the converted inhabitants of insular India, the doctrines of Shafaai, of whose works as well as those of some of the most celebrated doctors of his sect, they possess copies (Crawfurd 1812: 250).

> The extreme *kolot santri*, despite the fact that he is often called 'orthodox', is not actually the most Islamic of Javanese Moslems but the least. It is he who has made the minimum shift from the traditional religious system in which the 'animistic', Hindu-Buddhist and Islamic elements found a stable balance toward the situation where Islam and the world view associated with it have been fully taken up into the self, have been internalized in the individual psyche so that they actually control behaviour rather than merely putting a gloss on it to hide the values which are really determining individual action (Geertz 1960: 125).

> ... we should recall the general consensus of ethnographic studies that the Javanese traditionally view the world as composed of spiritual energies contained in forms and images, such as magically potent swords, sacred shrines, deities, teachers, and rulers; the Javanese syncretistic world is what Weber termed a 'garden of magic' - indeed, an animistic jungle. (Peacock 1978: 42-43).

The first of the above accounts was written by Crawfurd, who drew on his experience of Muslims in India. Crawfurd was the British Resident at the court of Yogyakarta during the Raffles administration (1811-1816) and, though he found the Javanese somewhat lax in their observance of Muslim prohibitions against gambling, opium smoking and drinking alcohol, he thought them orthodox. The opposite view, however, was advanced in certain anthropological studies, particularly those of Geertz, which claim that Islam never really took root in Java except among the mercantile class, the *santri*. According to Geertz, Islam had little influence on the Javanese nobility, the *priyayi*, who retained their Hindu-Javanese heritage and the *abangan* peasants and small traders. The *abangan* religious tradition comprised complex spirit beliefs, practices of curing and magic, and represented a stress on the 'animistic aspects' of Javanese syncretism (Geertz 1960: 5-6).

Many scholars accepted Geertz's contention that the Javanese were nominal Muslims, though details of his hypothesis were criticised by several Dutch and Indonesian scholars (Woodward 1989: 2). Geertz's division of Javanese society into three primary groups - the nobility, the orthodox Muslims and the animist peasantry - was also adopted by other scholars, often with only minor amendments. Geertz's theory, though undoubtedly influential, did not meet with universal approval, especially among specialists in Islamic studies. Hodgson, for example, who relied on Geertz's ethnography and Javanese texts translated by Dutch scholars cast doubt on Geertz's analysis. Hodgson argued that if one considered Javanese Islam from the perspective of the Muslim tradition as a whole, rather than from the viewpoint of modern reformists, then it bore a distinct resemblance to the Islam of the Middle East and India.

> ... influenced by the polemics of a certain school of *shari'ah*-minded Muslims, Geertz identifies Islam only with that which that school of modernists happens to approve, and ascribes everything else to an aboriginal or Hindu-Buddhist background, gratuitously labelling much of the Muslim religious life in Java 'Hindu'. For one who knows Islam, his comprehensive data - despite his intention - show very little has survived from the Hindu past even in inner Java and raises the question of why the triumph of Islam was so complete (Hodgson 1974: 551).

Despite the above reservations, Geertz's perspective remained largely unchallenged within the social sciences until the publication of Mark Woodward's book, *Islam in Java*, in 1989. Woodward not only attempted to address Hodgson's question concerning the success of

Islam in Java, but also helped to locate Javanese religious beliefs within the wider Islamic tradition. Woodward had some training as an Indologist before conducting research in Java, but his efforts to trace the Hindu elements in Javanese rituals and ceremonials proved unrewarding. Likewise he made little progress with trying to identify the Hindu or Buddhist precursors of traditional Javanese mysticism and in frustration he turned to the study of Islamic ritual and doctrine. On completing his research in Java, Woodward returned to the United States and continued with his religious studies, an endeavour heightened by having to teach an introduction to Middle Eastern Islam. Woodward concludes that Islam is the predominant religious force in Java and that it shapes the character of social interaction and daily life in all sectors of Javanese society (Woodward 1989: 3).

In his book Woodward traces the processes by which Islam became predominant in Java and places emphasis on the role of saints within the Indonesian context. Saints are said to perform miracles, are a source of blessings and help to bridge the intellectual and popular traditions. Although there is an extensive indigenous literature concerning saints, these beliefs are not uniquely Javanese since saints are as much a part of Sufism, the branch of Islam adopted in Java, as metaphysical speculation and the interpretation of religious texts. According to Woodward, Javanese Muslims not only revere saints, but also stress mystical practice and experience, as well as ritual. In court formulations, however, it is held that aristocrats need only be concerned with mysticism and the veneration of saints; the Sultan of Yogyakarta rarely worships at the state mosque on Fridays. In contrast, the non-royal orthodox Muslims, *santri putih*, are more concerned with ritual observance, conforming to the court view that the ideal society is one '... in which the sultan is a mystic and his subjects are devoted to normative piety' (Woodward 1989: 150). This ideal is impossible to realize because there are also lower class non-*santri* Javanese who show no more enthusiasm for piety than the nobility. Low class Javanese rarely attend local mosques and are seldom able to either recite or comprehend the Arabic of the Koran.

Woodward also asks why Islam triumphed in Java, which possesses an ancient Hindu-Buddhist heritage, whereas it failed elsewhere in Buddhist South-East Asia? Although Sufis are usually more willing than other Islamic sects to come to terms with non-

Muslim thought, they rarely accept certain theories such as reincarnation, caste and the Buddhist denial of the existence of the soul. Woodward accepts that many of the processes by which Islam became established in Java are shrouded in mystery, but suggests that it was the absence of a well-developed caste system that facilitated the spread of the religion. Moreover, Islam was established as an imperial religion, a development which '... involved the destruction of much of the existing Hindu-Buddhist religious culture ...' (Woodward 1989: 54). Woodward also compares Java's 'top down' conversion with that of India where Hindu states survived the onslaught of Islam. In contrast, the fall of Majapahit, the last Hindu-Javanese kingdom, eliminated state patronage of Hindu-Buddhism, and therefore adherents could not flee to neighbouring kingdoms when faced with forced conversion. Only Bali provided sanctuary for the Hindu-Javanese and the sacred literature on which their religion depended (Woodward 1989: 243). Bali steadfastly retains its Hindu-Buddhist heritage and the island's royal families continue to trace their origins to the Majapahit princes who fled the advance of Islam.

One question that Woodward does not address is that if the Hindu-Javanese refugees could escape to Bali, then why did they go no further east? Since vassal kingdoms of Majapahit are mentioned on islands such as Lombok and Sumbawa in the *Nagarakertagama*, then why did the refugees not establish dynasties east of Bali? One likely explanation is that Majapahit never exercised effective political control east of Bali; another is that Islam drove a wedge between Bali and Lombok in eastern Indonesia. Although there are several versions of the Islamization of Lombok, it seems likely that this religion was introduced from Java during the early 16th century, around the time of the demise of Majapahit (Cederroth 1981: 32, van der Kraan 1980: 2-3). Neighbouring Sumbawa succumbed to the powerful Sultanate of Makassar in south Sulawesi, and by the early 17th century the last non-Muslim ruler of Bima had been deposed (Noorduyn 1987: 339). Despite the success of Islam, eastern Indonesia remained a battleground between Muslim and non-Muslim forces for the next few centuries. Lombok became a buffer zone between the expansionist kingdoms of Bali and Makassar, a conflict that also spread to Sumbawa. The first large-scale clash took place in 1677, but it was not until 1847 that the Balinese consolidated their control over the largely Muslim population of Lombok (van der Kraan 1980: 4-6).

Perspectives on race and ethnicity

Given the focus on Islam and identity, it is necessary to consider briefly how anthropologists have approached this subject, especially with regard to race and ethnicity. It should be stressed, however, that this is not intended to be a definitive account since more comprehensive studies of race and ethnicity can be found elsewhere (e.g. Rex & Moore 1967; Barth 1969; Rex 1986; Erikson 1991). Since popular usages of the terms 'race' and 'ethnicity' vary greatly and are open to a wide range of interpretations, it is worthwhile outlining the development of the anthropological perspective. The United Nations, through its UNESCO branch, endeavoured to resolve some of the main questions concerning race by commissioning first biologists and then social scientists to provide a scientific definition. The biologists, after reviewing a mass of complex material, concluded that the human species had a single origin and that the so-called races of mankind were only statistically distinguishable as groups (Rex 1986: 18-19).

In contrast to the biologists, the social scientists working with UNESCO came up with three different perspectives. First, they realised that racial and ethnic problems were essentially similar and therefore concluded that these issues belonged to the same broad category. Second, it was recognized that racial differences did exist and that they often acted as markers for the differential apportionment of rights, though there was no justification for this. Third, the term 'race relations' was applied to situations characterized by racism and, broadly-speaking, this is how many social scientists continue to perceive these issues (Rex 1986: 19). Racism is widely regarded as a form of ethnocentrism based on physical criteria, in which the ethnocentric group feels that it is at the centre of the social world and all others are evaluated with reference to it. Thus, for many social scientists race is a version of ethnicity, albeit one based on physical criteria; but, if race is a socio-cultural issue, then what is meant by ethnicity?

Numerous definitions of ethnicity have been offered by social scientists, especially anthropologists, and, though an overall assessment of their relative merits lies beyond the scope of this chapter, it is worthwhile summing up the main points. Generally-speaking, theories of ethnicity can be described as 'primordial', in that identity depends on a series of 'givens' (e.g. Geertz 1963), or 'situational', in that identity may be invoked according to circumstances (e.g. Barth 1969; Wallman 1979). According to the former view ethnic identity stems from being born into a particular community, eventually becoming enculturated by adopting its values (religion etc.) and speaking its particular language, or even dialect of a language, and following a set of social practices which are deeply associated with that community. Ties of ethnicity are not closely linked to, or are dependent on, class or political phenomena; they usually cross-cut them. Ethnicity, therefore, has a life of its own and an internal dynamic which exists independently of the other elements in the political process (Rex 1986: 27). In certain contexts, such as in class conflict, it may be misleading to speak of ethnic groups, or quasi groups, even when grievances are expressed in terms of ethnicity.

The situational perspective, which was advanced by Barth, offered a more dynamic view of identity that placed greater emphasis on ethnicity as a set of processes and social relations. What distinguished Barth from earlier writers on ethnicity was his rejection of the view that culture was a fixed, monolithic entity and his refusal to identify ethnicity as the property of cultural groups. Barth sought to avoid any notion of cultural determinism and implicitly dismissed the concern of certain cultural anthropologists with national character as crude and misleading (Erikson 1991: 128). By focusing on social relations between and within ethnic groups Barth, and later Eidheim (1971) and others, developed a set of formal concepts for dealing with interpersonal ethnicity. The adoption of the formalist approach, which conceives of ethnicity as a social process in which cultural differences are communicated, facilitates comparison and enables us to account for ethnic phenomena without recourse to simplistic definitions of cultural groups (Erikson 1991: 128).

My intention is to show how the adoption of a world religion, especially one as universalistic as Islam, has a profound influence on identity and inter-communal relations. It questions, however, the notion that an ethno-religious identity has to be interiorized before it becomes meaningful. Although belief as an interiorizing concept is relevant in many social contexts, it is not applicable to all aspects of ethnic identity (cf. Tooker 1992: 799). Along with recent studies of ethnicity in the social sciences, this book rejects simplistic conceptions of cultures as bounded entities for study, and places emphasis on ethnicity as a set of social relationships and processes by which cultural differences are communicated (cf. Erikson 1991: 127). It will be stressed that in order for an identity to be understood, it must be shared and therefore has to be constantly created and re-created through intentional agency. This study also shows how signifiers of identity may change in different contexts and that fundamental to the notion of ethnicity is the very act of communicating and maintaining cultural difference (Erikson 1991: 129). It is also argued that in order for such expressions of identity to be understood in inter-personal encounters, there must be shared agreement as to what is significant.

It is accepted that, although the social communication of cultural difference can be observed and described, these activities are elusive and almost impossible to quantify. As formalist studies of ethnicity have shown, culture is a difficult concept to deal with analytically, not least because it cannot be reduced to a fixed system of signs (Erikson 1991: 130). But as this book demonstrates, the pursuit of cultural identity and social autonomy does involve the manipulation of symbols as boundaries are defined and maintained. What this study does is to examine one of the most obvious manifestations of this kind of communication - the use of material culture as a visual expression of identity. Physical products provide concrete reference points and, given the emphasis placed on the tangible in many cultures, are central to the art of communication. The meaning of a particular visual art form may be difficult to tease out, but what should not be overlooked is the readiness with which people identify with them (cf. Bowden 1992: 80). Although it is accepted that this symbolic discourse may take many forms (e.g. music, food, language, etc.), it is argued that material culture provides a highly significant medium of communication in South-East Asia, a part of the world that is renowned for the elaboration and complexity of its physical products. While this approach provides only a partial view of a highly complex area of human interaction, it deserves to be considered alongside more conventional approaches within the social sciences.

Miller's approach to the study of material culture has shown that there can be a direct link between an artefact and expressions of difference or similarity. By choosing to adopt or avoid certain things, the actor can be interpreted as conveying an association with, or an association against, a particular identity. Artefacts and the skills needed to produce them are significant boundary markers, communicating subtle messages about whom one wants or does not want to be identified with. Processes as well as products contribute to the social construction of identity with the aid of material culture. Varying degrees of relatedness may be signified, and material culture may be used to represent histories and events. Objects created by the members of one generation shape the environment in which future generations are constructed as subjects (Miller 1985: 204).

It will be argued in this volume that Miller's observations can fruitfully be applied in the Indonesian context with the appropriate modifications. We know from the ethnographies of the region that human handicrafts are not only associated with identity, but are also deemed to have their own life force. This point has been illustrated with admirable clarity in Roxana Waterson's wide ranging study of the 'living house' in South-East Asia (Waterson 1990). Similar observations have been made regarding the notion of 'property-as-talisman' in the Malay and Polynesian world, and the Pacific in general (Mauss 1990: 10).

Studies of material expressions of identity are also of particular relevance within the Indonesian context because of the widespread adoption of Islam, a religion which has strong views on representation. Prohibitions on idolatry are, for example, encountered in Islamic thought, but the extent to which they have influenced the symbolic and aesthetic traditions of Indonesia remains controversial. What will be argued here is that, although these restrictions were never applied uniformly, they have modified the ways in which identity is understood in certain contexts.

No matter how an ethnic group is defined, it must be aware of its own existence and this usually means having a name for itself, an ethnonym. Ethnic identities can, however, be externally imposed and the anthropological literature on South-East Asia contains many examples of names which have been bestowed on people by other groups. Terms such as *Naga* (Assam hill person), *Dayak* (upriver non-Muslim in Borneo) and *Bajau* (sea nomad) originated in this fashion and need not necessarily reflect real ethnic affinities. Some ethnonyms are so situational that an individual may possess two or more of them, as appears to be the case with the Lom of Bangka Island in Indonesia. According to Olaf Smedal, a Lom may become a Malay by refraining from non-Muslim habits such as eating pork, but can revert back again to observe non-Muslim habits (Smedal 1985: 19-35). A close association between a religious and ethnic identity is also encountered in Borneo where the ethnonym 'Malay' is applied to heterogeneous indigenous peoples who have adopted Islam (King 1978). Ethnonyms may disappear as a people assimilates with a more dominant or numerous group in order to fulfil political aims, as has been well-documented in highland Myanmar (Burma) by Sir Edmund Leach (1954). Their disappearance may, however, be only temporary as the latent ethnonym re-emerges at a later date when circumstances change and new allegiances come to the fore. Sometimes amalgamation occurs when different groups combine under a new ethnonym while retaining their old identities.

Islamic anthropology

Islam is highly significant within the context of race and ethnicity, not least because of its longlasting universalistic traditions. Islam teaches that all human beings are equally God's creatures and, that by acknowledging one creator, Muslims accept the unity of mankind. As can be seen from the Koran, the notion that humanity is indivisable is fundamental to Muslim thought:

> O mankind, we created you from a single male and female, and made you into nations and tribes that you may know one each other (49: 13) (Haneef 1979: 171).

What is also significant is that the Koran does not appear to distinguish between race and ethnicity, and simply refers to the linguistic and physical variety of human beings as if they were related phenomena:

> And among this signs in the creations of the heavens and the earth, and the variations in your languages and colors. Indeed, in that are signs for those who know (30: 22) (ibid).

Muslim writers like to remind their readers that the first muezzin to call the faithful to prayer was Bilāl, a black Ethiopian (Cragg 1975: 122-123). The Ethiopian argued that he was the brother of all pious Muslims, even though he was a slave (Waddy 1976: 106). Justice before the law in early Muslim society was expected to be

strictly impartial without regard to religion, race or class (Haneef
1979: 117). As Arnold Toynbee has observed the '... extinction of race
consciousness as between Muslims is one of the outstanding moral
achievements of Islam' (Waddy 1976: 105). According to some
scholars (e.g. Cragg 1975: 122), the major tensions in the Muslim
world have been political rather than racial.

Islam's universalistic creed has attracted attention within social
anthropology, though not perhaps as much as it should have done.
This situation has, however, been changing since the 1970s with the
work of scholars such as Akbar S. Ahmed who have sought to
develop a distinctive branch of the subject known as Islamic
anthropology. Working within the context of Islamic revivalism,
Akbar S. Ahmed set out to use his experiences as a sociological
resource to interpret what was happening around him (Akbar S.
Ahmed 1992: ix). In seeking to understand why Islam should be able
to transcend ethnic and racial barriers Akbar S. Ahmed has identified
three key concepts. First, universal and easily-identified symbols
have been introduced into even the most remote Muslim societies.
The Ka'aba is the visible symbol of God's unity and every day
millions of Muslims around the world turn to face the same central
point in prayer. Second, Muslims share a broadly-based cultural
heritage which includes common words, common festivals and
shared normative values. Islam places grave emphasis on the *hajj*;
pilgrimage not only brings together people from different cultural
backgrounds, but also keeps open channels of communication. Third,
Muslims around the world identify with the wider Islamic
community, especially if one part of it is seen as under threat.
Muslims have at times turned inwards to confront crises arising from
problems of identity, as was particularly the case in the 19th century
with the growth of European imperialism (Akbar S. Ahmed 1976: 84-
85). Akbar S. Ahmed regards the concept of *ummah*, the Muslim
brotherhood, as excellent but undeveloped, and argues that it needs
to be pursued with more vigour than is currently exhibited by
Muslims (1992: 45-46).

Field of anthropological study

In his book, *Islam in Java*, Woodward describes how Islam supplanted
Hindu-Buddhism and provides a detailed analysis of the Indic

elements of Javanese culture (Woodward 1989: 215-240). Many of these elements, such as the Indian epics used in the shadow theatre, have been transformed through contact with Islam and Woodward concludes that the significance of these Indic elements in Javanese religious philosophy has been over-estimated. Woodward does not, however, devote much attention to the pre-Indic beliefs of the Javanese and it remains unclear how Islam has affected the autochthenous culture of the island. This makes it difficult to locate Java within the wider social and geographical context of South-East Asia and ask whether or not the Javanese have retained much of their pre-Islamic, but non-Indic culture? Woodward is primarily concerned with the world religions and therefore does not analyse his Javanese material with reference to the considerable literature which exists concerning the indigenous religions and social systems of South-East Asia. When considering Woodward's study it might be appropriate to ask, in the manner of Valeri in Bali, if an 'Austronesian' heart beats beneath Java's Indic veneer (Valeri 1991: 142-143)? Similar questions will be raised in this book concerning the Islamization of an eastern Indonesian society, especially with regard to material culture.

Much of the literature concerning the autochthenous cultures of South-East Asia was inspired by Dutch structural anthropologists and is, therefore, particularly strong on Indonesia. The Dutch were especially concerned with symbolism and devoted attention to the interpretation of the thoughts and actions of Indonesian peoples within the contexts of their own cultures. Their thematic specialization arose out of attempts to apply insights derived from sociological theory to the study of indigenous peoples in the Dutch colonies in Indonesia (Teljeur 1990: 1). The theoretical roots of this Dutch anthropology can be traced back to the publication of Mauss and Durkheim's *De quelques formes primitives de classification* (1903); but was not given an institutional base until the appointment of J.P.B. de Josselin de Jong to the Chair of Indonesian and General Anthropology at the University of Leiden in 1935. That year also saw the defence of F.A.E. von Wouden's influential thesis entitled *Types of Social Structure in Eastern Indonesia* (de Josselin de Jong 1984: 1). This branch of anthropology developed into a separate school within the confines of cultural anthropology, which is inaccurately referred to as the Leiden School because not all its adherents were from Leiden (Teljeur 1990: 2).

This school of thought might be more accurately called the Dutch School to acknowledge the work of scholars such as H.G.

Schulte Nordholt who studied at Utrecht, but the term Leiden School continues to be used informally. The school reached a watershed in 1949 when J.P.B. de Josselin de Jong introduced Levi-Strauss to the Netherlands and from that point onwards the school became associated with structuralism. P.E. de Josselin de Jong refers to this school as 'structural anthropology', though this is only partially correct since some anthropologists prefer the more thematic term 'symbolic anthropology' (Teljeur 1990: 4). The school attracted interest in universities in other countries, most notably in Oxford, and, as its theoretical basis became more clearly defined, some of the unnecessary colonial intellectual baggage, such as social determinism, was jettisoned. The school continued to be admired for its work on classification and, in particular, the body of theory known as the Field of Anthropological Study, which was launched by J.P.B. de Josselin de Jong in 1935 (Niessen 1985: 1).

From the 1930s onwards the Dutch came to regard the cultures of the Indonesian archipelago as different varieties of the same general, hence the use of Field of Anthropological Study (*ethnologisch studieveld*) to describe the region (de Josselin de Jong 1984: 2). Despite the fact that there were hundreds of distinct ethnic groups in the archipelago, J.P.B. de Josselin de Jong believed that they were united by a common cultural substratum, which he labelled the 'structural core'. The preliminary assumptions of Dutch anthropologists were based partly on the ethnographic studies available at the time and the knowledge that the languages of the Indonesian archipelago were closely related to one another. In 1935 it was known that the Indonesian languages were also related to the Melanesian and Polynesian branches of the Austronesian family and from the outset the boundaries of this field of study were difficult to define. It remained unclear whether the limits of the field of study were marked by the Indonesia, Austronesian or even Austric languages (de Josselin de Jong 1984: 5).

From the outset the concept of the Field of Anthropological Study (FAS) was a flexible one that was neither tied to specific cultural phenomena nor to particular geographical or linguistic units (de Josselin de Jong 1985: 257). But this flexibility raises problems, not least because it blurs the boundaries between comparative linguistics and cultural anthropology. What J.P.B. de Josselin de Jong probably had in mind, though he never made it explicit, was the comparative study of societies that are genetically related to one another, an

Fig. 1 Villagers in Ntobo, an important weaving centre.

Fig. 2 Wooden house in Salama village. Rice is pounded in the mortar and pestle. Worshippers wash in the terracotta bowl before praying. A sarong is drying on the bamboo fence.

assumption based on the proven links between the languages of the archipelago (ibid). As the body of knowledge grew, the linguistic term 'Austronesian' began to be applied more generally to cultural phenomena. Customs that appeared to have survived from the pre-Indic era could therefore be labelled as 'Austronesian', as could whole societies that lay beyond the sphere of Indic and Islamic influence. The exponents of FAS began to realize that comparative research in the vast geographical area encompassed by the Austronesian languages would prove unwieldy and, therefore, they devised practical guidelines for more manageable research. P.E. de Josselin de Jong eventually recommended dividing the archipelago into two research areas delineated by the Western Austronesian and Central-Eastern Austronesian areas, '... the boundary between the two beginning, at its southern extremity, in Sumbawa' (de Josselin de Jong 1985: 257). Linguistically-speaking, Bimanese is genetically closer to, for example, Fijian and the Polynesian languages than it is to neighbouring Sumbawanese (Blust 1984: 30).

What is significant is that the island of Sumbawa should be regarded as occupying an intermediate position between western and eastern Indonesia and two fields of study. The Bimanese are clearly linked to the east and this is acknowledged in Sumbanese myths of origin. The ancestors of the Sumbanese are said to have travelled from the base of the sky via a route which includes Bima and Dompu, the Mbojo-speaking parts of Sumbawa (Forth 1981:91). In contrast, the people of the west of the island, the Tau Semawa, are culturally and linguistically affiliated to the west, especially with the Sasak of Lombok, whereas the Bimanese are oriented to the east and are potentially members of the 'Groote Oost' field of study delineated by van Wouden in 1935 (Le Bar 1972: 62; Jasper 1908: 100; Schulte Nordholt 1972: 69). In keeping with the proposal outlined by van Wouden a great deal of attention has been devoted to the peoples of Flores, Sumba and Timor, and the smaller eastern islands, and the last few decades have seen an active programme of ethnography and comparison by Dutch, British, French and American anthropologists (Fox 1980; Barnes 1985; de Josselin de Jong 1985). Much of this research has focused on the systems of prescriptive and preferential marriage alliance that van Wouden regarded as prototypic for the region (Just 1986: 21). Sumbawa, however, remained comparatively neglected and extended anthropological work was confined to the west of the island until the late 1970s. Brewer has suggested that

Sumbawa in general, and Bima in particular, tended to be overlooked because it was not only transitional, but was complicated by a long history of Islam (Brewer 1979: 2-3). The island was too marginal to attract scholars interested in the 'mainstream' cultures of the west, and yet too influenced by Islam to engage the attention of those involved in research in the eastern Indonesian FAS.

Anthropological research has been conducted on Sumbawa only five times since the Second World War. The late Dutch scholar G.J. Held carried out research in Bima and Dompu from 1954 to 1955, but he died before publishing his results. His fieldnotes are available in the manuscript collection of Koninklijk Instituut voor Taal-, Land- en Volkenkunde (Held H1220) and Michael Prager has taken responsibility for publishing the manuscript. Between 1954 and 1956 Peter Goethals conducted a study of Tau Semawa social organization and village politics which led to two substantial publications which laid the foundations for research on the west of the island. The first extended programme of work in the east was carried out by Jeffrey Brewer between 1975 and 1976; he made a comparative study of agriculture and decision-making in two Bimanese villages, one that was primarily engaged in irrigated rice farming, and one that subsisted mainly on swidden cultivation. Brewer's study made an important contribution to the ethnology of agriculture and was not intended to provide a comprehensive account of Bimanese social organization (1979a), though he filled some important gaps with papers on Bimanese teknonymy (1981) and nomenclature (1978; 1979b). My own research between 1980 and 1982 concerned Bimanese material culture, but was not designed to provide an ethnography of lowland Bima, though special attention was paid to court culture (1983). During the course of the research I made an extensive collection of Bimanese textile technology for the Pitt Rivers Museum in Oxford (Hitchcock 1984). This research was followed by Peter Just's authorative study of Dou Donggo social organization from 1981 to 1983 which resulted in a thesis and a series of highly informative publications on highland society in eastern Sumbawa (Just 1984; 1986; 1991). The time that has elapsed since the initial research and the preparation of this monograph is not excessive as compared with other books on the region such as Hose's *Natural Man: A Record from Borneo* (Durrans 1988: x). There has also been the need to take into account the rapid increase in publications on eastern Indonesia in the last decade.

My first intention was not to make a study of Islam in Indonesia but, as my research in Bima progressed, I became intrigued by the marked difference between the material culture of Muslim Sumbawa and the non-Muslim islands to the east. It was not so much the everyday technology that caught my eye, but the symbolic material culture, that is sometimes referred to as 'art', which is closely associated with identity in maritime South-East Asia. The peoples of the 'Groote Oost' are famed in the literature for their elaborate ikat textiles (Adams 1973), the figurative statuary, richly adorned swords and ceremonial jewellery (Taylor & Aragon 1991) and their traditional houses laid out according to socio-cosmic principles (Cunningham 1964; Waterson 1991). But in Bima, which is linguistically oriented to the east, one encounters all the hallmarks of a Muslim court-based society: sacred kris, silk and silver brocade cloth, houses and palaces built on raised platforms, and the virtual absence of figurative designs. The difference is as marked as it is in Borneo where the material culture of the so-called coastal Malays can readily be distinguished from that of the non-Muslim *Dayak* peoples. The Bimanese are, however, not Malays, though they are Muslims and possess a Malay-type material culture. Straightforward explanations couched in terms of Makasar influence (Gittinger 1979: 53) or the introduction of Islamic prohibitions on idolatry (Hitchcock 1987: 54) cannot alone account for the complex differences between the material culture of Sumbawa and the islands to the east. Although the Makasar connection is undoubtedly important, there are other processes at work, especially the ongoing experience of Islamization.

This book deals with the processes by which the identity of the Bimanese, a Muslim people in Indonesia, is being created and re-created over time. It examines the processes by which an eastern Indonesian people have been both Islamized and Malayanized without adopting a Malay identity. The book provides a discussion of Islamization in eastern Indonesia set against a backdrop of history, commerce and the development of a court society, and pays particular attention to the use of material culture in boundary definition and maintenance. The emphasis is not on the instrumental use of material culture to govern action, but its use in a conditioning sense, providing both options and inherited limits. Bima makes a particularly interesting case study within this context because it lies within the sphere of both Indic and Islamic influence, and yet shares a linguistic heritage with the eastern Indonesian societies that lie beyond this sphere. This work is neither a comprehensive discussion of Bimanese social organization nor a definitive account of the traditional technology of Sumbawa, but a study of material culture and religious affiliation in relation to identity. The book is grounded in an ethnographic study of eastern Sumbawa, but the frame of reference is much broader and contains a discussion of the wider Islamic community in maritime South-East Asia.

II

Geographical and Historical Background

The varied terrain of the Island of Sumbawa is best appreciated from the air. During the wet monsoon one only catches a glimpse of the lush rice fields when the plane descends from the thick cloud cover to land near the administrative centre of Raba-Bima. Should the flight be made in the dry season, however, when the island is parched by winds originating to the south-east, then one is immediately struck by the extent and ruggedness of the mountain ranges. Small villages perched well up the mountain sides are also clearly visible from the plane, their isolation contrasting markedly with the dense clusters of settlements in the verdant irrigated valleys.

Geographical background

The island of Sumbawa, which looks deceptively small on maps using the Mercator projection, does not have an indigenous name. The local people simply refer to the island in terms of its three regions - Bima, Dompu and Sumbawa; the modern form of the last name is derived from Portuguese sources. The Portuguese appear to have named the whole land mass after the kingdom of Sumbawa (*Cimbava*) on the western half of the island, which is known in the Sumbawanese language as Semawa (Pires 1944 [1515]: 200). The autochthonous name for the eastern half of the island is Mbojo; but, since the name Bima is acceptable to the local people and more widely known than Mbojo, Bima will be used here. Interestingly, both the names Bima and Sumbawa may have Hindu-Javanese origins: the former appears to be linked to Bhima, one of the heroes of the Mahabharata epic, whereas the latter is possibly related to Shamba (the God Shiva) or the Sanskrit *sambhawa* (Noorduyn 1987: 316-317).

The absence of an indigenous name for the whole island is not surprising when one considers that Sumbawa is located in a vast archipelago where the very existence of islands is commonplace. Local people tend to think in terms of domains which are, in their eyes, socially and politically meaningful and usually eschew the somewhat artificial categories devised by cartographers. The Bimanese say that they live in the land of Mbojo, which means 'high ground' according to the folk etymology. When a local person talks about Sumbawa he means the western half of the island (i.e. the territory of the old kingdom of Sumbawa) and the residents of Dompu and Bima, which lies on the east of the island, are still mildly offended by visitors who insist on generalising and say they are in Sumbawa. Modern political boundaries reinforce local perceptions since all three former kingdoms have the status of *kapubaten* (district or regency) in the Indonesian province of Nusa Tenggara Barat (NTB) (*nusa*, island; *tenggara*, south-east; *barat*, west). The modern political divisions follow the boundaries of the former kingdoms.

The densely populated island of Lombok comprises the other half of the province of NTB. Mataram, the provincial capital, is located in the extreme west of Lombok, and is linked to Bima by a regular air service. Ferries ply between the two islands and there is an arterial road which snakes across Sumbawa from the port of Labuhan Tano in the west to the town of Sapé. To reach Sapé on the east coast, the road crosses the Wawo mountains at Maria, where there are the remains of a Dutch hill station and defensive works erected by the rulers of Bima. Sapé and the port of Bajo handle most of the east and southbound shipping and are popular departure points for tourists bound for the Komodo National Park. The island's main smaller roads join the main thoroughfare and connect Bima's ten *kecamaten* (subdistricts) to the district capital, which is also known as Bima.

Each subdistrict has its own capital, usually comprising a cluster of government buildings, a mosque and a market surrounded by shops and residential dwellings. The district capital, however, is more imposing and is divided into two halves: to the east lies Raba, the administrative centre which was moved inland during the colonial period to avoid the mosquito-infested coastline; to the west lies Bima, the old seat of Sultanate government.

The capital is located on the eastern shore of Bima Bay, a good natural harbour, and has long been an important commercial centre. The entrance to Bima Bay is very narrow and the remains of stone fortifications can be seen beside the channel which links the anchorage to the Flores sea. Bima's natural defences are strengthened by steep-sided hills and mountains which encircle the fertile heartlands of the old kingdom. Little is known about pre-Islamic Bima, though it seems likely that it flourished as a trading centre before the Islamization of the kingdom in the seventeenth century. The existence of various Old Javanese remains in Bima indicates that before the coming of Islam, the island was in contact with the islands to the west. According to Tomé Pires, who was writing in 1513, Bima lay along a shipping route that went from Malaka to the Moluccas via Java. Ships sold their trade goods from Java and bought cloth destined for Banda and the Moluccas (Noorduyn 1987: 316). This trade declined during the colonial era, but the harbour is still frequented by ships from throughout the archipelago. The bay which is fed by several rivers is slowly silting up and the large ferries are beginning to find access to the port difficult.

The climate and vegetation of Sumbawa is similar to that of the neighbouring islands of Nusa Tenggara. Because of their proximity to the arid continent of Australia, these islands bear the full brunt of the south-east monsoon and therefore annual rainfall is much lower than in western Indonesia. The midday temperature seldom drops below 28°C and there is often a pronounced dry season. Although the south-east monsoon usually lasts from May to October, the drought may continue into November, often with serious consequences for the islanders. In highland areas goats have to be killed to conserve resources (Just 1986: 29) and in coastal districts the incidence of water-borne diseases rises as the people huddle around dwindling supplies of fresh water. The island's forest cover, though much depleted by a combination of logging and farming, is well-adapted to cope with fluctuations in rainfall. The monsoon-fed woodland lacks the dense green canopy of the rainforests of western Indonesia and, because light filters through to ground level, the vegetation is often multi-layered and impenetrable. Certain species grow better in the more exposed woodlands of Sumbawa than they do further west, and the island has long been a source of economically-prized forest products such as teak, sandalwood and sappanwood, a source of dye.

Sumbawa Island lies east of the Wallace Line, the imaginary line running down the Lombok Strait between the island of Bali and the islands of Lombok and Sulawesi. The line was identified by the naturalist Alfred Russell Wallace as separating the Asian and Australian biogeographical regions. Sumbawa Island, however, is also located west of the Weber Line and therefore forms part of a transitional zone which has a mixed Asian and Australian fauna. Thus there are no large Asian wild animals, such as tigers, but smaller Asian mammals such as civet cats and macaques. The woodlands are home to Timor deer, as well as feral dogs and pigs, the descendants of escaped domestic animals. The deer were prized by the Sultans of Bima and were caught and kept in the palace gardens. But the local population gave up keeping dogs and pigs after the adoption of Islam, though some sandy-coloured dogs are still retained for hunting. Both dogs and pigs are regarded as vermin: the former scavenge around villages at night, while the latter raid the fields and gardens and are especially partial to young rice shoots.

A wide variety of birds is also found on Sumbawa, though they tend to keep clear of the more densely-populated areas. Lowland farmers zealously protect their crops and scare off all kinds of birds, though some trap songbirds and sell them in local markets. Egrets are often seen along the coast, while in the uplands there are kites, parakeets, guinea fowl and finches (Just 1986: 30). Eagles are esteemed symbols of majesty and are said to inhabit isolated craggy peaks. One of these creatures, which was much admired by the local people, used to be kept in a menagerie belonging to a Chinese doctor. On the neighbouring island of Komodo monopods build vast nests from jungle debris.

There are also many species of arachnids, ranging from large, hairy spiders to transparent scorpions that lurk in washrooms and outhouses. Some of the myriapods are potentially dangerous, such as the brightly-coloured centipedes, though the maroon millipedes are harmless. There are green praying mantis, multicoloured moths and butterflies, and wild bees, a valued source of honey. The islanders clean their houses daily, but despite their fastidiousness they are troubled by bed bugs, cockroaches, lice, ants and mosquitoes.

Fig. 3 Wild pigs are hunted with spears and semi-feral dogs in the hills above Bima.

Fig. 4 Ploughs are drawn by water buffalo at the start of the wet season.

There are numerous varieties of reptiles which also live in and around houses. Nimble geckos scamper across walls and ceilings while the larger toké lizard stays in the shadows and announces its presence with a distinctive call. Villagers count the number of calls to see whether there will be good or bad fortune. Clusters of snakes can be seen sunning themselves on forest trails at dawn, and occasionally one catches sight of a monitor lizard.

The island forms part of a volcanic belt which runs through Sumatra, Java and the islands of Nusa Tenggara. The chain curves north towards Ternate and then re-appears in northern Sulawesi from where it continues on to the Philippines. There is frequent seismic activity and many islanders live within sight of a volcano. The largest of these is Tambora (2775 m), the remains of the immense volcano which erupted in 1815. The top third of Tambora disintegrated in what was probably the world's greatest recorded release of energy, outclassing even better-known Krakatau (Bridge *et al* 1981: 21-52). The noise of the eruption brought people flocking on to the streets in Java and ash rained as far west as Ceribon and as far east as central Flores, thrown against the prevailing wind (Bickmore 1868: 108-109). Volcanic debris rained on southern Lombok, damaging crops and causing starvation, while in Sumbawa as many as ten thousand islanders perished in the ash-covered countryside (Goethals 1961: 18). The effects were felt worldwide as a dust cloud circled the earth causing climatic disturbances.

The eruption took place during the period of British rule in Java (1811 - 1816) and the governor-general, Sir Thomas Stamford Raffles, dispatched a ship to the beleaguered island. The British found the islanders hungry and impoverished and the scale of suffering overwhelmed their resources (Raffles 1830: 244-250). Stripped of vegetation the peninsula of Tambora was virtually de-populated and living conditions remained harsh for those that survived. The eruption also changed the political structure of the island as the three small kingdoms of the peninsula - Tambora, Papekat and Sanggar - disappeared almost without trace. By the time the Swiss explorer Heinrich Zollinger visited the island, the Sultan of Dompu was laying claim to Tambora and Papekat (Zollinger 1856: 245), whereas Sanggar appears to have come under the sway of Bima, though it was not formally annexed until 1928 (Ahmad Amin 1971: 10). Although the island appears to be under no immediate threat, Sanggiang, which erupted in 1964, smoulders away to the north-east.

The fertility of many Indonesian islands is due to the volcanic eruptions which have periodically coated the land in layers of rich ash. Sumbawa is no exception, but because of its comparative aridity agriculture is restricted to well-watered regions. The islanders make good use of available resources and Bima was in the past a rice-exporting area. The United East India Company (*Vereenigde Oostindische Compagnie*), for example, learned of Bima's agricultural wealth and sent ships to eastern Sumbawa to buy rice. The Dutch traders had to feed their employees and became particularly dependent on Bimanese supplies when their rice granaries in Java were raided and destroyed by the Javanese in 1618 (Noorduyn 1987: 331-332). Bima's rice-growing hinterland comprises the valleys of the subdistricts of Rasanaé, Belo, Bolo and Woha, all of which are irrigated by river systems. Stone weirs and brushwood diversion dams are used to re-direct the water into paddy fields by means of irrigation channels. The average yield is two harvests a year, though some farmers grow three crops, especially around Tenté. Swidden cultivation is practiced on hillsides, but this has resulted in soil erosion above Bima town. Swidden farmers clear the fields where the forest has been allowed to re-generate and burn the debris before the arrival of the wet monsoon. Rice is also grown on rain-fed terraces in the highlands, though yields are not as abundant as in the valleys. Some hill peoples harvest rice cutting single stems with finger knives to avoid weeds on the uneven ground. Sickles are used in the valleys where the land is level and the spread of weeds is kept in check by the water used for irrigation. Highlander farmers store the sheaves in granaries - de-husking the rice with a mortar and pestle when it is needed for cooking.

The uplands provide grazing for livestock and hill farmers, particularly those of Wawo, rear water buffalo for export. From time to time water buffalo are driven through the streets of the capital and are packed on to ships bound for the Javanese port of Surabaya. Water buffalo are also used as draught animals to pull ploughs and harrows, and in the past status of landowners was measured in terms of the size of herds. In the festivals which precede the rice harvest water buffalo are decked out with ribbons; after praising God and the lowly buffalo are thanked for their services. Animal husbandry is also important along the dry coastal plains of Wera and Sapé where, in addition to water buffalo, Bali cattle and goats are kept. Goat saté is popular, and though water buffalo are rarely slaughtered for their meat, a version of *rendang*, Sumatran beef stew, is prepared locally. Neither goats nor buffalo are milked in the valleys, though the Wawo highlanders are said by lowlanders to be fond of milk. Ducks are kept wherever there is sufficient water and are penned in under the house at night. Chickens forage everywhere and are sometimes trained to climb bamboo ladders so that they can roost in safety under the eaves at night. Water-filled earthenware pots may be sunk into the ground to keep eels.

In recognition of the islanders' skill as horse-breeders, the modern Indonesian crest of the District of Bima bears a horse. Small, sturdy horses have long been exported to Java, where they are used to pull carriages known as *dokar*. The Bimanese are passionate about horse-racing and large crowds gather to watch boy jockeys gallop around Bima's dusty race track. The chariot races in *Ben Hur* caught the local people's imagination when the film was shown on the island and horse-drawn taxis are still called *benhur* in honour of filmstar Charlton Heston. In the past horses were used in hunting and warfare, and were probably included in the tribute which was paid to the rulers of Makassar in South Sulawesi; explicit mention is made of the grooms who had to be supplied as part of the annual tribute (Noorduyn 1987: 319). According to local tradition the Bimanese also honoured a request for cavalry horses by Diponegoro (his mother was half Bimanese) during the Java War (1825-1830); but the horses arrived too late. Until the mid-twentieth century the royal grooms of Bima resided in their own quarter, known as Salama, on the outskirts of the capital and enjoyed special privileges.

In addition to rice farming and animal husbandry, the Bimanese cultivate a wide range of fruits and vegetables. They grow tomatoes, onions, soya beans, peanuts and sugar cane in rain-fed fields, and plant maize as an additional crop after the rice has been harvested. There are orchards with citrus trees, as well as coconut groves near the coast. Breadfruit, jackfruit, papaya, custard apples and salaks are among the fruits grown on the outskirts of villages. Kitchen gardens may contain banana and acacia trees, as well as vegetable patches for cassava and yams. Lontar palms are tapped to produce sugar and palm wine and the leaves are used to make mats and baskets.

The local diet includes a great deal of seafood, especially in the lowlands. Large double-hulled canoes, called *bagan*, are moored at sea and serve as fishing platforms. Fishermen in double-outrigger canoes fish with dip nets using lamps to attract prey at night in Bima

Bay. In coastal shallows fish are caught with cast nets and sometimes poisoned bait is issued. Lines hung with string and seaweed are also used to fish and drive them towards men waiting with harpoons. Shrimps are scooped up in fine nets to make *terasi* (shrimp paste) and lobster pots are set regularly. Although the marine life is diverse, large shoals are not found in these tropical waters. Overfishing is a problem in Bima Bay and fish is often brought from as far away as Komodo and it has to be salted to prevent decay.

Historical background

Little is known about Bima before the fourteenth century AD, but it is reasonable to assume that eastern Sumbawa has a long history of human habitation. During the Ice Ages when the sea level was much lower than today, the Indonesian islanders were linked by dry land, though sea still separated the Australian and Asian continents. Hunter-gatherers passed down this land bridge and some went on to make the sea-crossing to New Guinea and Australia between 60,000 and 40,000 years ago. Sumbawa lay along this route and was almost certainly settled by proto-Australian peoples, though sustained archaeological research has yet to be undertaken on the island. The inhabitants of Sumbawa are predominantly farmers and fishermen, but some coastal dwellers continue to supplement their incomes by hunting and foraging on small outlying islands. They take along their hunting dogs in their canoes to forage on offshore islands, a reminder, perhaps, of how dogs were originally introduced to Australia from South-East Asia.

The populations that remained in the archipelago mingled with later arrivals from the Asian mainland, most notably the speakers of Austronesian languages. The ancestors of the Austronesians are thought to have originated in southern China and to have come to Indonesia via the Philippines between 2000 and 500 BC. Not only were the Austronesians adventurous seafarers, they were also farmers who knew the arts of pottery and weaving. The distribution of Austronesian languages overlaps with that of a rectangular axe culture and Robert von Heine-Geldern was the first person to link the languages to these artefacts (1932). H.R. van Heekeren, however, has warned against associating the spread of languages with migrations, especially since the origins of the Austronesians remain unclear

Fig. 5 Harvest in the village of Salama.
The rice is stored on sheaves in granaries.

Fig. 6 Locked rice granaries with rat baffles.

(1957). Interaction between different peoples, as well as migration, could have facilitated the spread of Austronesian languages, and trade was also undoubtedly important. Although it remains uncertain when Austronesian languages were introduced to Sumbawa, it is clear that they must have replaced any pre-existing languages since all the indigenous languages are Austronesian.

Bimanese is a member of the Central Malayo-Polynesian branch and is thus related to the Austronesian languages of Nusa Tenggara, the southern and central Moluccas, the Aru islands in the east and the Sulu archipelago in the north-west. The distribution of these groups suggests that the settlement of Indonesia by speakers of Austronesian languages involved at least two major north-south migrations, one into Borneo and Sulawesi, the other into the northern Moluccas. The latter branch may have split into the Central and Eastern divisions, giving rise to the languages of eastern Indonesia and Polynesia. Some of the descendants of the Eastern branch appear to have remained in the northern Moluccas and the neighbouring parts of New Guinea, whereas the others fanned out to settle the furthest reaches of the Pacific. The ancestors of the Central group may have spread southwards and then westwards across Nusa Tenggara, where their expansion was eventually blocked by the Western Malayo-Polynesian languages. Bimanese marks the limit of the westwards distribution of the Central Malayo-Polynesian languages (Blust 1984: 30).

Contact between the peoples of the archipelago and the Asian mainland in later periods may also have led to the transfer of material culture. The angular and maze-like patterns that appear on Indonesian artefacts, notably textiles, have been compared with the so-called Dong-son type. The geometric Dong-son designs appear on bronze kettle drums which are associated with a culture which flourished in northern Vietnam around two thousand years ago. Kettle drums of this type have been found in many locations throughout the archipelago, one of the most recent discoveries having been on the island of Sanggiang just off the north coast of Bima. In 1983 Dr Henri Chambert-Loir, who was working with the Archaeological Centre in Jakarta, unearthed a two thousand year old kettledrum, which is now in the National Museum. Although von Heine-Geldern linked the Dong-son designs to patterns which survive today (1937), ornamental designs which pre-date those of Dong-son have been found on pottery from Kalanay Cave in the

Philippines, Manuggal Cave in Palawan and Lie Srie Cave in Timor (Barnes 1989: 132). Dong-son is no longer seen as the source of these designs and is thought to be part of a continuum within a wider South-East Asian context.

In the absence of the appropriate documentary or archaeological evidence it is not possible to say much about eastern Sumbawa's early history. The first reference to Bima occurs in the *Nagarakertagama*, a fourteenth century poem composed by Pranpanca, a courtier in the Kingdom of Majapahit (AD 1293 - c.1520). This Kingdom was the last in a succession of Hindu dynasties which had tried to consolidate their control over Java and neighbouring islands. The poem lists Majapahit's tributaries and Bima is mentioned along with three other places on Sumbawa: Dompu, Sapé and Taliwang (Pigeaud 1962: 33). It seems likely that Bima with its good natural harbour would have been established as a port-of-call along the old spice trade route long before the rise of Majapahit. Eastern Sumbawa also possessed commodities, such as sappanwood, which were in demand in Java, and it would appear that Bima was gradually drawn into the Javanese sphere of influence. The *Nagarakertagama* probably lists the places the Javanese knew about through trade and it seems unlikely that Majapahit exercised effective political control over all the places mentioned.

There are a few Javanese remains in Bima that date from the pre-Islamic era. One of the most important of these is a large carved boulder, known as Wadu Tunti, which was described by Rouffaer in 1910 and van Naerssen in 1938 (Noorduyn 1987: 94). Eprigraphists have so far been unable to completely decipher the inscription on the stone and hesitantly classify it as late Old Javanese. A seated dignitary wearing a *wayang*-style head-dress is depicted on the stone, along with three smaller human figures and an animal. The seated figure has one hand raised, while two of the smaller figures crouch before him with their palms pressed together in what may be a Hindu greeting. The other small man is shown holding a pole which may have suported an umbrella, a symbol of authority. The boulder is located near the village of Padendé and according to local tradition is associated with Gaja Mada, the prime minister of Majapahit, and is the scene of 'ghostly apparitions' (Just 1986: 95).

A second inscription, in what seems to be Sanskrit script, has been reported at Wadu Paa by Henri Cambert-Loir (1985: 91). Wadu Paa is situated beside a spring on the shore of a small inlet close to the mouth of Bima Bay (cf. Rouffaer). It comprises a low cliff, roughly 2.3 m high, which has two niches and panels with small pillar-like relief carvings. There is a second carved cliff, which also has niches and a small chamber flanked by columns, the entrance to which has been blocked by a landslide. There are more carved recesses behind a small ridge, including a badly worn representation of a standing human (approximately 70 cm high) and a seated figure (approximately 49 cm high). Although the second figure is badly eroded, the lower part of the face projects outwards, suggestive of a mask or trunk, a depiction perhaps of the Hindu elephant god Ganesha. These carvings resemble shrines from east Java and are possibly associated with the veneration of Bima in the late Majapahit period (see, for example, Stutterheim 1956: 114). The fact that Wadu Paa is located beside a source of fresh water near the entrance to a port may link the spread of Javanese influence to maritime trade.

According to the Bimanese dynastic myth the royal family of Bima also has Javanese origins. The first King of Bima was a son of Sang Bima who, after conquering Java, sent his sons to eastern Sumbawa. This myth is only known in its post-Islamic form, though there are local versions (Chambert-Loir 1985: 77-82). Some of the popular versions resemble the legends of the prince and the naga princess which are found elsewhere in South-East Asia. According to one version, for example, Sang Bima is said to have been shipwrecked on the island of Satonda where he became the consort of a golden dragon woman. The princess gave birth to two sons, Indera Jambrut and Indera Kemala, who were endowed with magical powers and were thus able to fly to Bima on reaching maturity. The two brothers landed on a rock near the village of Dara, where the local *ncuhi* (chief) paid homage to them and invited the princes to live there. The rock of Dara is still regarded as sacred and an ancient kris, known as a *kris majapahit*, is kept in the nearby village. What is also interesting is that the Sang Bima legend is widely accepted by educated Bimanese as a mythical account of Bima's incorporation into the empire of Majapahit (cf. Just 1986: 93).

Although Bima was commercially and culturally linked to the islands to the west, notably Java, the situation changed radically with the coming of Islam. The new religion was introduced from Makassar in the seventeenth century and for the next century Bima's court culture was oriented northwards to southern Sulawesi. The local sources concerning the Islamization of eastern Sumbawa are incomplete and, in order to decide when these events took place, it is necessary to refer to contemporary Makasar and European sources. Noorduyn, for example, has argued that this process was not completed in 1640, as Bimanese sources claim, but almost two decades earlier (1987: 338-339). The Bimanese chronicle, *Bo*, was written long after these events took place and it would appear that names and dates have become confused. Some Bimanese records do, however, fit well with other sources as is the case with the Bimanese story of the accession of Abdul Kahir, the first Sultan of Bima. According to this story the Sultanate was founded in 1621 and therefore the establishment of Islam may be linked to the decisive Makasar expedition of 1619 (Noorduyn 1987: 339).

Although the Makasars introduced Islam by force of arms, the Malays also played a crucial role. The Malays were among the first Indonesian peoples to accept Islam because this religion was introduced along the trade routes to Sumatra via the Coromandel Coast and Malabar. By the 9th and 10th centuries AD the Arabs were exploring the furthest reaches of the Indian Ocean and their exploits were captured in both scholarly and popular works, most notably the group of stories known as 'The Voyages of Sinbad of the Sea'. Some of them were educated men who fled Gulf cities such as Hadramaut to escape the political strife in the Arab world. Their legacy includes Arabian administrative and mercantile loan words (e.g. *wakil* and *wali*) in Malay-Indonesian, the trading *lingua franca* of the archipelago. The Arabs became established in ports throughout Indonesia and their fortunes became intermingled with coastal Malays who were also traders and seafarers. Like the Arabs the Malays had their own extensive trading networks and, following their conversion to Islam in the 13th and 14th centuries, they played an important role as Muslim prosyletisers, especially in eastern Indonesia. It is not surprising therefore that when the Sultan of Makassar wanted to bring Bima into the Islamic fold he called upon the services of Malay intermediaries. Malay emissaries were sent to Bima where they established a settlement close to the capital which later became the centre of Islamic instruction in eastern Sumbawa (Syamsuddin 1980: 297).

As a consequence of their defeat the Bimanese had to pay an annual tribute to Makassar. Although the nature of these payments is not recorded, they probably comprised the principal products of the island: sappanwood dye, cloth and horses (Noorduyn 1987: 319). As vassals the Bimanese may also have been obliged to supply auxiliary troops for wars waged by their overlord. The presence of slaves from Sumbawa in the ranks of the Makasars is mentioned in the *Sja'ir Perang Mengkasar* (Skinner 1963:149). Bimanese-Makasar relationships were soon put to the test during the long struggle with the Dutch for control over the spice trade. The Dutch initially avoided attacking the powerful mercantile city of Makassar, but in 1660 they succeeded in storming one of the city's redoubts and forcing a treaty on the Sultan. The Dutch, however, attempted to curtail the Makasars' involvement in the spice trade and the agreement was soon broken and hostilities were resumed. The Dutch exploited local enmities and joined forces with the Bugis, the rivals of Makassar. Using reinforcements from Ternate and local Bugis troops, the Dutch admiral, Cornelius J. Speelman, crushed Makasar resistance in 1668 (Hall 1976: 321-322). The Dutch consolidated their control by blockading the port of Bima and preventing aid from reaching Makassar.

The Dutch emerged as the foremost mercantile power in the archipelago, after the collapse of Makassar and rapidly enlarged their trading network. The VOC established a trading fort in Bima, the site of which is still called Benteng (fort), and maintained a permanent presence in eastern Sumbawa from 1701 onwards (Jasper 1908: 70-74). Despite Dutch supremacy the Makasar-Bimanese relationship endured and was strengthened by a dynastic marriage. In 1727 a Bimanese prince married a Makasar princess and, as part of the dowry, the Bimanese acquired the overlordship of Manggarai in neighbouring West Flores (Noorduyn 1987: 54). The acquisition of Manggarai greatly enhanced Bima's reputation, though it remains unclear how much control they really exercised over West Flores. During the eighteenth century Bima assumed the role of the leading kingdom of Sumbawa, especially since its most powerful rival, the Sultanate of Sumbawa, was severely weakened by the depredations of the Balinese kingdom of Gelgel (Goethals 1961: 10-12).

In addition to the threat from Bali, the Sultanate of Sumbawa had to cope with the constant scourge of piracy. This is partly because the western peninsula of the island has few natural defences and is therefore more vulnerable to sea-borne raids than Bima. The situation appears to have deteriorated in the wake of the Dutch defeat of Makassar when the ranks of local pirates were swelled with refugees from southern Sulawesi (cf. Ricklefs 1981: 63). Despite its

defences, Bima was also affected, and the Bimanese chronicle
mentions the help provided by the Malays in driving off some of
these predators (Syamsuddin 1980: 296). The Dutch also tried to deal
with the problem, but their efforts to enlist Bimanese help were not
always successful, perhaps because of Bima's continuing links with
Makassar. Raiding remained a problem until well into the nineteenth
century, and when Zollinger visited he was told that pirates
sometimes sheltered in Biu Bay near Tambora (Zollinger 1856: 237).
He also reported abandoned rice fields and villages in the south-east,
deserted because of the fear of piracy (ibid.: 241).

Bima remained the leading court on Sumbawa throughout the
nineteenth century. The Sultanate retained its grip on Manggarai and
claimed suzerainty over the island of Sumba to the south. The
relationship between the Sultanate of Bima and Sumba dates from
the third quarter of the 17th century (Needham 1987:21). In 1675 the
Dutch came to an agreement with the Sultan of Bima concerning the
purchase of sandalwood, providing Bima renounced its claim to
Sumba (ibid.: 22). Mamboru in north-west Sumba, however,
maintained links with Bima and even had a special quarter where the
Bimanese built themselves houses (ibid.). Not only were the
Bimanese accomplished traders but they were also brave soldiers and
fought in West Flores and Sumba. Through trade with the Dutch they
acquired firearms, though they continued to rely on their traditional
light cavalry and foot soldiers armed with spears, shields and kris. A
ditty to be sung by young women as the men prepared for war
serves as a reminder of this martial heritage:

> *Didi ku kisi*
> *Mampanggé di tendé*

In the refrain the women urge the men to go forward in battle so that
arrows in their shields can be brought back and used as heddles.

After the defeat of Makassar the VOC was content to protect its
interests in eastern Sumbawa through a series of agreements, known
as 'contracts', with the Sultans of Bima. Trade was channelled
through the company's fort and European settlement was largely
restricted to the coast. The contracts were revised periodically and
new terms and conditions were added, a practice that continued into
the colonial era. In 1798 the imminent collapse of the VOC on the
Amsterdam stock exchange prompted the Dutch government to take

control over its assets - the Netherlands East Indies was born (Hall 1976: 342). The emerging colonial power did not initially have any imperial ambitions in Sumbawa and Dutch-Bimanese relations continued to be defined by contract throughout the nineteenth century.

The situation changed in 1905 when Bima was incorporated into the Netherlands East Indies. Sultan Ibrahim remained in control of local affairs but had to relinquish his rights to foreign trade; taxes also had to be paid to the colonial authorities. Transition to colonial rule did not pass smoothly and rebellions broke out as the news spread. Ambonese troops were brought in to quell the uprisings and, according to local sources, a Dutch officer was killed in a skirmish near the village of Nggali (Ahmad Amin 1971: 13). The highlanders of Donggo also refused to recognise the new regime, and the story of how a punitive expedition was lured into an ambush near Kala has been recorded by Peter Just. Resistance eventually petered out, and Bima remained under colonial jurisdiction until the Japanese invasion of 1942. There were, however, periodic outbreaks of strife and in the nineteen thirties the Dutch exiled the Bimanese prime minister, Abdul Hamid, to Timor to prevent him from challenging the Sultan's authority.

The Dutch ruled their maritime empire from Batavia (now Jakarta) in West Java and Bimanese cultural life and trade was reoriented to the west. A regular steamship service from Surabaya was introduced and seaplanes landed in Bima Bay in order to re-fuel. The colonial regime also re-drew local borders and the modern boundaries are largely based on those set down by the Dutch. Manggarai and Komodo were removed from Bimanese control and were placed under the jurisdiction of the Resident of Timor, while Sanggar and Dompu were annexed by Bima (Ahmad Amin 1971: 10-15). Work also began on a highway across Sumbawa to link together the major commercial and administrative centres. But before the road could be completed the island was overrun by the Japanese.

Although the Bimanese were awed by the military might of the Japanese occupying forces, they were shocked by their excesses. Bimanese women were harassed on the streets by Japanese soldiers and some were taken to work in military brothels. The Bimanese, however, do speak of the kindness which ordinary soldiers showed towards local children. Bima lay on the outer limit of the Japanese conquest of South-East Asia; and there were supply problems and imperial troops were reduced to foraging for themselves. As part of their war effort the Japanese attempted to boost cotton production; such was the demand for yarn that Bimanese men were forced to take up spinning, normally a female occupation. *Sirih* (betel) sets were melted down to make brass cartridges, much to the dismay of the islanders for whom these possessions had greater ceremonial significance. The Japanese occupation was mercifully shortlived. In 1945 the Royal Australian Air Force bombed Japanese military installations and leaflets were dropped, written in Malay and English, announcing the Allies' intention to restore the government of the Sultan of Bima and the Netherlands East Indies. The Sultan, who had evaded capture by hiding in the valleys near Dodu, returned to the capital after it was liberated by the Australians.

Colonial rule was never effectively restored and, following rumours that the Japanese had capitulated, three Indonesian nationalist leaders, Sukarno, Hatta and Wediodiningrat, proclaimed Indonesia's independence on 17 August 1945. The British were responsible for occupying Indonesia but because of the shortage of transport were unable to begin moving their troops until the end of September. The Allies were also overwhelmed by the problems that confronted them: in addition to disarming 283,000 Japanese soldiers, they had to cope with 200,000 Allied prisoners of war and Dutch internees (Hall 1976: 850). The proclamation of independence was followed by similar declarations on the other islands as news spread from Java. In Bima, supporters of independence gathered in a school room and swore allegiance to the nationalists' cause. Despite Dutch attempts to hive off eastern Indonesia from the new nation through the creation of a puppet state, Negara Indonesia Timur, Bima joined the Republic of Indonesia in 1950. The last Sultan, Muhammed Salahuddin, died shortly afterwards, but his son Abdul Kahir was persuaded to remain in Java by the nationalists. The discontinuation of the royal line is said to fulfil the ancient prophecy that the Sultanate of Bima was destined to last from Abdul Kahir to Abdul Kahir (Just 1986: 60).

Bima remained a *swapraja* (autonomous region) within the republic until 1958, when it became part of the newly-organised province of Nusa Tenggara Barat. Abdul Kahir returned as *Bupati* (district head) in 1960 and, though popular with the people of Bima, many of whom retain a great affection for the royal family, did not find favour with the national administration. In 1964 Abdul Kahir was recalled to take up a job in the Ministry of the Interior in Jakarta, and in the following year Indonesia entered its worst period of post-colonial strife. Abdul Kahir's Bimanese successor was unable to maintain order in the chaos which followed the alleged communist coup in Jakarta, and communists and suspected sympathisers were turned on with great ferocity. The army under General Suharto restored order and since then all the district heads have been military men from outside Bima. Abdul Kahir, however, re-appeared for the 1983 general election when he stood as a candidate for the government's party to undercut the local popularity of the Islamic party (Just 1986: 66). He entered parliament with a substantial majority.

III

Trade and Islam

The adoption of Islam in Bima and the neighbouring kingdoms on Sumbawa in the 17th century, is closely linked to the history of Makassar. Indigenous sources record that Islam was introduced to Bima by the Kingdom of Goa by force of arms not long after they themselves had been converted to Islam. After Islamizing the greater part of the peninsula of South Sulawesi between 1605 and 1611, the Makasars turned their attention to the south and sent expeditions against the rulers of Sumbawa (Noorduyn 1987: 312). Although the records on the Bimanese side are confused, it would appear that the Islamization of eastern Sumbawa was effected shortly after the decisive Makasar attack of 1619 (ibid. 339). The extent to which Bima was Islamized around this time remains unclear, but the fact that the monarch adopted Islam means that it was not just a personal but state act. The accession of Sultan Abdul Kahir marks the beginning of the Islamization of the whole area. By becoming a Sultan, Abdul Kahir became a member of an exclusive circle of Muslim rulers.

What is significant about the conversion of Bima is the way in which this new faith almost entirely supplanted all other belief systems. According to royal genealogists, Bima was ruled by a succession of Hindu rajahs; generations of Hindu-Buddhist traditions were swept away with the adoption of Islam. While it remains uncertain whether the Islamization of Bima occurred rapidly, as local sources would have it, or was a much more protracted affair, the fact remains that little of eastern Sumbawa's Hindu-Buddhist heritage has survived, other than a few place names and crumbling effigies. Why was the transformation so complete? Some insights into what happened in Bima can perhaps be drawn from the example of Java where Islam also triumphed. Mark Woodward, for instance, has argued that Islam achieved predominance not only because of the lack of a strongly developed caste system, but also because Islam became the state religion (1989: 54). Hindu hereditary castes, ranked according to degrees of purity and impurity and often with members following the same trades did not become firmly established in Indonesia. 5-6% of the population of Bali bear hereditary titles and are equivalent to the twice born castes of India, but Geertz has argued that this is in reality a system of titles (Geertz 1959). Something similar seems to have taken place in Bima. Although we do not know how deeply the Bimanese were influenced by Hindu-Buddhism, we do know that Islam became the official faith with the accession of Abdul Kahir. It also seems likely that the Bimanese were exposed to the Javanese version of Hinduism because they had little direct contact with India. The Bimanese did, however, have well-established trade links with Java, and it is perhaps more helpful to regard the island as having been Javanised rather than Hinduised before the adoption of Islam.

The promise of enhanced trade opportunities may also have helped the Islamic cause in Bima. Through the work of the *ulama*, the experts on contracts, Islam provided a legal framework that was good for business. Islam began as a trader's religion in Indonesia, having arrived in the archipelago possibly as early as the 8th century. The religion appears to have been introduced via the south-east coast of India to the islands of Indonesia. South Indian and Gujarati Muslim merchants and seafarers became established in North-East Sumatra whence the religion spread eastward to the other coastal areas of Indonesia. The religion was adopted by the rulers of mercantile states and, encircled by Muslim principalities, the last major Hindu-Buddhist dynasty, Majapahit, went into a slow decline.

Strengthened by religious ties, the link between Sulawesi and Sumbawa, if not always peaceful, proved to be longlasting, and it is not surprising that both Makasar and Bugis influences can be detected in Bima. Certain material cultural features, for example, such as the panelled walls and roof trusses of Bimanese houses appear to have originated in southern Sulawesi, as did the distinctive pink and mushroom-coloured checked Bimanese sarongs. Many

Bimanese kris resemble those of southern Sulawesi, and it seems likely that both trade and the formation of political alliances led to the exchange of ceremonial weapons. Certain Bimanese titles (e.g. *dieng* - lord; *gelarang* - village headman) are derived from similar Makasar or Bugis titles. Moreover, according to Bimanese tradition a kind of reciprocal relationship developed in which the Bimanese travelled as merchants on Makasar ships in order to trade in the islands of eastern Indonesia. Although Bima became oriented to the north, one should not lose sight of the wider Islamic context because the Bimanese also consolidated their links with other Muslim peoples. The Bimanese seem to have been in contact with the Muslim state of Banten in West Java and a Bantenese sheikh, known locally as Umar al Bantami, is popularly credited with converting many Bimanese to Islam. According to folk histories, an Arab called Sheik Maubarak was also involved in the conversion of Bima. Perhaps the most important people in this regard were the Malays who not only served as go-betweens for the rulers of Bima, but also established permanent settlements in Sumbawa.

The Malays

The Malays were among the most influential of the various seafaring peoples who settled along the coast of eastern Sumbawa from the seventeenth century onwards. In contrast to other maritime groups such as the Makasars, the Malay contribution to Bimanese culture has received comparatively little attention (see for example Gittinger 1979: 153 and Just 1986: 105). While it remains unclear precisely when the Malays first came to eastern Sumbawa, it would appear that they were closely associated with the Makasars, at least initially. According to Bimanese chronicles two Muslim teachers, Datuk Dibanda(ng) and Datuk Ditiro, came to Bima as emissaries of the Sultan of Goa. The teachers were not Makasars but Malays from Sumatra, Dibanda being a Minangkabau nobleman (Syamsuddin 1980: 294-296). Local folk histories also mention a Sumatran called Raja Lelo who came to Bima to teach Islam via Sulawesi, and Ahmad Amin refers to a man called Muballiq-Muballiq in this context (Ahmad Amin 1971: 9); but precise date and nature of their activities remain obscure. These teachers seem to have been followed by other Malays whose numbers must have been reasonably substantial because they managed to establish villages on the western and southern shores of Bima Bay, as well as near the capital. Although the Bimanese records are open to interpretation, there are indications that the Malays did not want to be confused with the Makasars, despite their close links. The Malays appear to have regarded themselves as staunch allies of the Bimanese and the chronicle refers to the help provided by the Malays in driving off pirates from the coast of Sumbawa (Syamsuddin 1980: 297). These pirates were most probably Makasars whose numbers had been swelled by refugees from the defeated kingdom of Goa-Tallo.

The Malays may have become rivals of the Makasars because, like the mariners from Sulawesi, they depended on the sea for a living. The Bimanese records show, for example, that when the Sultan offered the Malays rice fields, they declined politely, saying that they were sailors and traders and not farmers (Syamsuddin 1980: 296). The Malays clearly found favour with the Bimanese court as, in addition to the offer of agricultural land, the Bimanese chronicle mentions other privileges. The Malays were given the right to organise their affairs according to Islamic law and were granted exemption from taxation on their merchandise. In recognition of the services they had provided, the land on which the main Malay settlement was built was granted to them in perpetuity (it is still known as Melayu) (Syamsuddin 1980: 296-297). The Malay quarter became the centre of Islamic education where young Bimanese went to learn to recite the Koran. A children's song translated by Helius Syamsuddin recalls this tradition:

- Satusamasatu.	- Satusamasatu (sic.) [one with one].
- Mu lao ta be?	- Where are you going?
- Lao weha elaku ese Semili	- I am going to fetch my friend at Samili.
- Di au-mu ela?	- Why do you need a friend?
- Di ma muna wea-ku tembe teja	- I need a friend in order to weave me a sarong *teja*.
- Di au-mu tembé teja?	- Why do you need a sarong *teja*?
- Di lao kai-ku ngaji.	- I am going to wear it to learn to recite the Koran.
- Ngaji ta be?	- Where do you want to learn to recite the Koran?
- Ipa Mbojo Malaju	- Across (the bay of) Bima at the Kampong Melayu (the Malay Kampong).
	(Syamsuddin 1980: 292).

Although the mosque in the middle of the capital eventually replaced the Malay quarter as the centre of Islamic instruction, the Bimanese still regard the settlement of Melayu with respect because of its association with Islam. The leading role played by the Malays in converting the islanders to Islam is commemorated by a festival held in honour of the Prophet's birthday. Known as *sirih puan* (betel dish), this festival flourished until the outbreak of the Second World War (Damsté 1941), but was discontinued in the postcolonial era. It was revived briefly in the early 1980s, but proved difficult to hold regularly because of the expense involved. The festival begins early in the morning when four girls, wearing jewellery and brocade sarongs, are taken by sedan chair to the village of Melayu. The girls, who represent royal handmaidens, are joined by four boys from the Malay quarter, and then both groups are borne to the palace as part of a large procession. On arrival the children perform a series of dances, after which the assembled company is invited by a man taking the part of the Sultan to partake of refreshments. The members of the procession are seated in three rows representing the three-fold division of power in the old Sultanate of Bima.

Another symbolic representation of this threefold division of power can be seen in the capital's easternmost palace, the former residence of the prime minister. There is a carved *naga* head above the main doorway of this palace, behind which lies a pole representing the backbone or body of the dragon. The naga belongs to the island's pre-Islamic tradition and its continued use is significant. Like Islamic rulers elsewhere in the archipelago the Bimanese did not completely lose touch with their non-Muslim heritage; the naga not only provided continuity with the past, but represented a continuing bond with neighbouring non-Muslim peoples.

The naga pole carries the roof of the palace's entrance chamber and is supported by three carved pillars symbolising: *sara* (administration), *hukum* (Islamic law) and *adat* (customary law). According to Bimanese tradition, the senior officials in each of these divisions exercised a certain amount of independence, though the Sultan retained overall authority for the affairs of state. In theory, the most powerful person after the Sultan was the prime minister; he was responsible for the first of these divisions, *sara* or administration. The prime minister was referred to as the Sultan's younger brother, *ari ba raja*, though he was usually not related and the post was not hereditary. Descent, however, was important since prime ministers were not elected but were chosen from among the ranks of the higher nobility by common assent. The two other divisions appear to have had a more advisory role and were not greatly involved in the day-to-day administration of the state, though they were expected to pronounce on religious and legal matters. The specialists in Islamic jurisprudence, many of whom were of Malay descent, were based in the central mosque, whereas the head of customary law resided in the village of Dara, the arrival point of the mythical founders of the royal dynasty of Bima.

The Malay community comprised not only merchants and missionaries, but also scribes who revolutionised Bimanese record-keeping through the introduction of the Malay language and Arabic script, *jawi*. The Bimanese had their own script, which resembles the Bugis-Makasar script, but this was replaced by *jawi* as the Malays became responsible for compiling the Bimanese chronicles known collectively as *Bo*, a name which is etymologically related to the Malay *tambo* meaning 'annals'. The Malays also served as go-betweens and drafted the various treaties and trade agreements which the Sultans of Bima negotiated with the Dutch. The rulers of Bima realised that in order to communicate effectively with either foreign traders or neighbouring Indonesians they had to use Malay, the emerging *lingua franca* of the archipelago. The royal family themselves began to learn Malay and when the Swiss explorer Zollinger visited the island in the 19th century he was able to report that Sultan Ismail spoke it fluently (1850: 18). The use of Malay also expanded the Bimanese's cultural horizons since it brought them into contact with the wider world of Malay literature and poetry. The epic poem concerning the kingdom of Bima, *Syair Kerajaan Bima*, was composed around 1830 by Khatib Lukman. The poem was written in Malay and a copy was made in 1857 for the Dutch resident, Meneer Misor, of the trade fort near Bima Bay. The *syair* (narrative poem) comprises 487 stanzas and resembles other Malay texts of the same period, especially those of Java and Sumatra (Chambert-Loir 1982: 73-74). Despite Bima's distance from the main centres of Malay culture, the author of the *syair* was not divorced from what was happening elsewhere in the Malay world.

The Malays of Bima, many of whom intermarried with local families, served as the state record keepers for many generations.

What remains unclear, however, is precisely when they were incorporated into the Sultanate's administrative system and how they were remunerated for their services. It was the Bimanese custom to allocate paddy fields to Sultanate officials in lieu of payment; but the chronicles relate that when the Malays were offered irrigated land they steadfastly refused it and retained their connection with the sea. But in spite of their independence, some Malays were given the Bimanese noble titles of *bumi* and *dari* (Syamsuddin 1980: 297) and these resemble the titles of Sultanate officials in later periods (see Ahmad Amin 1971: 61-67). Scribes seem to have been held in as high esteem as other Sultanate professionals such as precious metal-smiths, royal carpenters and other court officials. Although the Malays do not appear to have had access to government land in the early days of settlement, perhaps their exemption from taxation on trade provided more than adequate compensation. Despite their initial reluctance to farm land, what is clear is that some of the descendants of the original Malay seafarers eventually acquired irrigated rice fields, often through judicious marriages with Bimanese families.

The Malay legacy in Bima is considerable, particularly with regard to language and literature. Most town dwellers speak *Bahasa Indonesia*, the modern form of Indonesian Malay, as well as Bimanese. Local poets and playwrights are also bilingual and use both languages in their creative work. Malay elements can be detected in the musical traditions of eastern Sumbawa: *lenggo*, one of the most esteemed court dances is said to be of Sumatran origin and Bimanese shawms, *surunai* resemble those played by Malays. Through their contact with the Malays and other seafaring peoples, the Bimanese were drawn into the wider world of maritime South-East Asia. For example, the pan-Indonesian tree-of-life symbol is used in coastal areas to herald the arrival of a newborn child. Hangings decorated with couched thread are suspended above the baby's bed; the bed posts symbolise trees and the hangings, the leaves. Fish mobiles are also hung above the bed, so that the child will have enough to eat, and moon mobiles are displayed to ensure the adoption of Islam in adulthood. Like maritime Muslims throughout the archipelago, the lowland Bimanese weave brocade textiles decorated with gold and silver yarn and make fine filigree jewellery. The ubiquitous checked sarong, worn by Muslim seafarers from the coast of East Africa to the ports of eastern Indonesia, is also popular in Bima.

Fig. 7 Mosque in Sumbawa Besar.

Fig. 8 A Bugis *pinisi* in Bima Bay.

The coastal economy

Although the Malays have largely been assimilated, coastal society is still heterogeneous and Bima Bay continues to be used as a port-of-call by ships from all over the archipelago. Some of the most commonly seen are ships such as the Madurese *leti-leti*, with its curved lines and lateen rigged sails, and the fore-and-aft rigged *lambo* from south-west Sulawesi. But perhaps the most frequent visitor is the Buginese *pinisi* with its steeply-raked masts and thrusting bowsprit. The *pinisi* is a ferry-cum-cargo ship which is used for transporting anything from copra to water buffalo between Indonesia's numerous islands. It has a shallow draught and is suitable for small ports and rivers and, though quite broad in the beam, it usually has elegant lines. Not all the *pinisi* in Bima harbour hail from southern Sulawesi, since many are built by itinerant Bugis and Makasar shipwrights around Bima Bay.

Surrounded by huge logs and bundles of sappanwood, the shipwrights work beneath the shade of a thatched awning. They split great balks of timber on the ground with the aid of wedges or cut them to size using two man saws and a sawing platform. Straight timbers are curved with the aid of hot embers and powerful levers, and adzes are used to transform the rough wood into the gracious lines of the ship. The sides of the hull are gradually built-up on an iron wood keel with planks that slot on to specially prepared sappanwood pegs, each section being caulked and driven into place with massive mallets. Sappanwood is thought to be lucky, and the Bugis sailors are reputed to drink a beverage made of it to give them courage. The ribs are added later to strengthen the hull; thus when one peers over the edge of a ship nearing completion one sees a network of knees and ribs making its way up the inside. When finished, the hull is given a coat of lime mixed with coconut milk which is pressed into the wood with bare hands. Additional protection from wood-boring sea creatures is provided by several layers of marine paint. The *pinisi* is then floated down a specially dug channel to the bay, with empty oil drums strapped to its sides as stabilisers. The shipwrights gather on the eve of the launch to share a ritual meal of sticky rice. Only if the launch is successful are the rigging and cabin added. With its high topsails, gaff sails and jibs, the distinctive *pinisi* is well-adapted to the prevailing conditions of the Java and Flores seas and is popular because of its versatility

(Horridge 1981). The modern *pinisi* is usually equipped with an engine and, being broad in the beam, is less elegant than it used to be.

The double-hulled *bagan* is another sailing craft that is commonly seen around Bima Bay. The separate hulls are joined together by transverse beams and usually comprise dugout canoes with raised washstrakes to keep out the water. Each hull may be equipped with a small mast and sail to enable the *bagan* to sail out to the fishing grounds. The *bagan* is often moored at sea and the crew sleeps in a cramped cabin on the platform between the hulls. A large windlass is used to raise the net and small launches visit the *bagan* to take the catch to market. Following the introduction of the engine, a single-hulled version of the *bagan* was developed, and many of these can be seen in the Straits of Sapé (Horridge 1981). The Bimanese outrigger canoe may also be used for fishing; like the *bagan*, it is essentially a dugout with raised sides. The outriggers are lashed to the main structure and comprise a pair of straight booms, to which floats are attached by means of curved elbows. A curved crutch, often elaborately carved, is used to hold the rudder, and the tilted rectangular sail may be moved around to take advantage of variable breezes. Plastic string bindings have, however, replaced traditional materials and sails are often patched with the remnants of gunny sacks. Indonesian sailors plan voyages across the Java and Flores seas with reference to the monsoons, while inshore fishermen make use of local changes in the air flow between the land and sea.

Sea fishing has long been one of the island's most important economic activities. Seafood is sold in all the lowland markets and is sometimes taken by peddlars to remote highland areas. In addition to many varieties of small fish, the islanders eat sharks, swordfish and rays, shrimps, prawns, crabs, squid and the occasional octopus. The fishing industry is not, however, solely the preserve of the mixed coastal populations since many inland Bimanese also engage in fishing. Their equipment comprises gill nets with bamboo floats, dip nets and barbed hooks and lines, and they can be seen wending their way through lowland villages at dusk with their lamps. The involvement of inland peoples in fishing dates back to pre-independence times when, according to Sultanate law, both sea and river fish were free. But fish trapped in weirs belonged to the owners of the land beside the river banks and therefore many poorer people resorted to sea fishing to supplement their diet.

Fish like rice is a symbol of plentitude and farming and fishing are accorded equal status in Bimanese culture. But, as the following story from the Sang Bima legend illustrates, fishing is a hazardous operation involving skill and luck. The story concerns the underwater adventures of one of the sons of Sang Bima and explains why a particularly delicious fish, known as a *tampoli*, is difficult to catch.

> Shortly after their arrival on the island the two brothers, Indera Jambrut and Indera Kemala, began to receive instruction from the headman of the village of Dara. Jambrut learned how to farm and Kemala to fish; but Jambrut became impatient to learn his brother's skill and borrowed his hook. Jambrut, however, lost the hook when a large sea creature broke his line. Jambrut went below the waves in pursuit of the hook where he met some agitated shrimps. The shrimps told him that their king, a whale, was sick and Jambrut swiftly realised that the hook was the cause of the problem. Jambrut offered to cure the king and a fish, known as a *pari*, agreed to take him to the whale on the condition that his descendants would never eat the *pari* (a taboo observed by the royal family). On reaching the whale's court, Jambrut craftily persuaded the fish courtiers that the cure would only work if they shut their eyes. Believing that he was not observed, Jambrut removed the hook and concealed it, and then held up a piece of seaweed as the culprit. But a suspicious fish, known as a *tampoli*, kept his eyes open and witnessed the removal of the hook - to this day the Bimanese have difficulty in catching the *tampoli*.

Bima Bay, though still a source of much of the capital's fresh fish, is gradually silting up. Fishermen may, therefore, go as far as Komodo to fish, though the catch often has to be salted to survive the return journey (Hitchcock, 1993: 309). Seafood may be used in soup, grilled over a charcoal brazier, deep-fried in coconut oil or stir-fried in a wok, with garlic, peppers and soya sauce as condiments.

In addition to fishing and ship-building, trade has long been a mainstay of the economy of Bima. Indonesian trading patterns are very ancient and it seems likely that, given its strategic location, Bima, has a long history as a port-of-call. Although little is known about pre-Islamic Bima, it is reasonable to assume that it enjoyed trade relations with other Indonesian islands, most notably Java. Eastern Indonesian products are mentioned in Old Javanese sources: these probably included Bimanese commodities such as sappanwood and sandalwood. Eastern Sumbawa was also drawn in to the Kingdom of Majapahit's sphere of influence, though its status in the *Nagarakertagama* as a tributary may well reflect economic rather than purely political factors, since Bima traded with Java. It seems likely that Bima was already well-established as a trading centre by the time the Europeans arrived in the archipelago. Writing in the 16th century, Tomé Pires noted that the shipping route from Melaka to Maluku went via Java and Bima, where the ships sold Javanese goods and purchased cloth for Banda and Maluku (Pires 1944: 206-207; Noorduyn 1987: 316). The Dutch also showed an interest in trading with Sumbawa Island since they knew that the Portuguese went to the north coast to collect dyestuffs and that it was a rice-growing region (Noorduyn 1987: 331).

In order to feed its growing personnel, the VOC needed to be assured of a continuous supply of food from local sources. Bima was not only a potential source of provisions, but also lay between the Dutch headquarters in Java and their trading posts in Malaku. The knowledge that Bima was a rice exporter proved to be invaluable when the VOC's granaries were destroyed in Java in 1618 and the Dutch were forced to look for alternative supplies in Bima and elsewhere. To help redress this setback the Dutch decided to send a succession of ships to Solor, the first of which was to drop a merchant and some men in Bima with instructions to collect rice for the ships that followed. But the men who were left behind in Bima were later murdered by Portuguese sailors, though the chief merchant survived and was later exchanged for Portuguese captives. The Dutch initially suspected the Bimanese but, on hearing the Bimanese version of events, they entered into an agreement of eternal friendship and mutual help with Bima. The agreement, which was known as the Sumpa Ncake treaty, was concluded with the Dutch near the village of Cenggu (Noorduyn 1987: 332-334).

Bima became politically oriented to the north during the seventeenth century, but it remains unclear how this affected trade with Java. The Dutch had become increasingly involved in this trade and, after the fall of Makasar, the VOC was able to strengthen its position in eastern Sumbawa. Despite the ravages of piracy, Bimanese goods continued to flow along the sea trade routes to the Dutch-controlled ports of Jakarta and Surabaya. Bimanese exports included dyestuffs and beeswax for the Javanese batik industry, handwoven textiles, lumber (especially teak), livestock, rice and other agricultural products, tamarind, honey, swiflet nests (used in Chinese cooking), sulphur and saltpetre. Modern cash crops such as coffee were introduced in the 20th century and plantations were established on the Tambora peninsula. In return the Bimanese imported European goods such as factory-spun yarns, crockery, guns and gunpowder, as well as luxury items from other Indonesian islands (e.g. Makasar silk sarongs) and alcohol (despite their Muslim faith). Eastern Indonesia provided a market for Bimanese craft products, especially silverware and pottery, and local merchants prospered on the trade in ivory, gold and pearls. Following incorporation into the Netherlands East Indies, the port of Bima continued to flourish, though Sumbawa, like many Indonesian islands, suffered badly during the depression of the 1930s. Conditions became so harsh that Bimanese potters from Raba Nggodu were forced to move east in search of work. The Japanese occupation of the Second World War provided a brief boost for the local economy, especially the cotton industry, but was offset by the depredations of the troops.

Islam in Bima

The Bimanese, like the majority of Indonesian Muslims, are Sunnis. They subscribe to the *Sunna*, the collection of laws based on Prophet Muhammad's words and deeds. As Sunni Muslims, the Bimanese oppose the Shiah branch of Islam whose predominantly Iranian adherents regard Ali as Muhammad's rightful successor and reject the authority of the first three Sunni Caliphs. Some Bimanese maintain that Shiah Muslims are not true members of the faith, though the Bimanese have little direct contact with Shiah believers. All Sunni Muslims belong to one of four schools of jurisprudence; the Bimanese, in common with most Indonesians, are followers of the School of Shafa'i. This school traces Islamic jurisprudence to divine inspiration, thereby elevating the status of the *Hadith*, the moral and legal commentaries (Guillaume 1956: 97-98). The School of Shafa'i originated in Cairo and Egyptian teachers of Islam continue to play an active role in Indonesia.

As has been mentioned, Indonesia has also strongly been influenced by Sufism and its ascetic mysticism. The spread of Sufism was accelerated by the fall of Baghdad in 1256 and Indonesia became one of a number of havens for Sufi teachers (Rauf 1964: 65-67). Saints are very important in Indonesian Islam, but these practices are not uniquely Indonesian since saints are as much part of Sufism as metaphysical speculation and the analysis of religious texts (cf. Woodward 1989). As in Java, the names and deeds of saints are well-known in Bima and this knowledge helps to unite the intellectual and popular traditions. Saints are believed to perform miracles and function as a source of blessings; Bimanese craftsmen try to emulate the example set by saints when trying to accomplish certain tasks. The Bimanese not only revere saints but stress mystical practice and experience, as well as ritual. Spritualy gifted leaders, known as syékh (sheikhs), also played a key role in the Islamization of Sumbawa.

As compared with Java, the processes by which Islam became established in Bima are reasonably well understood. Following military intervention by Makassar, Bima's last Hindu-Buddhist ruler was de-throned and Islam became the state religion. Very little of Bima's Hindu-Buddhist past has survived, perhaps because this religion was only established at the court level and never exerted much influence among the wider population. From the 17th century onwards, Bima was ruled by a succession of sultans and became one of Indonesia's most self-confessedly Muslim regions. Bimanese religion does not have a strong local identity, as is the case in Java where adherents may describe their version of Islam as *Islam Jawa* (Javanese Islam). But as in Java, Bimanese traditions include a belief in angels and jinns, and mysticism is important. Differences in religious observation are not as marked between the classes as they are in Java, though the royal family, known as the *sangaji*, whose ancestors were held to be heavenly-born, were traditionally expected to be mystics. The main divide occurs between the highlanders and lowlanders, and, if one takes Friday mosque attendance as a basis of comparison, the former are clearly less pious than the latter (Brewer 1979: 42). This division is not acknowledged in the local terminology as is the case in the neighbouring island of Lombok where orthodox Muslims are described as *waktu lima* and those who combine Islam with indigenous beliefs as *waktu telu*.

Fig. 9 Sultanate tomb in Dantaraha.

Fig. 10 Sultanate tombstone in Dantaraha.

Some indication of the strength of religious convictions in Bima can be drawn from the numbers of people making the pilgrimage, *hajj*, to Mecca. According to the Department of Religious Affairs, 750 pilgrims made the journey in 1981 at a cost of two million rupiah (£1 = Rp 1100) per person - no mean undertaking in one of Indonesia's less developed regions. Farmers sell land and household possessions in order to pay for the journey, but they defend the undertaking by saying that the outlay is soon recouped, such is the will of God. The *hajj* is accorded high prestige, and the wearer of a white pilgrim's hat exercises a great deal of authority on his or her return. The annual commencement of the pilgrimage is a major event, and on the eve of departure friends and relatives gather in the houses belonging to embarking pilgrims. Special foods are packed for consumption on the way and one dish in particular, a sweet dry porridge, is regarded as 'pilgrim's fare'. At this time of year the muster points at airports and bus stations are a sea of white. The pilgrims travel in groups to keep down the costs of transport and are not presented with many opportunities to interact with Muslims from other countries. Bimanese and Indonesian are the main languages of Islamic education in eastern Sumbawa and, though many pilgrims are able to recite passages from the Koran, few are able to speak Arabic. Many pilgrims, therefore, find that the language barrier reduces effective communication with Muslims from the Arab world. Better-educated pilgrims do, however, take the opportunity to inform themselves of the theological changes taking place in the Arab world and have long been aware of the Wahabi orientation of the Saudi regime; most return impressed by the scale and diversity of the Muslim world.

Bimanese children of both sexes receive some instruction in reading the Koran between the ages of six and ten. There is an extensive network of part-time teachers, especially in urban areas, who provide courses for small groups of children in the early evening. Islamic education is included in the curriculum of state schools where emphasis is placed on the national philosophy of *Pancasila*, which stresses religious tolerance. Some children, however, attend Islamic schools where the girls wear white veils, and are taught separately from the boys. The Koran is the word of God and its aesthetic qualities are admired and the best students go on to take part in public recitals which are very well-attended. The Bimanese value higher education and many aspire to a place at the provincial

university in Mataram or at one of the more famous universities in
Java. The range of subjects they study is diverse, though law, science
and engineering are popular. A few receive scholarships to study
abroad; the most favoured destinations being Japan, Australia and
the United States of America, the Pacific Rim nations. There are also a
small number of theology students who progress to Arab seminaries
and colleges, the Al-Ashar University at Cairo being especially
highly-regarded.

Much of Bimanese village life revolves around the mosque,
usually a lime-washed brick structure with a corrugated iron roof
and dome. Shortly before dawn the population are called to prayer
by muezzin to make the first of the five daily observances expected
of Muslims. Worshippers wash according to a prescribed formula
and then prostrate themselves on hands and knees and touch the
ground with the forehead in the direction of Mecca. They are not
obliged to go to the mosque, though many do, and may pray
wherever they happen to be: inside the home, on board a ship or in
the middle of a market. On religious holidays massed ranks of
Bimanese Muslims can be seen praying in the open square to the
west of the Sultan's palace. Although the villages are run by elected
headmen who preside over a collection of hamlets known as a *desa*,
the mosques provide an alternative administration and forum for
discussion. The mosque elders have both spiritual and temporal
duties and are responsible for supervising the collection of the
Muslim tax *zakat*, in theory one-fortieth of personal assets. In practice
they rely on donations, usually in the form of rice or cash, which are
used to maintain the mosque and provide a welfare system for the
needy.

Bimanese values and codes of behaviour have been strongly
influenced through contact with other Muslim Indonesians. The
Bimanese recognise that security and hospitality facilitate trade
within the house of Islam. In accordance with Islamic custom the
Bimanese bestow lavish hospitality on visitors, though discourteous
guests are not encouraged to overstay their welcome. Bimanese
dress is modest and the minimum requirement for men is to cover
themselves from their calves to their armpits; but shorts may be
worn when working in the rice fields or when playing sport. Women
are expected to clothe their bodies from their shoulders to their
ankles and to cover their hair in public, usually with a light gauze
scarf. Rural women coming into market may veil themselves with

checked sarongs, secured with a fold known as a *rimpi*, to preserve their modesty and to keep the dust out of their hair. The Bimanese are abstemious, and though beer, gin and palm toddy are available, they do not tolerate drunkenness and refrain from eating pork. Like good Muslims everywhere, they regard dogs and pigs as unclean, and the fact that they refrain from eating these animals is closely associated with their Muslim identity. The dog, in particular, is so distasteful that an infringement of the food taboo is given as the reason for the eruption of Tambora in a folktale from the Dompu district.

'Shortly after the islanders had been converted to Islam, a sheikh arrived from overseas at the fort of Doro Cana on the Tambora peninsula, which was ruled by the Makasars. Upon entering the local mosque, the sheikh noticed that his fellow worshippers had brought along their dogs, a practice strictly forbidden under Muslim law. The sheikh remonstrated with the local people, but they were wary of the newcomer and unconvinced by his piety. That evening they decided to test the sheikh by serving him a dish comprising the front half of a goat and the back half of a dog. After the meal the visitor was informed about what he had just eaten, whereupon the sheikh commenced praying. Suddenly the dog appeared in complete form and at that instant the sheikh vanished as the volcano erupted with God's vengeance'.

Although the Bimanese are very conscious of their Muslim identity, they have not completely abandoned their pre-Islamic heritage. It would appear, for example, that despite the adoption of Islam as the state religion, the new religion did not completely supplant existing traditions because *adat* was not always incompatible with Islam and the rulers of Bima retained the services of a specialist in customary law until well into the 20th century. After three centuries of Islamic rule, state ceremonials continued to reinforce the notion that *adat* was one of the founding principles of the Sultanate of Bima. This suggests, on first examination, that the process of Islamization sets in motion a long process of cultural change involving a struggle between the demands of Islam and what was in conflict with it. From this perspective it makes sense to write about three hundred years of

Islamization in Bima in much the same way as Ricklefs has written about 'Six centuries of Islamization in Java' (cf. Noorduyn 1987: 313). Bimanese Muslims, however, see it somewhat differently and regard their conversion to Islam, not so much as a continuing process but as a precise event with a fixed date of completion. Few educated Bimanese would dispute the fact that it took time to modify the existing corpus of beliefs and laws known as *adat*, but they do not conceive of it as a struggle to bring it in line with Islam. Islam and *adat* are not invariably mutually exclusive since they are often concerned with issues which lie outside each other's sphere of influence. There is a whole series of *adat* practices associated with herding water buffalo which do not come into conflict with Islam, because Islam has little to say on the matter. Islam is, however, pervasive, partly because it is relatively easy to Islamize existing traditions by grafting on Muslim elements without obliterating the local character of these traditions. Any non-believer can become a convert by sincerely pronouncing the belief that there is but one God and Muhammad is his prophet. But just because many Bimanese customs are a synthesis of Islam and *adat*, it does not make the Bimanese any less Islamic than other Muslims, both inside and outside Indonesia.

In order to appreciate how Islam has become an integral part of the Bimanese way of life, it is helpful to look more closely at one of the most important local rituals, the *doa*. Although the ritual has an Arabic name, it has much in common with rituals found elsewhere in Indonesia, notably the *selamatan* in Java. The *doa* takes place inside the house with the men sitting near the front entrance or on the verandah and the women in the interior, the symbolically female part of the home. Neighbours, friends and relatives are invited and there are usually between twenty and thirty guests. In wealthier homes the proceedings may begin with a reading from the Koran, but usually the men simply recite Muslim prayers in unison by heart. The women do not join in and are generally more festive than the men, though they usually fall silent when the prayers are offered. The guests then relax and chat among themselves while the hostess and her daughters serve sticky rice and cakes, followed by sweet coffee and clove cigarettes for the men. The ritual is usually held on the eve of an important event such as the departure of a pilgrim on the *hajj* or the erection of a new building. The *doa* also forms the basis of a whole series of other rituals, especially those which mark salient points in the life cycle.

The first life cycle *doa* is held during the seventh month of pregnancy when prayers are offered for the safe delivery of the child. In the event of miscarriage the aborted foetus is accorded the same respect as a living child, providing four months has passed since conception, the age at which the soul is said to enter the unborn child. Shortly after birth the child is wrapped in a white cloth, *malanta*, a symbol of purity, and the placenta, which is likened to a sibling, is taken outside and buried. A week later the child is wrapped in the white cloth again and has its head shaved, though this ritual may be delayed for up to forty days if either the mother or child is ill. The removal of the hair marks the end of the child's association with the womb and, until the completion of this ritual, the mother must refrain from eating spicy foods, which are thought to harm the milk. The next rite of childhood, circumcision, is thought to be the most important, since it differentiates Muslims from unbelievers. Boys are usually circumcised in groups between the ages of six and ten, and later rest in beds with raised canopies, a Malay Muslim custom. Although the boys parade through the village wearing new sarongs and fez, female circumcision attracts far less attention and is rarely discussed with outsiders. In the past a pre-pubescent girl would wear a silver chain between her legs to protect her vagina from witchcraft, but this custom died out on Bima in the post-independence era.

Pre-Islamic elements can, however, be detected in lowland Bima, though they are today contained within an Islamic framework. Tutelary spirits, known as *parafu*, are said to inhabit large trees, boulders and springs; these spirits are usually benevolent, but may wreak havoc if ignored. When the Bimanese pass graveyards, they usually utter a short Muslim incantation, though the practice of leaving offerings beside boulders, springs and large trees had almost completely disappeared by the early 1980s. There are also shaman-herbalists known as *sando*, who mediate between the human and spirit worlds and provide health care based on local remedies. Garlic, chilli peppers and turmeric are administered to cure stomach and intestinal disorders, and rice is thought to aid recovery. Massage is used to move pain to the extremities of the body, such as fingers and toes, from where it can be 'pushed out'. Illness is thought to be caused by an imbalance among the four humoral fluids of the body which may be distinguished by colour; red is associated with blood and vitality; and black with earth and death; white with conception and yellow with bile and anger. The *sando* knows the appropriate rituals by which the balance can be restored and is able to determine which, if any, of the ancestral spirits should be placated. The intervention of the healer must, however, take place before the sickness has gone beyond the neck and penetrated the head, the centre of goodness and purity. The association of the head with purity is possibly a Hindu-Buddhist concept that was introduced during the Majapahit era.

IV

Islam and Ethnicity

The newly arrived visitor in eastern Indonesia is often struck by the diversity of peoples in trading ports such as Bima. There are seafarers, countrywomen selling market produce, Muslim pilgrims in white skullcaps, Indonesian officials, and Arab and Chinese shopkeepers. Occasionally, one catches a glimpse of a highlander from the interior of the island selling baskets or herding livestock. On witnessing similar scenes in Burma and Java, J.S. Furnivall, the British colonial administrator– turned–social scientist, concluded that the various groups were not bound together in a single unit by normative bonds.

> In Burma, as in Java, probably the first thing that strikes the visitor is the medley of peoples - European, Chinese, Indian and native. It is in the strictest sense a medley for they mix but do not combine. Each group holds by its own religion, its own culture, its own ideas and ways. As individuals they meet, but only in the market-place, in buying and selling (Furnivall 1968: 304).

According to Furnivall, these peoples live alongside one another, but separately within the same political order; and labour is often divided on ethnic or racial grounds. Furnivall depicts a situation in which separate peoples or ethnic groups organize their own communities by what Geertz would describe as the primordial bonds of ethnicity. This attachment depends on the assumed givens of social existence that stem from being born into a particular religious community, sharing the same language and customs (Geertz 1963: 109). Furnivall describes multi-ethnic societies that were brought together in the market-place under the control of a state system that was dominated by one of these groups (Barth 1969: 16). In the larger society the pure laws of the market apply, unhindered by moral control, though large areas of cultural diversity remain in the religious and domestic spheres. 'The market' is what we might call the 'villain' of Furnivall's account, though he did not draw attention to the fact that economic relations in the colonial market-place often involved the intersection of the political and the economic, and the use of force (Rex 1986: 33).

Like the multi-ethnic societies described by Furnivall, Bima's different populations are brought together in the market-place. Historically, it was the sultans of Bima who regulated trade and set the standards that governed the conduct of inter-personal relations. In accordance with Islamic practice, the sultans aimed to establish an 'abode of peace', *dar-es-salaam,* in which different peoples could go about their business without let or hindrance. Punishments for disturbing the peace were severe and the Islamic courts could sentence trouble-makers to banishment and, ultimately, death. Since independence, responsibility for policing inter-ethnic relations has devolved to the Indonesian authorities, though appeals to loyalties that date from the sultanate era are not unknown when the republican government tries to tackle particularly intractable inter-communal problems. In disputes involving Muslim peoples belonging to different ethnic groups, the Indonesian authorities are also not averse to using local religious leaders as intermediaries. Not only do Muslim peoples mix in the market-place, but they also combine, and intermarriage between Muslims from different ethnic groups does occur (Hitchcock 1995: 238).

Ethnic Groups and Boundaries

The majority of the population live in lowland villages of between 1,500 and 4,000 inhabitants or in the urban centres of Raba-Bima and Sapé. Paddy rice is grown both on hillsides and in valleys, though swidden farming is also practised in highland areas. Animal husbandry is important on the dry northern and eastern plains, while many coastal dwellers depend on fishing and trade. Urban people pursue a wide variety of occupations ranging from street trading to shopkeeping and public administration. There are artisans, such as carpenters and blacksmiths, in both urban and rural areas, though there tends to be less specialization in the more remote villages.

Although Bima is multi-ethnic, the majority of the population speak Bimanese, an Austronesian language belonging to the Central Malayo-Polynesian group (Blust 1984: 29). This language is spoken as far west as the Dompu-Sumbawa border; thereafter Sumbawanese, a member of the Bali-Sasak group, is spoken. The inhabitants of Bima and Dompu recognize both cultural and linguistic affinities and refer to themselves as Dou Mbojo, literally 'people of Mbojo'. The origins of the word 'Mbojo' are obscure, though etymological explanations have been offered by local scholars. Some say that 'Mbojo' means 'high ground' whereas others argue that it is a corruption of the word 'Majapahit', a reference to the Hindu-Javanese kingdom (AD 1293 to c.1520), which claimed Bima as a tributary in the fourteenth century. What is significant is that the Bimanese switch to the term 'Orang Bima' (people of Bima) when speaking Indonesian, a change which may be attributed to the western Indonesian origins of the name Bima. The name 'Bima' appears to be linked to 'Bhima', one of the heroes of the Mahabharata epic, though the shadow theatre is not performed in east Sumbawa.

Bimanese lowland society was divided into three hierarchical classes under the sultanate and though this system was, in theory, abandoned during the post-colonial period, many people still reckon status in terms of class. At the top of the old social order was the royal family who did not usually take local spouses, but instead enhanced their political influence through judicious marriages with members of the ruling élites from other Indonesian states. The second tier was occupied by a large class of people who can be described as nobles. They were expected to find marriage partners belonging to either the same rank or the wealthiest section of the lowest class, the commoners. The latter group was sub-divided into upper and lower halves, while the bottom rung comprised slaves. There was some social mobility, usually through hypergamous marriages between the nobility and high commoners, and between the high and low commoners. But there is also some evidence that commoners could enter the ranks of the nobility on grounds of merit, and this applied in particular to the skilled craftsmen who made prestige goods for the sultan.

There are two distinct highland communities in Bima: the Dou Donggo of the western massif and the Dou Wawo of the southeastern hills. The former speak a language that resembles Bimanese (Just 1984: 31), whereas the latter are linguistically separate, though they share some vocabulary with the lowlanders (Hitchcock 1986: 23). To the northeast of Bima Bay there is a coastal group, known as the Dou Kolo, whose language may also differ from Bimanese. There are long-established Bugis and Makasar enclaves around Bima Bay and Sape harbour, where there has been much intermarrying with local Bimanese. Settled Bajau Lau communities are encountered in eastern Indonesia, as is sometimes reflected in the place name 'Bajau'. The inhabitants of Bajau, for example, to the west of Bima Bay may have Bajau Laut ancestry, though it would appear that they had become speakers of Bimanese by the early twentieth century (Jasper 1908: 103). Until the early 1980s it was widely held in Bima that the older members of the Bajau community to the east of Sape still spoke their own language. Bajau Laut identity had little significance in the 1980s and appeared to be a largely historical phenomenon. Malays have also been assimilated into coastal Bimanese society where bilingualism has long been common. The Malays settled the western and southern shores of Bima Bay (Syamsuddin 1980: 297), though their main village is located to the west of the capital near to the port. In contrast to the Bajau Laut, the descendants of the Malays are very aware of their distinctive heritage, particularly their role in the Islamization of Bima. Islamic revivalism as well as the sense of belonging to a wider Malay community in Indonesia may be factors in this case.

In addition to people of Malay and Makasar-Bugis descent, there are speakers of other Austronesian languages, especially Javanese, Sundanese, and Balinese. The majority are government employees and are concentrated in the towns, though there is a growing number of Balinese small businessmen, particularly hoteliers and skilled artisans. There are also many eastern Indonesians in the urban areas, such as Florenese and Timorese, some of whom originally came to Bima for educational purposes. Speakers of non-Austronesian languages make up a substantial proportion of the urban business community. Most prominent are the

Fig. 11 House building methods were introduced to Sumbawa Besar from South Sulawesi, as was the case in Bima.

Fig. 12 The *pinisi* is plank built on a keel using sappan wood pegs. Makasar and Bugis shipwrights build ships on the shores at Bima Bay

Chinese, a diverse people belonging to several dialect groups, including Hokkien and Cantonese. It is unclear how long the Chinese have been in Bima since many do not speak Chinese dialects. There has also been a certain amount of intermarriage with the indigenous population. Some Chinese migrated to Bima via Ujung Pandang, where they had relatives, whereas others came as indentured labourers during the colonial period.

The Arabs are another long-established group, though it remains uncertain when they first arrived in Bima. They are primarily of southern Arabian descent, and claim Hadhrami and Yemeni ancestry, though very few of the younger members of this community speak Arabic. Arab communities with kinship links to the Arabs of Bima are encountered elsewhere in eastern Indonesia, especially in Lombok. Many Arabs have married into local families, and entrepreneurs of mixed ethnic origin are not uncommon. Because of the increasing significance of tourism since the late 1970s, tourists also deserve to be mentioned in this discussion of Islam and ethnicity (see Chapter 10). Bird, for example, has noted that in the case of Langkawi (Malaysia), the uneven benefits derived from tourism, combined with inappropriate behaviour on the part of certain tourists, may eventually contribute to a decline in visitor-host relations (Bird 1989: 53).

In addition to ethnicity, many Bimanese groups subscribe to forms of classification based on other criteria, some of which cut across the ethnic boundaries mentioned above. These cleavages are in many respects idioms, as opposed to fixed categories, and are thus subject to reinterpretation over time. It is common, for example, for people to be ascribed various stereotypes on the basis of residence. Generally speaking, the population of Bima is perceived in terms of three distinct socio-geographic zones: the town (any urban area such as Bima-Raba, Sapé, and Sila), the countryside (lowland rural villages), and the mountain (highland settlements in Donggo, Wawo, Wera, and Sanggar). Most people, irrespective of origin, hold the towns in high esteem on account of their educational, technical, and commercial success. Non-urban residents, however, argue that townspeople are rude and that they only work for money as opposed to helping their kinsmen. It is often said that government investment is creamed off in the towns and that this accounts for the greater wealth of urbanites. In contrast, townspeople praise country folk for their generosity, but say that they are not clever and that they have to look to the towns for leadership. On account of their origins alone some townspeople expect to be respected by rural dwellers, though they do not always get it. Highlanders also sometimes conceive of lowland farmers in pejorative terms. Highlanders may argue, for instance, that lowlanders are lazy and that they only become wealthy through the good fortune of living on fertile land, but not as a result of their own endeavours. Some highlanders, particularly the Dou Donggo, pride themselves on their ferocity (Just 1991: 295) and despise what they see as the craven attitudes of lowlanders. While townspeople may regard highlanders as being incredibly rustic, even a source of amusement, many secretly admire mountain peoples on account of their adherence to old values and their expertise in traditional crafts. Lowlanders also fear the alleged magical superiority of the highlanders, and claim that mountain peoples, especially the Dou Wawo, are able to rustle livestock with the aid of charms.

Material culture provides one of the most immediately recognizable symbolic systems of identity, especially in contexts such as markets, where the different groups mingle with one another. It is widely held in Bima that it is possible to discern a person's regional or ethnic background from his style of dress, particularly the colour of his clothes. Rural Bimanese women veil themselves with sarongs tied over the head with a method of folding known as the *rimpi*. The veils simultaneously signify a Muslim and Bimanese identity. Tourists taken from cruise ships to the sultan's palace are encouraged to try this style of dress and, hopefully, purchase the cloth. Vivid red checked sarongs, for example, were worn in Bima town until the mid-twentieth century where they were regarded as symbols of urban sophistication. In contrast, blue sarongs, which are seen as embodying the positive ideals of rural areas, are associated with the countryside. Indigo-banded fabrics are closely linked to Dou Donggo cultural identity, though these textiles are also woven in some remote lowland areas. The Dou Wawo also make distinctive blue checked textiles that are associated with their region.

The Bimanese claim that they can distinguish Bugis checked fabrics from their own by the colour and size of the bands and stripes. Bimanese weavers occasionally imitate a style considered to be Bugis, which involves the use of broad bands of pink and mushroom-coloured yarns. Green is another colour that is connected with ethnic identity since it is associated with the Arabs. It is not clear, however, whether this stems from the green banner of Islam or the colour of the checked sarongs worn in the past by Arabian seafarers (Hitchcock 1989: 26–28). The ubiquitous sarong is worn in the countries surrounding the Indian Ocean and is closely associated with Muslim identity. Checked sarongs, known as *sarongi*, are, for example, popular with the peoples of Zanzibar and coastal Tanzania.

Religion is another kind of common identity that may transcend boundaries based on ethnicity. In addition to sharing similar values, members of the same faith, even though they belong to different ethnic groups, may worship together and participate in the same festivals. Thus the Bimanese, who are predominantly Sunni Muslims, have an affinity with both the Arabs and other Indonesian Muslims such as the Javanese, Sundanese, and Makasars. Muslims from other Indonesian islands pray in Bimanese mosques and observe holy days, such as Idul Fitri, alongside the local population. There are also political and economic, as well as cultural dimensions since it was through Islam that the Bimanese were able to consolidate their links in the past with other Indonesian peoples. The Malays, for example, are particularly highly-regarded in eastern Sumbawa because they were instrumental in spreading the Muslim faith in Bima and the Malay quarter became the centre of Islamic education. Up until the outbreak of World War II, parades were held annually to commemorate the role played by the Malays in converting the Bimanese to Islam. During the festival, girls representing royal handmaidens are taken by sedan chair to the Malay quarter, where they are joined by four 'Malay' boys. Both groups are then borne to the sultan's palace to the accompaniment of music and dancing. Parallels can be drawn with the invented traditions discussed by Hobsbawm and Ranger (1983) in relation to the formation of national identity.

Although Islam became the main faith in lowland Bima, Islamic law did not entirely supplant traditional practices. Customary law, *adat*, remained significant and the settlement of Dara, to the southwest of the capital, retained a leading authority on *adat* until the early twentieth century. The sultanate had to reconcile the conflicting demands of Islamic and customary law, as well as the question of political authority. A symbolic expression of the unity of the state, with its threefold division of power, can be seen in the easternmost palace, the former residence of the prime minister. Above the main entrance there is a carved *naga* head, behind which lies a pole supported by three pillars representing Islamic law, customary law, and administration. The rulers of Bima used other symbols, such as the ceremonial *kris* and ritual seating patterns, to reinforce the concept of unity, but were unable to prevent the kingdom splitting apart when it was subject to immense external pressure. Islam, for example, became the rallying point for lowland Bimanese who refused to accept incorporation into the Netherlands East Indies in 1905. The issue was not resolved peacefully and the Muslim rebels were eventually overwhelmed by colonial forces in a battle near the village of Nggali.

The Bimanese also use religion as a means of differentiating themselves from neighbouring eastern Indonesian peoples with whom they otherwise have much in common. Inter-religious relations often appear to be primordial in character, especially when ethnic identity is closely associated with a belief system. A common material culture also reinforces the Bimanese's identification with other Muslims, as is especially apparent on holy days when *fez* and sarongs are worn to the mosque by all believers, regardless of ethnic origin. Thus the Bimanese feel more affinity with the Muslim Sumbawanese, who belong to another language family, than the Christian Sumbanese, who are linguistically more akin. Likewise, Christians from other eastern Indonesian islands, such as Flores and Timor, are regarded with some circumspection by the Bimanese. The Bimanese also distinguish themselves from the Hindu Balinese in religious terms, though anti-Balinese sentiments are not as marked as they are on the west of the island where there is a history of Balinese incursions dating back to the eighteenth century (Jasper 1908: 72). The Balinese continue to be resented in west Sumbawa, partly because of their commercial success, particularly in the tourism industry. During the anti-Balinese riots of 1980, Balinese-owned hotels were attacked by the Tau Semawa and government troops had to be brought in to quell the disturbances. The trouble did not, however, spread to Dompu and Bima, where there are also many Balinese-owned hotels and guest houses.

Sometimes religion may reinforce boundaries based on locality, as is particularly the case with lowland-highland relations. The mountain dwellers are notably less Islamic than the highlanders and were widely held to be kaffirs until well into the twentieth century. As non-believers the highlanders were open to exploitation by Muslims, as was apparently the case with the Dou Donggo who built their settlements on easily defended sites, possibly because of the fear of slaving raids (Just 1986: 100–1). Furthermore, some Dou Donggo communities were converted to Christianity in the mid-twentieth century, and this later became another source of tension.

In view of Bima's social, geographical, linguistic, and cultural diversity, it is not perhaps surprising that inter-communal relations are characterized by ambiguity. The various boundaries overlap one another and relations between different groups are perceived locally in a variety of different ways, depending on the context. Thus a Bimanese will regard a Javanese as a member of another ethnic group, but will find common ground with him or her in terms of religion. If both live in an urban area they may share a similar outlook, especially if they belong to roughly the same class. Although there are numerous potential areas of conflict, the majority of inter-communal dealings are conducted on a fairly cordial basis with only minor disagreements, particularly when the participants recognize that they have much in common. There are, however, three major fault lines that divide the populations of eastern Sumbawa and these are not only sources of discontent but are the cause of occasional outbreaks of violence.

Conflict and conflict resolution

One of the most significant boundaries in eastern Sumbawa is that which separates the highlanders from the lowlanders. This division can be understood in varying degrees of differentiation based on ethnicity, locality, and religion, and to a certain extent class is a consideration, since it is only lowland society that is stratified on this basis. Historically, the ruling élites of Bima recognized the need to come to some kind of accommodation with the highlanders, despite the longstanding enmities, not least for reasons of security. The mountain zones were strategically significant because they encircled the rice-growing heartland of the old Sultanate of Bima, providing a natural defensive wall. As guardians of much of the kingdom's outer defences, the highlanders were held to be important by the Bimanese royal family who attempted to reduce inter-communal tension by absorbing disparate groups within the sultanate system. The crown prince, for example, became directly responsible for the administration of Donggo, and Donggo smiths, widely respected as *kris*-makers, were invited to settle in the capital. The identification of the crown prince with the highlanders suggests a situational approach to the wider identity of Bima; it could be invoked in times of crisis. Certain positions in the court, albeit lowly ones, were reserved for the Dou Wawo, though the dividing line between minor palace functionary and hostage was finely drawn. In some respects the means used by Bimanese rulers to stabilize lowland-highland relations resembled those used to accommodate the Malays in the seventeenth century. Although the Malays were granted several privileges, including a certain amount of legal autonomy, they did become part of the sultanate and served as record-keepers and go-betweens.

Within the context of inter-ethnic relations, it may be significant that the Sultanate of Bima was named after the legendary prince, Sang Bima, who founded the royal dynasty and not after the dominant ethnic group, the Dou Mbojo. Thus non-members of the largest ethnic group could identify with the sultanate while retaining their own ethnonyms.

There were, however, occasions when the court's means of conflict resolution, especially in the highland-lowland cleavage, failed. One of the best-documented breakdowns of law and order occurred shortly after the annexation of Bima by the Netherlands East Indies in 1905. In the Donggo highlands traditional rights and obligations were invoked by rebels who no longer accepted the authority of the sultan's government. According to highland sources the resistance fighters held out for two years against sporadic attacks by sultanate forces supported by Ambonese sepoys (Just 1986: 101). There were also outbreaks of trouble in the post-colonial era when Donggo highlanders aired their grievances with the central administration by demonstrating in the capital. Some local scholars have argued that the lack of recognition for traditional rights in this period exacerbated the situation. In accordance with republican practice, the Bimanese crown prince did not succeed his father on the death of the last sultan in 1950. In their drive to establish national unity, independence leaders appear to have underestimated the checks and balances within traditional structures, particularly with regard to conflict resolution.

The republican administration has also experienced problems in dealing with lowland-highland disputes, particularly with regard to the Wawo hills. Lowland farmers periodically accuse the Wawo highlanders of stealing livestock, sometimes with the aid of witchcraft, and have threatened to take the law into their own hands. In the early 1980s the authorities attempted to allay lowland suspicions by installing an army sergeant of lowland extraction as a headman in one of the highland villages. The local government also resorted to traditional channels of communication in this period when dealing with the Dou Donggo and invited the son of the last sultan, now an Indonesian politician, to act as a mediator.

Another source of tension is the somewhat ambiguous divide between the Bugis and Makasars on one hand and the Bimanese on the other. Although all the participants share the same religion and have numerous marital ties, this conflict is significant. The strife does not usually amount to more than exchanges of insults, often highly ritualized, between rival gangs of youths, though quarrels involving knives are not unknown. The assertion of ethnic identity in these contexts is situational and usually not long-lasting. Much of this inter-communal conflict takes place in urban areas and has, like the lowland-highland division, regional as well as ethnic elements. The Bugis and Makasars have their own settlements near the ports of Bima-Raba and Sape, and such is their numerical significance in the latter centre that Sape is regarded by many Bimanese as virtually a 'Bugis town'. The Sulawesi-Bima conflict has an historical dimension that can be traced back to the early seventeenth century when Sumbawa Island came under the sway of the sultanate of Makassar. According to the Bimanese chronicle, which was compiled by the Malays and their descendants, eastern Sumbawa was subject to raids from southern Sulawesi, which the Malays helped to fend off. As a reward for these and other services the Malays were granted special privileges, including the right to organize their own affairs in accordance with Islamic law (Syamsuddin 1980: 296–97). Although the Malays are attributed with converting the Bimanese to Islam, it is clear from a consideration of both Makasar and Bimanese accounts that Makasar intervention was decisive in the foundation of a sultanate in eastern Sumbawa.

Not all seafarers from southern Sulawesi came to eastern Sumbawa in search of plunder since many eventually settled along the coastline and around the main ports. The rulers of Bima, however, do not appear to have tried to incorporate these communities into the sultanate system, as they did with the Malays. Although it remains uncertain why the Bugis and Makasars were treated differently, it may be because the Bimanese still feared Makasar domination, given the proximity of Sulawesi to Sumbawa. The Malay homelands lay far to the west and, in Bimanese eyes, they may have posed less of a threat than the mariners from Sulawesi. Whatever the reasons, it is clear that people of Makasar and Bugis origin did rise to high positions in the Sultanate on an individual basis, usually after marrying into influential local families. Many Makasar cultural elements were absorbed by the court to the extent that the Bimanese say that the Makasars refer to them amicably as the *orang selatan* (men from the south). At the same time, however, the Bimanese claim that they are more *halus* (refined) than either the Bugis or Makasars, questions of refinement having long been important in the rivalry between the traditional Indonesian courts. Indonesians often conceive of ethnic differences in terms of relative refinement and coarseness, though the former is not invariably regarded as positive and the latter negative. The Bugis, Batak, Bimanese, and Dou Donggo will readily admit to being more *kasar* than the Javanese, Sundanese, and Balinese, but regard themselves as being more open and trustworthy than the so-called refined Indonesians (Just 1991: 295).

The third major fault line running through Bimanese society is the one that separates the Chinese from the various Austronesian groups. Despite the fact that many Chinese speak Bimanese and have lived for generations in the area, they are still perceived as being ethnically distinct from both indigenous and immigrant Austronesian populations. There are admittedly some Chinese who have managed to bridge the gap through intermarriage and the adoption of the Muslim faith, but they are too few in number to affect the overall picture. Not only do the Chinese differ in physical appearance from many Austronesians, but some also subscribe to cultural traditions, such as Confucianism, that cannot readily be categorized as religions by the Muslim majority. Furthermore, the Chinese are the most decidedly urban of all the ethnic groups and usually live in separate family houses around the main market areas. Chinese society is centred on the town, and immigrants to Indonesia, though often from rural areas in southern China, brought with them the image of life focused on the city (Evers 1984: 147). In contrast, urban Austronesians tend to live in quarters that resemble rural villages in terms of social organization. To a certain extent, therefore, the Chinese are separated from the majority population in terms of

Fig. 13   Women wear the sarong veil, *rimpi*, to travel to market.

Fig. 14 The local version of the Malay martial art, *silat*, is performed to music.

locality, and when combined with ethnic and religious considerations this helps to intensify inter-communal divisions. Bimanese grievances are expressed in terms of ethnicity, though the underlying reasons have much to do with resentment of the comparative economic success of the Chinese. It is when considering the position of the Chinese in Bima that one comes closest to the plural society envisaged by Furnivall.

As an easily identifiable minority who are widely believed to have control over a disproportionate share of the region's finances, it is perhaps not surprising that the Chinese have been victims of inter-ethnic conflict. There are occasional rumours of discoveries of pigs' heads or hides in mosques, and the Chinese, along with Christians and Hindus, have been accused of provoking local Muslims. In 1980 a Chinese transport operator was severely injured when he was dragged from his bus by a mob on the road between Sapé and Bima, though the reasons behind this assault remain unclear. There are also sporadic outbreaks of anti-Chinese rioting, which are often triggered by complaints about the high rates of interest charged by Chinese traders and moneylenders. Despite this history of strife there do not appear to have been any traditional means of resolving this kind of conflict. The rulers of Bima do not, for instance, seem to have tried to absorb Chinese communities into the sultanate system, as they did with the Malays and highlanders. This may be because the Chinese were, until the early twentieth century, a relatively small population who were not perceived as either useful or a threat by the Bimanese court. It also remains uncertain whether or not some Chinese managed to secure government positions on an individual basis like the Makasars and Bugis, and the members of other Austronesian groups. The Chinese did, however, periodically come into conflict with the majority population and they were forced to look towards the sultanate and colonial authorities for protection, a role that has passed on to successor republican regimes.

As can be seen from the above account of inter-communal relations in Bima, Sumbawa, conflict needs to be considered with reference to three main variables: ethnicity, locality, and religious affiliation. Class and economic differentiation are also considerations not least with regard to development and tourism. Although strife can and does arise in any of these three arenas, they are seldom, when taken in isolation, the cause of severe conflict. Prolonged inter-communal friction cannot, for example, be understood in terms of ethnicity alone since many inter-ethnic dealings are characterized by tolerance, particularly when the participants belong to the same religion or reside in the same area. Thus there is little discord between the urban Bimanese and the Javanese, though they differ ethnically, because they share roughly the same regional and religious outlooks. Similar observations can be made with regard to the Sundanese and other Muslims, though not with regard to the Bugis and Makasars who have long preserved a distinct maritime heritage, which does not always accord well with the agrarian orientation of much of Bimanese society. Historical factors, such as the rivalry between the courts, also need to be taken into account when discussing the relationship between the peoples of Sulawesi and Sumbawa.

When elements of all three factors - ethnicity, locality, and religiosity - are combined, the conflict may prove to be especially enduring, as is the case with highland-lowland relations. Likewise, the Chinese can be distinguished from other communities in ethnic, religious and, to a certain extent, residence patterns. The Chinese are also divided from the indigenous *pribumi*, Indonesians on account of their perceived wealth. Furnivall's concept of pluralism does have analytical value in this context, though there are many grey areas. In contrast, people of Arab descent can less readily be separated from the majority population because they are Muslims, do not occupy a separate quarter, and have intermarried extensively with the local people.

According to local sources, the government of pre-independence Bima attempted to reconcile differences based on locality and ethnicity by absorbing the various groups into the sultanate system. The Sultanate of Bima was also named after a prince and thus 'Bima' is not strictly an ethnonym, thereby facilitating the absorption of minorities without complete loss of identity. Identification with the Sultanate has situational features, involving the mobilization of different people under the name 'Bima' to achieve certain social and political objectives. Religious tensions were also reduced through the recognition of both Islamic and customary law within the state system, and by keeping both apart from the administration. Through these means the sultanate was able to accommodate the Malays and the highlanders, though the position of the Makasars and Bugis was more ambiguous, possibly for political reasons. Members of the latter groups did, however, intermarry with local peoples, as did the Arabs, and as a consequence perhaps the sultanate was under less pressure to integrate them in a formal sense. Although it remains unclear why the sultan did not make special provisions for the Chinese, it seems unlikely that they were less readily absorbed into the traditional order for religious as well as other cultural reasons.

Like the Sultanate, the republican regime had to contend with inter-communal strife and they ran into difficulties in the early years of independence. This may be because the concept of citizenship of a vast and remote state was too abstract for the many peoples who had grown up as subjects of a local monarch. The sultan was not an absolute ruler and traditionally he was kept at one remove from the day-to-day administration of the state because of the existence of the prime minister. The republican leaders did not, therefore, have the ritual authority of a sultan who could appeal over the heads of different factions to the public at large. Unlike the sultan the new authorities were unable to demonstrate through court ceremonials what contribution the separate groups made towards the functioning of the state. Numerically weak peoples like the highlanders, who had at least some access to the centres of power under the sultanate system, were deprived of a forum for expressing their views as the new political procedures were introduced. The various attempts at democratic reform virtually disenfranchised minority groups because they were insufficiently numerous to influence the outcome of voting, leaving them no option but to resort to active, and sometimes violent, protest in order to make their opinions felt.

The Indonesian authorities have addressed some of these issues and emphasis is placed on tolerance and multi-cultural harmony within the compulsory *Pancasila* education programme in schools and colleges. The state-controlled television also promotes Indonesia's multi-religious identity and regularly contains features on non-Muslim peoples in the nation. State employees are obliged to participate in the work-place rituals introduced by the 'New Order' regime such as swearing allegiance to the republic and raising the national flag. Cultural revivals receive official sponsorship, though traditional dances may be modified to conform to what are considered to be national standards. Generally speaking, it is court culture that receives the most encouragement by the authorities. It is not only perceived as representing a cultural high point within the region, but is also more easily monitored than the cultural events that take place at the village level. Court culture is also easier to control and package in response to specific demands and is thus more likely than other genres to be influenced by tourism (Hughes-Freeland 1993: 153). Court culture itself is also being reinterpreted in terms of the integrative values of the wider state.

V

Court Society

The royal tombs of Dantaraha provide an excellent vantage point from which to survey the capital. This abode of spirits is located to the south of Bima on a bare, sun-drenched hill which is rarely visited by the local people. The first structure which catches the eye in the valley below is the Sultan's palace. With its cream-coloured walls, green woodwork and horned roof, it dwarfs all the other buildings including the more recently-constructed administrative and commercial complexes. The palace dates from 1931 and was designed by a Dutch-Indonesian architect, though it was built mainly with local materials and labour. It housed the Sultan's extended family and their descendants, who had hitherto lived in a wooden palace on raised piles. Both the old and new palaces are surrounded by a walled park with gatehouses on the eastern and western approaches. The central mosque, with its onion-shaped dome, is found in the immediate proximity of the palace, though it lies outside the walls. The market and port are some way off the centres of religious and political power and are separated from the mosque and palace by a large square, *padang*. This open space is usually windswept and deserted, but may be crammed with the massed ranks of Muslims at prayer on holy days.

Up until the mid twentieth century the palace was, much like a Javanese *kraton*, surrounded by royal villages inhabited by retainers and artisans who served the court. Members of the same profession, often linked by kin and ethnic ties, resided in the same quarter and this is reflected in the place names. Thus the Malay settlement is known as *Melayu*, and the dwelling place of noblemen, *Bumi Naé*, is called *Naé*. The capital is located in a valley surrounded by easily defended hills and was never walled, though the boundary between the town and the countryside remains culturally significant. Despite this distinction urban and rural dwellings resemble one another, though the wooden houses of the capital are rapidly being replaced by substantial brick buildings. Some of the traditional houses in the capital are, however, much grander than those in the countryside, most notably the prime minister's palace in Pané. The building comprises several small houses placed side by side which have been brought together under one roof. There is a carved naga above the doorway whose spine extends into the roof of the entrance hall and is supported by three pillars representing the threefold division of power in the Sultanate of Bima. Although this palace lies outside the Sultan's walled enclosure, it was the administrative heart of the realm.

In many respects the Bimanese pattern of settlement resembles that of other South-East Asian peoples, most notably the Malays. According to Evers, for example, the Malay cities developed primarily through Chinese and Indian immigration and in fact the Malays lack a truly urban concept of space. The Malay terms for town, *bandar* and *kota*, should strictly-speaking be translated as 'port' or 'stockade' respectively and it would appear that the Malays do not have a precise definition of 'town' or 'city'. The Malays, by popular definition, live in villages (*kampung*) and it is the mosque and palace that provide the focus for national sentiment and identity (Evers 1984: 146). Like the Malays the Bimanese live in villages, even though the settlements lie within municipal boundaries, and many urban dwellers have strong links with the countryside. Nevertheless, the parallel should not be taken too far since the residents of urban Bima do think of themselves as town or city people. There are also Bimanese, the descendants of craftsmen and administrators, whose lives have always been closely associated with the fortunes of an urban centre which, at its height, was the capital of a major eastern Indonesian Sultanate. There urban identity is strengthened by their town's trading past and Islamic heritage; but in order to appreciate this it is necessary to refer back to the sociopolitical conditions of pre-independence Bima.

Fig. 15 The original wooden palace before restoration work was carried out.

Fig. 16 The entrance to the prime minister's residence.

Sociopolitical organization

The most important sociopolitical unit at the local level up until the demise of the Sultanate was the village. Each village usually had a mosque and was administered by a headman, *gelarang*, assisted by a deputy and a council of elders. The term gelarang appears to have originated in southern Sulawesi, suggesting a Makasar pattern of government, though it also has affinities with Javanese (cf. Jav. *gelar*). A striking feature of this type of organization was the division between *hukum* (Islamic law) and *adat* (customary law); but as Islam gained ground at the expense of the indigenous belief system the latter became primarily concerned with secular administrative affairs. Although this pattern was replicated in the capital, with the wards taking the place of villages, responsibility for overseeing *adat* was devolved to a lord of the realm known as the *Bumi Luma Rasanaé* (*bumi*, soil; *luma*, a title; *rasanaé*, large village). He resided near the sacred rock of *Dara* (*dara*, blood) and presided over an *adat* council comprising commoners and nobles which met periodically in the goldsmith's ward in Paruga. This council was directly accountable to the Sultan and lay outside the state's administrative structure. In times of war a military council, with representatives from all strands of government, would meet in the village hall in Paruga.

Each village or ward had a kind of foreman (Ind. *mandur*), who was responsible for implementing orders and an official (Sumb. *malar*), who was the custodian of the land (cf. Goethals 1961: 118). The custodian was responsible for agricultural rituals and the distribution of land, especially irrigated rice fields. Parallel with this organizational system was that of Islam. The Muslim religious head at the village level was the *lebé naé*, or head of the mosque, who oversaw the annual festivals in the Muslim calendar and the rites of the agricultural cycle. He was assisted by the members of the mosque council, known as *cape lebé*, who took charge of the building and related administrative matters. There was also an official (Sumb. *ketip*) who organized mosque services and the recitation of sermons. based on the holy scriptures, *kita* (cf. Goethals 1961: 64). Bimanese life in the capital tended to be focused on the central mosque because it overshadowed the ward mosques, some of which were very small due to lack of space. Up until the 1980s the mosques also provided an effective communications network. Drums made from hollowed-out tree trunks were housed in the courtyards and verandahs of mosques, and were used to transmit messages between the villages.

Islamic law was introduced when Bima became a Sultanate, though it did not totally supplant the indigenous customary law. Like the Malays the Bimanese subscribed to the doctrine of Shafa'i in regulating such matters as commerce, property, marriage and court procedure (cf. Hurgronje 1906a: 196). This code included penalties for various offences and governed the treatment of slaves, and was adopted by the state. These rules were introduced through the medium of Malay from translations of the original Arabic, though a simplified code was adopted for the guidance of the judge, known locally as the *kali* (Ar. *qadhi*). While Islamic law prevailed with regard to many domestic matters, customary law remained influential, especially in the political domain. However great the authority exercised by judges and Islamic teachers, the Bimanese continued to be guided by *adat* and to respect the traditional bearers of political power (cf. Rauf 1964: 86).

Although *adat* continued to influence the affairs of state, Islam became closely associated with Bimanese identity in much the same way as among the Malays (Hussin Mutalib 1990: 31). Islam became an integral feature of Bimanese culture and exerted a strong influence on the Bimanese world view, especially with regard to their relations with other peoples. Despite their varying degrees of personal commitment the Bimanese like other Muslims know the five tenets of Islam: the declaration of faith (*shahadah*), the five daily prayers, fasting and alms-giving, and the pilgrimage to Mecca (*hajj*). Ethnicity and religion have, however, a dialectical relationship and at times the Bimanese lean closer to one than the other. Bima has long been multi-ethnic and within this context Islam played a vital role in bringing together disparate communities. The use of the title 'Sultan' by the rulers of Bima symbolized the adoption of Islamic rule, thereby guaranteeing the rights of all Muslims regardless of ethnic affiliation. Islam provided a common religion where none existed before and through its institutions generated a sense of solidarity that transcended cultural barriers. The process of socialization and communication was aided by the activities of the mosques and the common legal framework, thereby creating a strong sense of common purpose. This was particularly marked in the towns, the most ethnically diverse areas.

In addition to the Islamic functionaries, each ward or village (often a cluster of hamlets in rural areas) had a headman who was assisted by a council. Decision-making depended on consensus and the members of the council were, in theory, selected by the villagers on account of their wisdom, though they were often simply the major landholders. The headman was answerable to officials working under the direction of a lord who was known in Bimanese as the *Tureli Nggampo*. This high-ranking aristocrat was also called the *Ruma Bicara* (*ruma*, lord; *bicara*, speak), and was sometimes known as the *Raja Bicara* in Malay. He was also referred to as the Sultan's younger brother, *ari ba raja*, though he was of noble rather than royal origin and was not related. Although the Sultan was the highest authority, he was primarily concerned with spiritual matters and executive power was vested in the *Ruma Bicara*, the prime minister or secular monarch. It was said that although the two rulers' water buffalo were marked differently, it was not necessary to check their ear notches (a hole for the Sultan's and a single slit for the prime minister's) to tell them apart because they rarely mingled with one another in the common pasture.

The Sultan's power was likened to the cool shadow, *flawu ninu*, cast by a parasol and on ceremonial occasions the monarch's head was shaded by a gold painted parasol, a symbol of authority. The boundaries were well-defined until the introduction of colonial rule when the Sultan was persuaded by the Dutch to become more involved in practical administration. The concentration of more power in the Sultan's hands led to discord and eventually to the banishment of the prime minister. But until the colonial authorities tightened their grip, the prime minister made the day to day executive decisions, and met regularly with his council of ministers in the hall with the three carved pillars. On these occasions the prime minister would sit to the west of the group in the direction of both Mecca and the ancestral home of Sang Bima.

Seating patterns in state ceremonials also helped to reinforce the notion of a tripartite division of power. After the parades which marked the end of Ramadan, for example, the Sultan would sit in state on his verandah facing three rows of courtiers. The Sultan sat to the east of the gathering who were arranged in three lines going from east to west. The prime minister and his council sat in the northern row, the mosque officials in the middle and the head of customary law and the nobility to the south. These ceremonies were designed to confirm the court's view of the official order, but it remains unclear when they came into use. The court ceremonies are reminiscent of the 'invented traditions' described in other contexts by Hobsbawm and

Ranger (1983). Sitting cross-legged in an upright posture with his hands on either side, the Sultan would discuss the affairs of state with individual courtiers. Negative answers to the monarch's questions would not be tolerated, the nearest possible response being 'not yet'. When replying the lower ranking person would place his hands in his lap, avert his eyes and incline his head downwards. While executive power remained in the hands of the prime minister this questioning was largely ritual and was intended to remind the courtiers that all were ultimately subject to the sacred authority of the Sultan. The monarch also sat to the east of his courtiers, the exact opposite of where the prime minister was located when he discussed state business in the palace with the three carved pillars.

Islamic and pre-Islamic notions appear to have fused with regard to this westwards orientation, which is also encountered at the village level. According to a former Sultanate minister, A.D. Talu, devout Muslims liked to sleep on the west side of the house, preferably with the feet pointing to the west so that when they awoke they would face Mecca. There are, however, good reasons for considering alternative explanations, especially since other eastern Indonesians express a strong preference for the west. The Savunese, for example, claim that their ancestors originated in the west (Kana 1980: 255), whereas the Ema of Timor see the sun as an ancestral personification and build their houses with entrances to the west so that the sleeper will not set eyes on the rising sun when he awakes (Clamagirand 1980: 130). In Indonesia the Muslim prays west to Mecca and this practice was probably easily absorbed in Bima because it was already part of the local culture in another guise. The invented traditions of the court presumably arose out of the need to re-affirm the ruler's power within the new Islamic context.

As many as thirteen ministers are recorded in colonial sources, though Ahmad Amin, the local historian, lists only four (Ahmad Amin 1971: 61, cf. Couvreur 1917, Elbert 1912). Ahmad Amin's account of Bimanese history deserves serious consideration, not least because he was in a better position to describe the workings of the Bimanese state than many colonial commentators. A. Amin was born in the Malay quarter, into a family of Sultanate record keepers, and his account accords well with local oral histories, though it is possible that the constitution of the council changed over time. In A. Amin's version the council of ministers comprised the *Tureli Belo*, *Tureli Woha*, *Tureli Sekuru* and *Tureli Parado* and, although two of them bore regional titles (i.e. *Woha* and *Belo*), they were not, as members of the central executive, directly responsible for districts. The officials entrusted with the latter task were the ten district heads, known as *jeneli*, who were each assisted by a nobleman *Bumi Naé* (*bumi*, soil; *naé*, big). According to local folk etymologies the term *tureli* is derived from *turu*, to point, and *eli*, voice (i.e. one who gives orders), and the term *jeneli* from *jena*, work, and *eli* (i.e. one who tells people to work).

Like rulers elsewhere in maritime South-East Asia the Sultan of Bima had to reward public employees for their services in what was a cash-deficient economy. To be sure, there were foreign coins in circulation - Dutch, Chinese and Arab - but they were few in number and were often hoarded, especially silver guilders. The Sultanate did not mint its own coinage and the basic unit of exchange remained the rice sheaf until well into the 20th century. Most goods and services could be calculated in terms of bundles of rices, which added together according to a decimal system, a custom which persisted in highland areas until the 1980s. The solution was to award public officials irrigated rice fields while they held office, the yield of which they were entitled to. The land would revert to the state should the official relinquish his post or die in office, whichever happened first. The land was worked by sharecroppers and slaves, or by rural relatives of the post-holder, leaving the official free to carry out his duties on behalf of the state. Ahmed Amin's *Sedjarah Bima* provides a list of these holdings ranging from 40 hectares for a minister to 10-20 hectares for a district head. The hectare was introduced by the Dutch and it replaced an indigenous unit of measure. the *ndo'o*, which was roughly equivalent to half an hectare. The *ndo'o* could be further subdivided into four or five equal parts known as *lobé*. The size of holdings was calculated with reference to the turning space of a team of buffalo and a plough in the valleys, and with regard to arm spans on rough hillsides.

Couvreur compared the structure of Bima to that of Sumba, which has close linguistic affinities but was never Islamized (1917: 12). In Sumba there is a similar division between the Maramba, the head of the community, and the Mangu Tanangu, the custodian of the land, and though Bima was subject to external influences the existence of a dual monarchy links it to other eastern Indonesian islands. The *maramba* class of Sumba claim descent from a miraculous woman who descended from the heavens by means of a golden chain

(Forth 1981: 222). The concept of heavenly derived rulers is a common idea in Indonesia, though each tradition has local features (ibid.:223). As van Wouden has shown the division between the spiritual and the temporal, corresponding to groups regarded as older and younger, is common in eastern Indonesia. The oldest members of the class are generally regarded as having the greatest spiritual power (ibid.: 238). But some kind of dual authority can also be detected in other Malay-Indonesian states, especially on the Malay peninsula, and it seems likely that foreign elements were grafted on to well-established local systems of government which had many pan-Indonesian features. This polarity is achieved in different ways in different historical periods and may be modified by external agency. The balance of power was irrevocably altered with the introduction of colonial power when the Dutch concluded a treaty with the Sultan as if he were the absolute authority. The Sultan took the opportunity to become such and more wealth and power were concentrated in his hands. Some appreciation of the relative importance of the two rulers before the advent of colonialism can be deduced from their respective wooden palaces; they do not differ greatly in size. The Sultan's larger brick palace was built after annexation by the Netherlands East Indies. As was also the case elsewhere in eastern Indonesia, the development of a strong kingly authority undermined other sources of authority (cf. Valeri 1991: 138).

Nas has argued that the Indonesian town has been largely overlooked in FAS related studies and consequently urbanization is a comparatively neglected phenomenon. What is significant is that the scattered references to the Indonesian capitals, especially the kraton or holy towns, suggest that the layout has been determined by cosmological principles. These urban centres symbolize the cosmological order and their most important elements are the kraton, the religious buildings and the residential districts of the different estates. The layout of these holy cities often comprises a series of concentric circles representing the cosmos. The core usually contains the kraton and the main temples surrounded by the dwellings of the nobility and the religious leaders. The residential area for the artisans surrounds the core, whereas the foreign traders live outside the city alongside the poor. The outer ring embraces the villages of the countryside, the abode of the peasants. A gradient runs from the core to the periphery, with status and power concentrated in the centre,

Fig. 17 The pillars symbolising Islamic law, customary law and administration in the prime minister's residence.

Fig. 18 Carved naga head above the entrance to
the prime minister's residence.

gradually declining as one moves to the outer rim (Nas 1984: 133). Given the fact that Bima is a kraton city, it is worthwhile enquiring how much it resembles the general pattern advanced by FAS theorists.

The Sultan was the ritual centre within the traditional system and was expected to be immobile and not venture outside his palace, though this changed markedly after the introduction of colonialism. The Sultan was held to be ritually pure and during Muslim festivals he attended state ceremonies dressed completely in white. His palace was also symbolically significant and a complex protocol covered how it was guarded. The outer gates were manned by *ananguru*, members of the military task group; but the discrete southern gate, which led to the goldsmith's ward, came under the auspices of goldsmith's *dari*. Although a military officer, *Ratu Parenta*, had overall authority over the guards, he was assisted by a civilian, known as the *Ompu Toi* (*ompu*, grandfather; *toi*, little), who represented the wider society. The perimeter wall marked the first boundary between the sacred centre and the profane outer world hence the division of authority between the two officials. The ratio of military to civilian personnel was reversed on the doors of the palace itself, since only the southern entrance was manned by soldiers, whereas all the rest were guarded by nobles. In view of their proximity to the innermost sanctum the rank of the guardians on the palace doors was higher than those on the outer walls.

The arrangement of the guards also reflected the division of authority within the realm. The district heads, for instance, were assisted by noblemen, *bumi naé*, who were as custodians of the land responsible for conducting rituals. In times of drought these 'lords of the land' offered sacrifices. They in turn were subject to the dual monarchy of the *Ruma Sangaji* and the *Ruma Bicara*. Likewise the officer in charge of the outer walls, a dignitary of the realm, was assisted by a commoner, a lower ranking custodian of the land and representative of the ordinary people.

A recurring theme in the Indic states of mainland South-East Asia is the capital as a symbol of cosmological order, and attempts have been made to apply this principle to the cultures of the Indonesian archipelago with mixed results (cf. Nas 1984: 125-138). Given the fact that local legends indicate strong links with Hindu-Java with regard to the foundation of the state it is tempting to apply these principles in the analysis of Bima. The myth of the prince and the naga princess is also present in Bima as it is in Indianized states of South-East Asia. The treatment accorded the centre in Bima could perhaps be regarded as a vestige of Hindu-Buddhism, but there are sound reasons for examining other parallels closer to hand. Ritual centres and elaborate protocols are found elsewhere in Indonesia, most notably in Timor among the Antoni (Cunningham 1964: 50-63). Not all these societies were subject to Hindu influence, especially that of the Atoni, and this strongly suggests that these customs are of indigenous derivation. Although Hindu influences cannot be entirely ruled out, the palace in Bima can be better understood in terms of the general Indonesian pattern.

Social rank

Up until the demise of the Sultanate Bimanese society was highly stratified. Although the class system was, in theory, abandoned during the early independence period many Bimanese are well aware of what rank their forebears belonged to. Former members of the nobility are proud of their aristocratic origins and the descendants of the last Sultan are held in high esteem. As late as the 1980s people of noble birth could still be addressed by their Sultanate titles, though these were being supplanted by the more egalitarian terms of the national language, *Bahasa Indonesia*. The use of titles such as *dieng* suggests strong Makasar influence and indeed the Bimanese class system resembles, in broad terms, that of neighbouring Sumbawa (Goethals 1961: 14) and southern Sulawesi (cf. Chabot 1967: 191). There are, however, other features that seem to be more generally Indonesian, which need not necessarily be ascribed to specific external influences. There are also elements which might be described as largely distinctively local, though parallels can sometimes be drawn with other maritime South-East Asian societies.

Before the establishment of the Hindu dynasty Bima was, according to legend, divided into three or four districts, each headed by a ritual leader known as an *ncuhi*. There arose a prince in Bima town who united the districts in what might be regarded as a federation. As the principality developed, the title of *ncuhi* fell into abeyance, though it continued to be used in the Donggo hills until the 1980s. The prince's family, who were known as the *sangaji*, comprised the social elite and were addressed by lower ranking

Bimanese as ruma (lord) through the Sultanate period, though the full title, *Ruma Sangaji*, was reserved for the ruler. This title lends support to the dynastic myth which links Bima to Java since, although the term *sang* (lord) is Malay, the address form *aji* (prince) is Javanese (Wilkinson *et al* 1963: 4 & 241).

The first rulers were born of a union between a prince and a naga and were thus spirits associated with heaven. The prince of Bima was also known as the *Dewa Sang Hien* or 'Lord of the Spirits', a title which he retained after the Islamization of the island. As can be seen in folk etymologies the notion that the rulers were heavenly-born persisted long after the Bimanese were converted to Islam. The term *sangaji*, for example, is said to be derived from sanga (branch) and a corruption of the Arabic word *jin* (spirit): hence 'descendant of a spirit'. The royal family eschewed marriages with lower ranking Bimanese apparently on account of the spiritual strength derived from their heavenly forebears, though there may also have been more pragmatic reasons since the rulers of Bima were able to marry into neighbouring royal families, thereby strengthening their dynastic links. Royal males were permitted to bear kris with gold sheaths, a right denied the nobility, as well as swords, *sondi*, with golden scabbards. Royal women were partial to elaborate jewellery set with rubies and pearls, and both princes and princesses wore silk sarongs brocaded with gold yarn. This standard of living was supported by the yield of irrigated land, which amounted to 266.33 hectares for the Sultan (Ahmad Amin 1971: 61), and the tribute from vassals and taxation, especially on trade.

Aristocrats known as *bumi naé* comprised the next tier of Sultanate society. What is interesting is that the term *bumi* is Sanskrit (Cooper *et al* 1963: 40) which suggests that it was either introduced through contact with Hindu-Buddhist Java or through the adoption of Malay by the court. Nobles were also addressed by the term *rato*, which is etymologically linked to the Javanese *ratu* (prince), though some aristocrats, presumably those of Makasar descent, were called *dieng*. After the royal family the nobles were the largest landowners, and though many owned no more than five hectares of rice fields, their holdings could be supplemented by government service. On ceremonial occasions the nobility wore silver and silk brocade sarongs, and bore kris with silver sheaths, though a gold and silver mix was permitted for nobles of the highest rank. Noblewomen were prevented from marrying commoners, as was the case in the neighbouring Sultanate of Sumbawa (Goethals 1961: 15), since any offspring would become commoners. Hypergamous marriages were, however, permissable, though a commoner woman who married a noble was not, in theory, eligible to be addressed as *rato*, though her children were nobles by birthright. In theory men were prevented from marrying well, but in practice the manipulation of genealogies ensured upward mobility for especially enterprizing young males. Genealogists were consulted when a low born man wished to marry a woman of a higher estate to see whether or not the male had anything in his family history that suggested noble origins.

The majority of the population belonged to the class of commoners which was subdivided into lower and upper halves. The higher commoners were wealthy farmers or skilled artisans and retainers who served the court. Higher commoner males were entitled to be addressed as *uba* and their wives could be honoured with the name *inantua* (grandmother), though there was no specific name for the stratum as a whole. Language also served as a mark of class distinction since Bimanese, like other Austronesian languages, has a graded vocabulary that communicates the relative status of speaker and listener. Higher commoners were free to marry lower commoners of either sex, though rich commoners often encouraged their daughters to marry into noble families, a practice that continued into the 1980s.

Although all lower commoners shared, in theory, the same rank, they were differentiated from one another in terms of land ownership. The richest who owned between one and five hectares of irrigated land were called *pertani*, whereas those who owned smaller plots were known as *burutani*. Landless commoners, *kulitani*, had to survive by share-cropping, though they were permitted to grow maize, subject to the approval of the headman, after the second crop of rice had been harvested on the land of wealthier villagers. In the urban areas landless commoners worked as labourers and were often dependent on rice collected in the wards as part of the Muslim tax known as *zakat*. Checked sarongs made of handspun cotton were worn by commoners, though the wealthier members of the class bore kris with wooden scabbards and owned silver jewellery. At the bottom of this social hierarchy were the slaves, comprising people who were temporarily enslaved as a result of failure to pay debts and permanent slaves, often prisoners of war, who could be sold.

The commoners, especially in the capital, were divided into a large number of groups known as *dari*. Elbert, following Jasper (1908:

98-108), refers to twenty-six of them, though some local scholars have claimed that the number was much higher. A. Amin made a list of *dari* (1971: 66), which he regarded as incomplete, and there is some disagreement in Bima with regard to his recollection of the titles. A *dari* was, as Goethals has argued (1960), a 'task group'. These groups have been likened to guilds (cf. Elbert 1912: 98), though they were not as independent as their European counterparts. All the *dari* were in the service of the court and each sent a representative to the Sultan. The representatives had noble titles and they and their assistants were treated as public servants and were given access to irrigated rice fields. Each task group did, however, hold some land independently of the Sultanate and therefore had a measure of autonomy. The *dari* also facilitated a certain amount of social mobility since it was possible for a higher commoner to become the leader of a task group and adopt a noble title. There was also downward mobility, though this is rarely discussed in Bima. Impoverished members of the nobility would find that they were unable to maintain the outward show of their rank and gradually they would find that they were no longer addressed with noble titles.

The members of each task or occupational group commonly resided in the same ward and were often related by kin ties or, as was the case with the Malays, by ethnic allegiance. The Indonesian term *suku* (a tribe or division of people) is sometimes offered locally as a translation of *dari*. *Dari* may also be translated as 'string' in the sense that each occupational group was attached to the court in order to carry out specific tasks. Interestingly, A. Amin treats the royal family as if they were also a task group (1971) and similar notions can be found in everyday speech when royalty are referred to as belonging to the *Dari Ruma* or *Dari Sangaji*. The task groups carried out a wide range of duties on behalf of the state in accordance with the general Indonesian pattern. Some *dari* were responsible for the armed forces, including cavalry, infantry and artillery, whereas others supplied the palace servants. There were *dari* for the different trades, such as blacksmithing, goldsmithing and carpentry, as well as task groups that had clerical and administrative responsibilities. The task group which supplied the grooms was located in Salama on the outskirts of the capital close to the pastures.

The occupational groups were principally responsible for tasks carried out by men, though many important activities at the state level were conducted by women. Although women's occupations were not regulated by the Sultanate in the same way as men's, it does not mean that they were small-scale and irrelevant. Indeed there was a flourishing trade in dyes, textiles and pottery, all of which were products made by women. Many female tasks were organized by the royal women, many of whom were accomplished in the arts of basketry and weaving. With regard to textiles, for example, the royal women exercised control by restricting access to the most important designs, which were kept on palm leaf lattices, and by monopolizing the import and manufacture of silk and gold yarn. These princesses were assisted by skilled noblewomen who worked under the supervision of a head woman known as the *Wai Naé* (*wai*, wife; *naé*, big). She managed the women in charge of the palace granaries, *Wai Oha*, basketry and storage, *Wai Baku*; and the chief femal circumcisor, *Wai Saraso*, as well as a wide range of other female functionaries. Although all noblewomen were expected to have a knowledge of music and dance, there were palace women who specialized in these areas. Leading practitioners were usually assisted by younger women, *ana wai* (*ana*, child), who were learning the various skills.

Indonesian Bima

The transition to an Indonesian-style system of government began after the death of the last Sultan, though it was not complete until Bima became part of the province of NTB. The monarch was replaced by a district head, *bupati*, and the administration was moved away from the palace to Raba. Bima's district heads began to be appointed directly by Jakarta following the assumption of power by Suharto's New Order regime. The next tier of government, however, remained largely in Bimanese hands, though the administrative system rapidly became Indonesianized. The subdistrict heads, *jenelis*, became known as *camats*, in accordance with the Javanese model, whereas the village headmen were given the Malay-Indonesian title of *kepala desa*. Although the headmen were, in theory, supposed to be elected, the New Order government was not averse to installing former military men, usually sergeants of Bimanese extraction, in areas where they perceived a threat to their authority. Government officials were expected to support GOLKAR, the government's party, a trend which increased during the 1980s, and by these means the Suharto regime assured loyalty at the local level.

The task groups fell into abeyance, though their former members continued to reside in traditional wards. Some of the heads of the task groups found employment at senior levels in the new government departments, especially when they possessed the appropriate skills and training. There were, for example, scribes from the Malay quarter who went on to pursue successful careers in the Department of Education and Culture, aided no doubt by their facility with Malay which is closely akin to the national language, Bahasa Indonesia. Less fortunate were the various craftsmen who, following the removal of royal patronage, had to find alternative markets for their goods. Some opened up small businesses with varying degrees of success, whereas others completely abandoned their heritage and sought other forms of employment, often as administrators and clerks in the expanding Indonesian bureaucracy. Generally-speaking it was the aristocracy who had had most access to education in the colonial era and it was they who went on to fill posts in the higher echelons of local government. There were, however, commoners who were quick to spot opportunities during this transitional period and who rose through the ranks. Likewise there were noblemen who did not adapt fast enough to the new system and who found themselves without a livelihood.

State employees were no longer awarded irrigated fields in lieu of payment and instead drew salaries. Although some members of local government continued to farm plots of land outside the capital, many began to lose contact with the rural way of life. To be sure, wealthy landowners often retained control of their fields by a variety of ruses, despite national attempts at land reform; but the majority of government servants became effectively landless and consequently more urbanized. The kris and sarongs of the old order were exchanged for a plethora of Indonesian badges of office (suits, banners, desktop ornaments, etc.), which were almost as symbolically complex as the ones they replaced. Following a cleaning and restoration programme in the 1970s, the Sultan's palace re-opened as a cultural centre, though, with the exception of the Ramadan parades, it was rarely used for state ceremonials. Increasingly the palace was supplanted by the new government buildings in Raba, where government employees worked and performed new national rituals devised by the New Order regime. Seated in rows of chairs the uniformed civil servants gather to listen to speeches by their superiors, and to applaud colleagues who have won promotions and awards. An elaborate protocol surrounds the raising and lowering of the national flag at the beginning and end of each working day. Office walls are dotted with posters proclaiming national targets (family planning, the electrification of villages, etc.) and statistics, as well as portraits of the president himself.

The emerging middle class of New Order Bima, increasingly dependent on government and commerce rather than agriculture, also became more mainstream Muslim in outlook. By the early 1980s the phone, and more importantly the television, were well established in urban areas and provided a conduit by which new developments in Islam could reach the population as a whole. Increasing numbers of Bimanese went on the *hajj* to Mecca and returned enthused by the scale and diversity of the religion to which they subscribed. Bimanese students went to study at seminaries in Java and abroad, and others found work in the oil rich Gulf states as drivers, security men and labourers. Increasing use of the national language Bahasa Indonesia facilitated access to newly-translated Arabic texts, and Islamic revivalism. The Indonesian authorities regarded traditional belief systems as backward, symbols of the countries underdevelopment, and, in accordance with the state philosophy of *Pancasila*, citizens were encouraged to re-affirm their allegiance to one of the world religions. The urban Bimanese duly obliged: the process of Islamization was intensified in the hills and more remote rural areas; new and better-equipped Islamic schools were opened; village mosques were enlarged or even entirely re-built. The Bimanese of the capital became simultaneously more urban, more Indonesian and more Muslim, and though ethnic ties remained strong the pendulum swung closer to an Islamic identity.

VI

Handicrafts and Gender

In spite of the archipelago's ethnic diversity, common cultural themes can be detected, especially with regard to gender. Broadly similar values are shared by the speakers of Austronesian languages, and nowhere is this more apparent than in the link between handicrafts and gender. Research by anthropologists and historians has revealed a fairly consistent division of labour across maritime South-East Asia, though there are some regional variations (cf. Adams 1975: 27; Du Bois 1961: 60; Raffles 1817: 168). Certain tasks are nearly always linked with one gender and the most common division is that between metalworking by men and the production of cloth by women (Adams 1973: 277). Men also tend to undertake such tasks as boat- and house-building, while women practise basketry and pottery. Many of the tasks connected with weaving (such as harvesting and spinning cotton, and dyeing) are also controlled by women, and the income derived usually belongs to them. Not only is the labour divided, but so are the products: goods made by women are symbolically female; goods made by men are associated with masculinity. It is the purpose here to examine Bimanese notions of gender with special reference to the concepts of Indonesian unity derived from Dutch structuralism and later formulations within the same tradition.

Such is its cultural significance that the division of labour is a common theme in the mythology of many Indonesian peoples. The Toba Batak, for example, possess a legend known as the story of

Tunggal Panaluan, in which the male-female opposition is described in terms of weaving (women's work) and writing/magic (man's work). In the story, boy and girl twins are born fully equipped with the tools of their respective professions: the boy with sacred texts and the girl with weaving implements. Later in life when their parents try to set them tasks that males and females do together the twins refuse: the boy wishes to devote himself solely to the magic arts, while the girl desires only to weave (Niessen 1985: 80-83). The link between women and textiles also appears in other Batak legends, such as the tale of the girl who was turned into an ape for refusing to spin yarn. Yet in another Batak legend the opposite happens: a young woman is exiled to the moon because she is more interested in spinning than marrying (Niessen 1985: 116). The latter myth emphasizes moderation when dealing with potent symbols of gender such as cloth. References to this division of labour may also be seen on the artefacts themselves, as is the case in Lamatera where textiles bear designs showing the harpooning of rays, a male task, and the preparation of ikat cloth, a female occupation (Barnes 1989: 68).

Among some Indonesian peoples craft processes, such as weaving, are seen as expressions of the interdependence of men and women, sometimes with sexual connotations. Thus the Batak liken the bamboo shuttle to the penis, as do the Bugis and Makasar who traditionally believed that if a man held a shuttle he would become impotent (Jasper & Pirngadie 1912: 6). There is also a Javanese myth that concerns a weaver who drops her shuttle and rashly promises to marry whoever retrieves it. When the shuttle is returned by a dog, the weaver fulfils her obligation and marries the animal (Derks 1983: 48). The shuttle is associated with the male in many Indonesian societies, but both cloth and yarn are commonly considered to be female. Among the Toraja, for example, the words for weaving and vulva are etymologically linked, and textiles are traditionally likened to the female sexual organs (Kruyt 1922: 415).

Because male and female tasks are complementary, the possession of craft skills enhances a young person's marriage prospects. Women, for example, were traditionally expected to advertise their skills to potential husbands, as was particularly the case in Java where young women worked in front of their homes (Raffles 1817: 80). Upon mastering the art of weaving a woman is considered to be ready for marriage, and looms and spinning wheels are widely associated with the rituals of courtship. In some societies, especially Muslim ones, it was inappropriate for a girl to work in full public view and, therefore, the weaver was expected to demonstrate her skill with the aid of noise-makers attached to her loom. The sound made by clappers and rattles not only indicated that the weaver was hard at work, but was also believed to help ward off evil spirits (cf. Ling Roth 1977: 82-85). Rattling looms that have romantic associations are also known in the Philippines and there is a model of a Bugis loom in the Cambridge University Museum of Archaeology and Anthropology that has a clapper built into the warp-beam.

Indonesian weddings are usually preceded by gift exchanges in which the bride's family provides goods associated with the female and receives in return objects that are symbolically male. The family that provides the wife may be socially superior, as is the case with the Toba Batak, who give spiritual, life-giving female gifts. The wife-takers show their respect by providing worldly support in the form of cattle and money, etc. (i.e. male goods). The generic term *ulos* (textile) is used by the Toba Batak for all gifts provided by the wife-givers, even if they are not textiles. Prestations of any kind made by the wife-takers are likewise referred to as *piso* (knife); the opposition of the cloth and the knife parallels the opposition of the wife-giver and the wife-taker (Niessen 1984: 67). Similar observations can be made with regard to the kris (male) and cloth (female) in Java, and elsewhere in the Malay-Indonesian world (cf. Rassers 1959).

The fact that common cultural themes could be detected in the Indonesian archipelago led Dutch scholars to argue that these peoples were united by common core elements. These societies were structured in varying but related ways, and this made comparative research, within what was known as a 'field of ethnological study', worthwhile. According to JPB de Josselin de Jong the nucleus of these core elements, which had some kind of organic link to the overall social structure, was socio-cosmic dualism. This dualism formed the basis of an all-embracing classifactory system in which human society was divided into two descent groups, two phratries, and two series of clans, etc. This was paralleled by a cosmic dichotomy that divided the heaven from the earth, and the upperworld from the lowerworld, as well as many other oppositions (e.g. superior-inferior; good - evil) (de Josselin de Jong 1977: 172).

It seemed to Dutch structuralists that this classificatory system also embraced the male-female dichotomy, and nowhere was this more apparent than in the symbolic link between certain handicrafts and gender, especially with regard to textiles and women. After perusing the literature for information on the social function of cloth, JH Jager Gerlings drew the conclusion that cloth is generally included in the sacred heirlooms, *pusaka*, of Indonesian societies, clans and families, and plays an important role in the ceremonies connected with birth, rites of passage, death and agriculture. According to Jager Gerlings, the use of cloth in these rituals formed part of the 'Indonesian world view' and was linked to the complex female qualities of life, namely fertility (1952: 105). Like Dutch scholars before him Jager Gerlings was also of the view that the dualistic Indonesian world view was reflected in social structure, though he did not pursue the matter.

In considering the underlying unity of Indonesian traditions – a theme that has been returned to on many subsequent occasions (cf. Gittinger 1975, 1975, 1978) – Dutch scholars were struck by the resilience of indigenous cultural systems. Despite the fact that these societies had been subject to a variety of foreign influences (e.g. Hindu - Buddhism, Christianity), the local culture did not appear to have been eroded. Foreign cultural elements were incorporated selectively and given an indigenous interpretation and, according to J.P.B. de Josselin de Jong, this reaction to external influence was one of the core features of these Indonesian societies (Niessen 1985: 3). On the basis of the information available at the time, these observations were appropriate, but they did not fully take into account what happened in Muslim societies. Islam is a pervasive and all-embracing religion and it was by no means clear from the Dutch structuralist perspective what happened when indigenous cultures were confronted with this vital religion. The data was not, in any case, always readily available, since much of the research conducted in the Dutch structuralist tradition, particularly in eastern Indonesia, was carried out in non-Muslim societies, though P.E. de Josselin de Jong worked on the Minangkabau and Malays of Negri Sembilan (1980). Bima is particularly interesting in this respect because it is both self-confessedly Muslim and yet has much in common with neighbouring non-Muslim regions.

Sexual division of labour

Bimanese children learn the skills appropriate to their sex largely through practical experience. A five- or six-year old girl may begin by learning crafts associated with the female by imitating her mother or grandmother, gradually extending her repertoire of skills. In cotton-producing areas, girls learn to spin between the ages of eight and eleven, and by her early teens a weaver is expected to be competent in the basic patterning skills. Unlike the boys described by du Bois in the island of Alor, young Bimanese males are often given responsible tasks before they become teenagers. While still very young boys learn gardening and lumbering, and often stay overnight in field shelters with older boys to help protect the crops from thieves and wild animals. All girls learn to prepare food and many are proficient cooks by the age of eleven.

Child labour is valued in Bimanese society, though children are not coerced into working. Children run errands, sweep out houses and tidy up yards, sell drinks and snacks, herd ducks and goats, help bring in the harvest, and lay out chairs for meetings. The Bimanese abhor glumness and children are encouraged to lighten the workload with cheerful conversation, banter and sometimes songs. It is unthinkable for a person to work alone; virtually all tasks are group activities. Even when learning to recite passages from the Koran, Bimanese children are expected to work in pairs. Since a great deal of work is divided by gender, group tasks help to reinforce identities based on sex. Young children are urged by adults and older children to carry out gender specific tasks and are rewarded with approval and, occasionally, small gifts. Adult roles are also acted out in children's games: boys playing the part of buffalo pull toy ploughs to the command of a junior ploughman; girls set up shops on crates and learn how to bargain. Culture may not be the only factor in determining gender behaviour, but it undoubtedly plays an important shaping role.

The way that craft skills are divided in Bima corresponds to the general Indonesian pattern. Men, for example, are associated with metal and metal-working, whereas women are the weavers and potters. There are, however, tasks that are carried out by both sexes (e.g. rice harvesting), particularly those in the agricultural sector, as well as occupations that are mainly, though not exclusively, the preserve of one sex (e.g. market trading). Tasks that have not long been established in Bima, which cannot readily be associated with an already existing occupation, tend to be ambiguous at first, though they may rapidly become the preserve of one sex (e.g. electrical repairs). The sexual division of labour as it existed in the 1980s may be summarized as follows:

Women	Men	Mainly Women	Mainly Men	Both
weaving	blacksmithing	water carrying	clearing	havesting
spinning	gold & silver	peddling	swiddens	animal
dyeing	smithing	market-	gardening	husbandry
pottery	carpentry	trading	tailoring	(ducks
basketry	house & boat	house	portage	chickens
grain storage	building	cleaning		goats)
clothes	brick-making	child minding		clerical work
washing	ploughing	traditional		
midwifery	irrigation	medicine		
household	fishing/			
finance	hunting			
	taxi driving			
	animal			
	husbandry			
	(horses &			
	buffalos)			
	electrical			
	repairs			

The Bimanese explain this division of labour by recourse to folk models which are shared by both men and women. It is held, for example, that men do the heavier and coarser work, and women the lighter and more refined tasks, and reference is often made to working with clay. Women are skilled artisans and make a wide range of fine pots, whereas men are responsible for producing rough tiles and bricks. Male and female methods of portage also serve as a folk paradigm; a man uses a carrying pole over the shoulder and can therefore lift twice as much as a woman who bears loads on her head. Bimanese men also say that as good Muslims they are expected to shoulder a heavier burden than women and profess to be shocked by the behaviour of Balinese migrants to the island. Hindu-Balinese women serve as hod carriers and labourers on building sites, tasks that Bimanese women would never be expected to undertake. Generally-speaking these folk models provide a rough guide to attitudes to gender since men do undertake heavier jobs (e.g. ploughing, blacksmithing) and women lighter ones (spinning, basketry). There is, however, a contradiction since men also carry out the comparatively light task of gold- and silversmithing; but in this case it is the ancient association of men with metals that is applicable and not the 'heaviness' folk model.

Tailoring is also a light task that is undertaken by men. In view of the use of metal sewing machines, it would be tempting to account for this phenomenon in terms of the man/metal link, but there are good reasons for considering alternative explanations. Although men are responsible for making and maintaining equipment (e.g. looms), they do not invariably use them (the women weave), and it does not therefore follow that tailoring should be a predominantly male preserve simply because men repair sewing machines. A more overriding concern is the fact that tailors usually have physical contact with their customers, especially when taking measurements. Muslims do not approve of this level of intimacy between males and females and therefore men are obliged to go to male tailors. Tailors tend to be male simply because it is men who make most use of their services; women usually run up their own tailored garments at home.

In accordance with another folk paradigm, it is held that women's tasks are those most closely associated with the home. Again the model serves as a rough guide to what actually happens since many women's tasks (e.g. weaving, spinning, cooking) are carried out at home. So close is the association between women and the home that the interior of the house, the women's quarters, are known as the *ina uma* (*ina*, mother; *uma*, home). The inner sanctum also includes the attic which sometimes serves as a workplace, especially for young women. The possession of craft skills traditionally enhanced a woman's marriage prospects and weavers, in particular, were expected to advertise their skills to potential husbands. In Bima it was thought unseemly for a girl to weave in full public view and therefore young women often worked in the attic. This seclusion, however, made it impossible to judge the young woman's abilities and the problem was overcome by attaching rattles and clappers to the looms. There are tales of young men reciting love poems to girls in attics, the success of their suit being gauged by the level of rattling coming from the attic.

Explanations for the link between women and the home are usually couched in Muslim terms in Bima; but there are grounds for considering alternative explanatory frameworks, not least because similar notions are encountered in neighbouring non-Muslim societies. On the nearby island of Lombok, for example, the Hindu-Balinese also say that women's tasks are those that are home-based, an outlook that corresponds with the wider South-East Asian pattern

(Duff-Cooper 1985: 235). It would appear that certain Bimanese attitudes to gender pre-date the arrival of Islam and, though they were strongly influenced by the new religion, the Bimanese did not entirely abandon their pre-Islam heritage, especially when it did not contradict existing social mores. What is also worth looking at in this context are the occasions when the folk model does not accurately reflect social realities, as is the case when going out of the village to plant and harvest rice. Such is the demand for labour during peak periods in the agricultural cycle, that women leave the household and work in the fields; certain economic factors may override cultural preferences. Likewise men took up the female occupation of spinning during the Japanese occupation because of the extreme shortage of yarn.

Both men and women subscribe to the view that women are primarily home-makers, while overlooking the fact that much of the island's commerce is in the hands of women. Women not only manage family finances, but also do most of the buying and selling, and consequently dominate the marketplace. Women travel freely from home to market, sometimes on a daily basis; they greet returning shoppers with the traditional *lao ta bé?* (where are you going?), a prelude to questions about prices and the availability of goods. By the time a woman reaches the market, she usually has a shrewd idea of current prices and rarely wastes much time in bargaining. Markets follow the bazaar pattern with groups of small traders selling similar products congregating in the same areas. It is more advantageous for women to gather together where they may be located by shoppers than to strike off on their own. The women do not pose much of a competitive threat to one another since they only have a limited number of goods to sell and leave when their stocks are exhausted. Profit margins are low, but so are the overheads, and the involvement of large numbers of petty traders spreads small benefits widely. The markets also provide security and friendship, and serve as an important source of information in a society where newspapers are rare.

Women do not rely on markets alone, and many also work as peddlars. They wrap traditional medicines, perfumes and handicrafts in colourful sarongs and carry them in baskets on their heads. Peddlars wend their way around urban backstreets, calling out their wares, or trudge down country lanes to serve outlying villages. Some brave hazardous mountain paths to sell coastal produce, including salted fish, in highland settlements. A few women rise to prominence as dealers in luxury goods such as gold, ivory, rubies and pearls. They travel the length and breadth of eastern Indonesia by means of the network of small buses, ferries and prohus. They rely on friends and relatives for food and accommodation, often staying in Muslim enclaves in the Christian dominated islands. Some travel as far afield as Singapore in search of a good bargain.

According to some Bimanese, the freedom experienced by women is a relatively new phenomenon dating from the late 1960s. They maintain that the island used to be more staunchly Islamic and that the main market traders were men because women rarely ventured beyond the confines of their villages. It remains unclear, however, whether or not the restrictions imposed on women were entirely due to Islamic prohibitions since other factors, especially poor security, need to be taken into account. Normal economic relations were severely disrupted by the alleged coup of 1965 and its bloody aftermath, and the Bimanese, like many Indonesians, retreated to the comparative safety of their villages. The women may simply have resumed trading as the security situation improved and therefore their involvement in markets need not have arisen because of a marked discontinuity in Islamic practice. The fact that Bimanese attitudes to gender conform to the broad Indonesian pattern strongly suggests that the involvement of women in trade is an old established custom.

Not all notions concerning gender have indisputedly Islamic origins, though explanations may be couched in Islamic terms. There are, however, some practices that are clearly derived from Islamic sources, and chief among these is the custom of veiling. Local women have long made use of handwoven sarongs to cover the hair, a custom which attracted the attention of Dutch scholars, though Islamic laws concerning dress were never applied with equal vigour throughout the island (cf. Ligtvoet 1876: 587). Women traditionally tie the sarong under the chin with a tuck, known as a *rimpi*, which leaves the face bare. Many women wear veils when travelling between the marketplace and home, but remove them immediately on arrival in an environment in which they feel secure, such as in the market itself. For many women the veil is not only a sign of faith, but is also a convenient way of keeping long hair clean when journeying on Sumbawa's notoriously dusty roads. Whether or not women wear veils is a matter of personal choice; the only people who wear them on a regular basis are girls attending Islamic schools and colleges.

In addition to using sarongs as veils, women wear them as skirts in conjunction with a Malay blouse, *kebaya*. In contrast to men women do not tie the sarong above the navel. Instead they press the cloth with the left hand on to the right hip and then use the right hand to pull a large fold of cloth across the stomach to the left hip. The end of the fold is then tucked under the tightly wrapped top of the sarong. This method of tying is closing associated with female identity, though it is also adopted by certain men. The men who wear sarongs tied in the traditional female manner occupy a special place in Bimanese society. Some of them weave high quality textiles and live their lives as women, short of marrying and raising children. These men may be called upon to organise life-cycle festivals and often provide entertainment during wedding receptions. The fact that some men choose a female identity is accepted and, though regarded with a certain amount of amusement, these men are not ostracized. A similar outlook is encountered in southern Sulawesi where men who adopt women's roles are also involved in arranging wedding festivals (cf. Millar 1989: 83).

South-East Asian peoples are generally tolerant of men with ambiguous sexual preferences, though they rarely distinguish between different types of behaviour. The fact that no distinction is made between transsexuals, transvestites and homosexuals is reflected in the use of catchall terms, such as *banci* (Ind.), to describe them. The question of female homosexuality is rarely entertained. In the eyes of many South-East Asians it is the desire on the part of certain men to act and dress like women that places them in this ambiguous category. Homosexual sex itself is regarded as a minor abhoration and a man who indulges in it is not necessarily regarded as a homosexual, especially if he is young at the time and later goes on to marry a woman and father children. Bimanese attitudes to homosexuality conform to the wider South-East Asian pattern and do not appear to have been radically altered by the introduction of Islam. Islam may, however, have helped to define gender boundaries more precisely, and the prominence of transvestisim in Bimanese society may be related to the sharp differentiation between the sexes.

Marriage and inheritance

As is the case in Bugis society, and the Malay world in general, marriage is the premier ritual of social location in Bima. From

Fig. 19 Dressed as a prince and princess the bride and groom
are congratulated by guests at a wedding reception.

Fig. 20 The groom's costume is based on court dress.
Bpk Abbas, a silversmith from Naé, demonstrates the outfit.
The bright colours symbolise health and prosperity.

childhood onwards the Bimanese are enjoined to marry well. The wedding day not only confirms complete adult status, but also represents the completion of the individual by bringing together the male and female halves. The Bimanese present cloths as gifts from the wife-givers to reciprocate the brideprice payments agreed between the two families (see Chapter 8). Masculine goods provided by the wife-takers may include gold coins, weapons, tools, jewellery and livestock, especially horses. During the wedding reception the bridal couple, dressed as a prince and princess for a day, sit in state to receive the congratulations of friends and relatives. The visitors bring small gifts, often coins wrapped in paper. The reception area may have stuffed mattresses and cushions, and the bridal bed may be festooned with embroidered hangings. Textiles that are believed to have talismanic properties are usually displayed behind the podium. After shaking hands with the newlyweds, the visitors file off to dine on sticky rice and fried chicken, washed down with tea and 'sprite'. Musicians may be brought on to entertain the guests at the end of the ceremony, and these may include bawdy songs sung by transvestites.

The information on Bimanese kinship is limited and we are largely dependent on Brewer's study of a village community in eastern Rasanaé. In an unpublished paper Brewer listed the kinship terminology of his village in Rasana, Raba town and the Rasanaé subdistrict generally (Brewer 1978). He found that the same terms were used across the region, an observation that has been corroborated by subsequent studies (Hitchcock 1983: 77). In accordance with the general Indonesian pattern, Brewer noted that the same core kin terms were used to refer to non-kin who occupied a similar generational position relative to the speaker (Brewer 1978: 13-14). Thus a man might address any male of his father's generation as *ama* (father). Brewer's study of eastern Rasanaé also showed that there was a bilateral recognition of kinship, in which children inherited from both parents, with all siblings receiving equal shares (Brewer 1979: 66). If a married couple had no children then the inheritance would go to the children of the couple's siblings (Brewer 1979: 14).

Wealth in eastern Rasanaé was evaluated in terms of agricultural land, large domestic animals, houses, granaries and gold coins. Among the most esteemed were gold and land because they were regarded as productive resources that could be put to use. For daily transactions the liquid assets of rice and money were used, though increasingly radios and tape-recorders were being used as easily convertible stores of wealth (Brewer 1979: 276). The preferred marriage rule was for kin of the same generation, who were not siblings, to marry (Brewer 1978: 14). The ideal match was that of a man and the daughter of a younger sibling of either of his parents. In accordance with customary law married couples were expected to own their own house and they usually resided somewhere inbetween the homes of both sets of parents (Brewer 1978: 14). Limited research by Brewer in Raba town also revealed a preference for cross-cousin marriage, that is marriage to the offspring of a parent's brother or sister of the opposite sex (e.g. the child of the sister of the father), suggesting that there were variations in Bimanese kinship patterns (Brewer 1978: 1-14). A parallel can be drawn with neighbouring west Sumba where means of regulating marriage and descent vary, though there are general principles of order which are understandable throughout the region (Needham 1980: 22-42).

In view of the paucity of data from many regions, it is not possible to identify general principles concerning Bimanese kinship; but what is clear is that patterns of marriage and descent do vary, particularly to the west of the area investigated by Brewer. The people of western Rasanaé are more urbanized and multi-ethnic than their eastern neighbours, and this accounts for some of the differences. Historically, they were also more involved in court affairs than the people further east, especially the members of the nobility. People in the west of the subdistrict do not express a preference for marrying cousins and have, in theory, a freer choice of marriage partners than their eastern counterparts. In practice, however, the poorer members of society tend to marry people from their own or a neighbouring hamlet and therefore tend to be locally endogamous. In contrast the wealthier members of society, often the descendants of the nobility, widen their circle of influence by marrying outside their local area. The network of contacts established through marriage enables those village exogamous families to play a leading role in local affairs, particularly when dealing with the outside world.

In western Rasanaé it is often the woman who moves into her husband's village on marriage. In contrast to the east of the subdistrict, the people of the west like to live virilocally after marriage. Men say that they prefer to have their sons live near them and it is customary for a father to provide each son with a house. Fathers like to build their sons' houses next door; but, given the shortage of land near Bima Bay, this may be impossible and parents have to contend with any available plot. Since married couples are expected to own their own homes, fathers struggle to provide the basic amenities, and only the poorest members of society continue to live with their parents after marriage. If a man is sufficiently wealthy to take a second wife he is obliged, in accordance with Islamic law, to provide his new spouse with her own home: wives expect equal treatment.

The ideal is for a man to begin constructing his son's home when the boy reaches adolescence. As the structure becomes habitable the boy starts to sleep there and gradually it becomes his permanent sleeping quarters. The eldest son often shares the building with his younger brothers until they move into dwellings of their own. The younger sons are expected to vacate the building on the marriage of the eldest brother. From the moment a boy moves into his new home it is known as a *ruka*; but it becomes a complete household, *uma*, when his bride takes up residence. The Bimanese customarily hold a wedding reception outside the *ruka*, though poor families who are unable to afford homes for their offspring have to make do with alternative venues. The term *ruka* is applied to any place where a marriage is celebrated, even if it is only a temporary arrangement (cf. Ahmad Amin 1971: 27). As is the case with the Bugis of South Sulawesi, the Bimanese attach great importance to weddings and the associated ceremonials are elaborate. Each wedding involves a series of rituals of social location which reaffirm the status of the bride and groom, and celebrate the appropriateness of the union.

The bilateral inheritance rule recorded by Brewer in eastern Rasanaé is also observed in the west; but only with regard to certain communities. Land, livestock, rice and money are inherited from both parents by male and female offspring, but craft tools are handed on from parents to children of the same sex. Thus a son will inherit his father's tools and a daughter her mother's. Although land is inherited bilaterally, there is often disagreement concerning the proportion due to children of each sex. Many men subscribe to Islamic law and argue that males should inherit twice the amount of females; others continue to abide by customary law and divide their property equally between sons and daughters. Women are disadvantaged by the application of Islamic laws of inheritance and it is not surprising that they stress *adat*. It is widely held that women are less strict than men in their observance of Islam and that they prefer to keep ancient customs and laws alive. A parallel can be drawn with the Makasar of southern Sulawesi who maintain that the '... ancestor cult is the religion of women, Islam the religion of men' (Chabot 1967: 203).

Basketry and pottery

Two important female occupations, basketry and pottery, which are not explored in detail later in the book are worth discussing here because of their historical significance. A prime example of Bimanese basketry is recorded in Jasper and Mas Pirngadie's comprehensive series on the arts and crafts of Indonesia (1912). Baskets like the one shown in the illustration were probably made in lowland Bima up until the mid 20th century, and some especially fine varieties were made by the women of the palace. Finely woven baskets were used as rice covers during state banquets and were often embellished with velvet and silver thread. By the early 1980s the lowland basketry industry was in decline and items of the quality described by Jasper and Mas Pirngadie were rarely being made. The Wawo highlanders remained some of the last exponents of a craft that was once widespread in lowland Bima, and thus it was possible to gain some insight into how the royal baskets were made (Hitchcock 1986: 26).

During the early 1980s Wawo highlanders could be seen making their way down the dirt roads with baskets destined for the lowland markets piled high on their heads. Some of the most popular baskets were the robust general purpose containers made from bamboo. The baskets were made by women from Tarlawi during lulls in the agricultural cycle when the demand for female labour in the rice fields was low. The Tarlawi baskets were made in the following manner. Bamboo strips approximately a yard in length were laid on the floor and were held in place with a slim stick under the weaver's foot. Using an under and over plait, weft strips of a similar length were beaten in with a hard wooden sword; the bamboo was moistened with water to keep it supple. The unplaited ends of the strips, approximately 8 inches in length, were turned up and then woven in to make the corners of the basket. A strip of bamboo on the inside rim was secured with rattan stitches to a willow-like lath around the outside. A short metal spike was used to punch holes in the bamboo for the rattan ties. Baskets could be made fairly rapidly,

Fig. 21 Basket makers use hard wooden swords
to beat in the bamboo wefts, Tarlawi.

Fig. 22   Potter in Raba Nggodu.

and a woman could make at least three and perhaps as many as ten per day. In 1981 these baskets could be sold for between Rupiah 150 (30 cents) and Rupiah 250 (50 cents) each.

Baskets were not made in the neighbouring village of lower Tarlawi, though they did have an interesting variant of this craft - rain capes made from pandanus leaves. The capes comprised two sheets, each made of five leaves compressed together along their long sides. The sheets were joined together end to end, and then folded in the middle and sewn along one side to make a roof-like structure that could be hung over the head. The sides of the cape reached as far as the upper back, and with its open front the garment was ideal for working in the rice fields when the wearer would be bent double. For children the garment was especially snug since it would almost envelop them. Another practical application for pandanus could also be seen in the village of Teta where hard-wearing house mats, the usual interior furnishing of highland homes, were plaited.

More delicate examples of the basket maker's craft could be seen in the village of Sombori where three main types were made. The *kaleru* was a soft plaited bag that was used for storing either a packed lunch of boiled rice or the owner's betel chewing kit. The *saduka* was used for carrying seeds or plants and therefore had a broad, round opening and a strap for suspending the baskets from the wrist. Dyed strips were incorporated into the third kind of basket, *kula baku toi*, which was shaped like a small hexagonal cylinder. Its lid was detachable and the basket could be used for carrying a woman's personal effects by stowing it in a fold in the sarong.

In contrast to basketry, pottery is largely a lowland occupation. The main pottery village, Raba Ngodu, is located close to a source of clay and fine river sand. Pottery is exclusively a female task, including digging for clay, though two transvestites were involved in this work in 1981. The women ensure that the clay is free of stones before kneading into a ball. The potter keeps a bucket of dry clay granules in a bucket to hand and uses a piece of sacking cloth as a work surface. She then pinches up the sides of the ball before beating it on a stone anvil with a wooden mallet, *bebe*. The surface of the clay may be moistened with water and smoothed with a rag, though the bases of straight-necked pots are left rough. A broad open-mouthed pot may be made with the aid of a circle of rattan, *binggi*, and the lips may be trimmed with a bamboo tool, *seduncu*. The pot may be left for up to two hours in the sun before the anvil is re-inserted and the sides are beaten again to make the pot larger. After drying in the morning sun, the pots are placed on a pile of firewood and are covered with straw. Coconut husks are inserted between the pots to protect them and ensure the passage of air. As many as thirty pots, stacked in three layers, may be fired in the kiln in one session. Firing lasts long enough to ensure that the pots glow bright red, though they may be scorched black by covering them with burning stalks. Approximately twenty large pots can be made ready for firing over the course of a few days.

The product range is based on variations of eleven or so basic types of pot. These include pots with spouts, pots for carrying water, several kinds of cooking pots, and water pots with bungs for washing before prayers. The latter are slightly porous and may sweat in sunlight, thereby helping to keep the water cool. A large flat pottery dish serves as a hearth for cooking in many Bimanese households. Flower pots with wavy necks are also produced, as are ashtrays decorated with clay birds. Plates are made by coiling strips of clay, which are smoothed together with a wet cloth. When the plate has dried some more, it is polished with a glass bottle.

Pottery is a female task, and unlike weaving, it is not assumed that all women are able to make pots. The potters of Raba Ngodu learn the craft as teenagers by watching their mothers and elder sisters. Various explanations are given as to why men do not make pottery: it is simply not their job; they are too lazy to learn; their work is insufficiently refined. Men do, however, help out and may fetch clay and sand, as well as tending kilns. Men are also involved in making tiles, as are some women, which are trimmed with a wire cutter, *rabi*. The villagers of Raba Ngodu recall an active trade in pots with the neighbouring island of Flores, where some Bimanese potters settled. The islanders of Sumba also purchased Bimanese pots, giving in exchange coconuts and palm sugar. There was an exodus of potters from Raba Ngodu in the 1930s because of drought, some of whom eventually took up residence near Kupang in Timor.

VII

The Sacred Kris

The Malay-Indonesian dagger known as the kris (*keris*) was the paramount prestige weapon of the courts of maritime South-East Asia. Forged by armourers gathered around the palaces of princes and rajahs, these prized heirlooms were made to the highest aesthetic standards. Kris were attributed magical powers and individual personalities, and craftsmen took care to ensure that weapons matched the temperaments of their owners, an especially meaningful consideration in societies where these daggers were closely associated with masculinity. In the literature on the archipelago, the male character of the kris is as much a recurring theme as the femaleness of the textile (cf. Adams 1975: 27, Du Bois 1960: 60, Gittinger 1976: 20). The huge linga sculpture with inset kris found at Candi Sukuh in Java links kris iconography to phallic symbolism (Ibbitson Jessup 1990: 150). So closely was the dagger identified with the male that a kris could be used as a substitute for a groom should he be unable to attend the wedding: the bride would marry the groom's kris (Raffles 1965: 318). Similar notions are encountered in eastern Indonesia where the Bimanese, like the Bugis and Makasars, consider the kris to be the '... inseparable brother of man' (Rassers 1940: 525). This weapon may rightly be regarded as one of the region's foremost cultural artefacts, a pan-Indonesian symbol of masculinity.

As the power of the courts declined in post-colonial Indonesia, the demand for ceremonial weaponry decreased and the armourer's art suffered accordingly. The new leaders increasingly preferred international status symbols - cars, watches, electrical goods, etc. - and though a few skilled armourers survived (cf. Solyom & Solyom 1978), the art of kris-making went into decline. Yet despite the change in values and the demise of kris forging, these weapons remain culturally significant, albeit on a diminished scale. Because of its ancient association with the male the kris is usually still worn as part of the groom's wedding costume, and it is kris of this kind that are inherited in the time-honoured fashion. Cultural revivals in various Indonesian regions have helped to re-awaken interest in the kris, especially, though not exclusively, in areas with a strong Islamic tradition. The art of kris making is strongly associated with the court cultures of the archipelago, and thus the non-Muslim Balinese, as well as the Muslim Javanese, possess fine kris traditions. But because the majority of the indigenous courts were converted to Islam, the kris eventually became closely connected to an Islamic identity. Interestingly, some modern bureaucrats and businessmen have acquired an antiquarian's taste for these weapons and have become enthusiastic collectors - the art of kris appreciation is still extant. The transformation of the kris, which began before the demise of colonialism, from mystical weapon to art object did not invariably meet with approval from Western scholars. Gardner, for example, in his study of Malay kris, clearly regretted the weapon's descent from royal symbol to '... mere curio' (1936: 63).

It is the purpose of this chapter to show how the kris was made and used in the Sultanate of Bima, and to trace its transformation from sacred weapon to item of private contemplation. As in many Indonesian societies kris served as markers of social status, and even badges of office, but as the old hierarchical values were swept away after independence, kris were no longer worn on a regular basis: There were also attempts to disarm the population, a process begun in the colonial period, and Bimanese males long ago gave up feeling 'undressed' in public without their daggers. The kris, however, forms an integral part of Bimanese ceremonial dress and continues to be worn during important festivals, such as the parades which mark the end of Ramadan. But the majority of kris are never taken out of the home, though they may be shown to friends, relatives and honoured guests. Despite the predominance of republican values, the reference point to kris evaluation on these occasions remains the Sultanate of Bima. Kris are ranked with regard to the Sultanate class system and aesthetic appreciation is closely tied to old social values.

The armourer's craft

The Bimanese kris, known as *sampari*, is similar to daggers from other parts of the archipelago. Its blade may be straight or wavy and the handle, which is held like the butt of a pistol, is set at an angle to the central axis of the weapon, a feature which, according to Gardner, gives the kris a longer reach in proportion to its length than more conventional daggers (1936: 9). Although when compared to a straight-handled dagger the power of a thrust with the kris is not high, this is compensated by the precision manner in which it is used. In other words, it is a piercing weapon which is well-adapted for personal combat in confined spaces: on board a ship, in the middle of a battle or beside a forest trail. The soldiers of the Sultanate of Bima were equipped with a variety of offensive weapons - including spears, swords, blowpipes, whips and muskets - and the kris was generally a weapon of last resort when all other means of killing the enemy had been tried. As was the case in other Indonesian societies, Bimanese men were known to run amuck in the streets, stabbing people with their kris, though this was a rare occurrence involving individuals suffering great mental stress. Frenzied troops, however, brandishing kris in battle behaved much like the beserks of the Viking age in Europe. In the Malay world the *amok*, a furious charge designed to scatter the enemy, was a key element in the attack (Reid 1988: 125).

The most prized characteristics of the kris are the tracery patterns, *pamu* (cf. Malay, pamor), on the blade, popularly referred to as damascening, which are made by a process called pattern welding (Maryan 1960: 25). Rods of low carbon steel and nickle rich iron are forged on either side of a central member, the blows of the hammer causing distortion. The metal is folded and hammered so that the different layers meld with one another. When the surface of the blade is etched a contoured pattern or damascene is revealed. The use of nickelous iron to sharpen the contrast between the metals dates from c.1600 and South Sulawesi was probably the source of much of this iron (Reid 1988: 110). The iron, known as *pamor luwu*, was often called 'white iron' because it was etch-resistant and left silvery patterns on the acid-darkened blade. Meteors provided another source of nickelous iron and because of their heavenly origins were thought to bestow magical powers on the kris. A meteor fell near Prambanan in 1749 and the Javanese probably began forging kris from meteoric iron towards the end of the 18th century (Frey 1986: 31). Meteoric iron, though esteemed, was always rare and accounted for a tiny percentage of kris production.

Bima was also short of iron and supplies were brought by *perahu* from Kalimantan (Borneo) and Sulawesi. By the 1980s scrap iron salvaged from automobiles was being used, steel suspension springs being especially popular. The Bimanese forge comprises an open-sided, thatched building containing a packed clay work surface and a trough made from a hollowed-out log. Charcoal, a by-product of the pottery industry, is burned in a crucible scooped out of the clay dias (cf. Reid 1988: 109). Oxygen is supplied by piston bellows which resemble those depicted in a relief carving on the 15th century temple at Sukuh in Java. Although kris are no longer made in Bima, many of the basic metallurgical skills are used to repair old weapons, and former courtiers and artisans, or their descendants, also recall how they were made.

The red hot iron is folded into a U-shape and hammered, and then the edge of the fold is cut away and reserved for the strip, *ganja*, that will cover the top of the blade. The tang, *edi*, is worked out of the blade and waves may be added by beating the metal over cylindrical anvils. At this temperature the iron may be cut and rough designs are chiselled through the edge of the blade where it spreads out near the tang. The base of the kris invariably widens to one side, suggestive of a stylized sword-catching device. The *ganja* is then shaped and slipped over the tang and because it is part of the blade material it has the same damascene (cf. Frey 1986: 39). While still hot the tang is slotted into a blank handle of wood, bone, horn or ivory which is later carved. A metal ring also helps to keep the hand grip in place; but the slimness of the tang renders the blade unsuitable for a lateral cutting action without impairing its performance as a stabbing weapon (cf. Maryam 1960: 32). The blade is then filed and shaped, the finer details being added with small chisels and files. Fine grit is applied with a bamboo pad to polish the surface of the blade.

After it has been polished the blade is treated with an acidic solution of citrus juice and arsenic, which attacks and darkens the iron but does not affect the nickelous patterns (cf. Frey 1986: 39). The blade is then washed and oiled to protect it from rust, and the damascene appears in silvery whorls and threads set against the lustrous darker metal. This damascene is considered by many to be the kris' finest feature. As is indicated by the wide contours, most

Fig. 23 Piston bellows used by blacksmiths in Nggarolo.

Fig. 24 Blacksmiths forging agricultural tools in Nggarolo.

Bimanese kris are made with decorative layers that lie parallel to the hard metal core which serves as the point and cutting edge. This kind of pattern welding is one of the most widely-distributed Indonesian damascenes and is therefore difficult to provenance. There are also kris in Bima that have four or five hollows on the blade which are thought to have been made with blacksmiths using their bare hands. According to local tradition smiths made the impressions with their fingers and thumbs while the metal was red hot. This type of kris is linked to the *kris majapahit* and may have Javanese origins (cf. Shahrum bin Yub 1967: 13). In Surakarta (Solo) there is, for example, a story concerning a female smith who forged a kris with her fingers. But there is also a legend in Sulawesi which claims that the art of making kris with the bare hands was introduced by a Bugis prince of supernatural parentage (Frey 1986: 14); a Sulawesi connection with regard to the Bimanese pinched kris cannot be ruled out.

Because blades that resembled one another were forged in many places throughout the archipelago it is often impossible to identify a kris by the blade alone. Kris makers moved to wherever there was a demand for their services taking with them the skills and styles of the court where they had learned their trade. Cultural exchange occurred as a result of trade between competitive and fashion conscious courts, and an important factor was the movement of Bugis seamen from Sulawesi to Sumatra, and through the Straits of Malacca to Penang. There was also a continuing intercourse between the Malay Peninsular and the island of Sumatra. Political allegiances were also significant since beautiful kris were given to honoured guests as symbols of mutual friendship (Moebirman 1974: 14). As far as the kris is concerned these ties have left their mark, especially with regard to the Malay and Bugis world. Consequently kris from Sulawesi, Sumatra, the Malay peninsula and coastal Borneo often look alike, and in order to provenance them it is necessary to study their hilt forms, sheath forms and hilt fittings (Frey 1986: 40). The same applies to Bima which not only came within the political orbit of Makassar, but also had strong Muslim ties with the Malays. Exogenous influences are detectable in Bimanese kris, indicative perhaps of the presence of foreign born armourers and a certain amount of imitation on the part of local smiths.

Bimanese kris are usually furnished with a sheath made from two strips of wood bound and glued together, which takes the long, slim portion of the blade. A single block of wood with a slot cut through is added to the top of the sheath to accommodate the broad upper section of the kris. This section is almost always carved with a curve on one side and a sharp angle on the other, and resembles the Malay and Sulawesi types described by Gardner (1936: 31). A wide variety of ornamental woods is used to make kris sheaths, one of the most esteemed being *kemuning* which has a lustrous flame or tiger grain effect (Frey 1986: 44). Sandalwood is available locally and not only has a pleasant odour, but is easy to carve. The Javanese value *kemuning* and sandalwood, and claim that the latter provides protection against rust (Solyom & Solyom 1986: 46-64). Sheets of silver embellished with the cold working methods of sinking and raising are also used to cover sheaths. Because silver may become brittle when worked, it is annealed with a mouth operated blowtorch, a process which uses heat to realign the metal's crystaline structure. Brass stamps and moulds in the shape of birds, leaves, stars and moons are used to emboss silver on a lead bench anvil, fine details being picked out by chasing with a punch and hammer. Wire is made by pulling silver through a draw-plate and is soldered into complex filigree designs; 'granulation' is used to attach small balls of precious metal.

The decorative metal ring that lies at the base of the Bimanese kris hilt is usually quite elaborate and has much in common with the hilt fittings of South Sulawesi. It comprises a flat cup on a short stem, with a thick metal ring and is usually engraved with flower and leaf patterns (cf. Frey 1986: 53). Most are made of brass, though royal kris have finely worked gold rings. Hilt rings in the Madura and Malacca styles are also encountered in Bima, as well as the Javanese type of *mendak*. The hilts themselves are usually made of wood, horn, bone or ivory and may be elaborately carved. The lost wax technique, which was used to cast brass or precious metal hilts, may also have been known in the Sultanate of Bima. Like the hilt rings, many Bimanese hilts are patterned on the Bugis or Makasar model and are abstract in design and sharply curved. There are, however, hilts with a less pronounced angle of inclination which resemble those of the Malay Peninsula, as well as hilts showing crouched figures which may have originated in either North Java or Madura (cf. Frey 1986: 48).

The state kris of Bima, *Tatarapa Sangajikai* or *Samparaja* (*sampa* (ri), kris; *raja*, prince), represents the finest example of the armourer's art. This diamond encrusted pusaka (heirloom) kris is one of the three treasures essential for the legitimization of the Sultan and symbolizes the unity of the realm. The others are the golden crown and the gilded palm leaf parasol, and together they represent the concept of the rajah upholding the state, *dou lao dana na* (*dou*, man; *lao*, go; *dana*, land; *na*, will) and recall the heavenly origins of the royal dynasty (cf. Ibbitson Jessup 1990: 261). The influence of South Sulawesi is apparent in the style of the sheath with its squared top, flared and flattened bottom, diagonal motif and braided gold hanging loops (cf. *Ensiklopedi Budaya Nasional* 1988: 180). The reddish hue of the gold, suggestive of a high copper content, is characteristic of Bima, though it can also be found on artefacts from Sulawesi and Sumatra (Ibbitson Jessup 1990: 262). The precise date of 1634, which is contained in the chronogram (*candra sangkala*), links the kris to the period of Makasar hegemony and the Islamization of Bima (ibid.).

Of particular interest is the anthropomorphic figure on the hilt of the state kris, which is said to be a representation of Sang Bima, the founder of the royal dynasty. Hilts like this have been identified as Balinese (Frey 1986: 48, Ibbitson Jessup 1990: 262), and a parallel can perhaps be drawn with Java where the five Pandawas are represented on some of the oldest pamor motifs (Rassers 1940: 518). Similar figures also adorn hilts from Makassar (*Ensiklopedi Budaya Nasional* 1988: 180) suggesting that they were either cast in South Sulawesi or obtained through trade with Bali. Armourers in South Sulawesi appear to have been willing to modify kris and Ibbitson Jessup has suggested that Bimanese blades originated in Java and were taken to Sulawesi where the tangs were cut short to fit sharply angled Sulawesian grips (1990: 262). The sheath of the royal kris of Bima is of Sulawesian style, but local historians maintain that the state kris was made in eastern Sumbawa. Although the Bimanese certainly possessed the necessary skills, monistic explanations are clearly unsatisfactory. As is indicated by the date there is a strong Sulawesi connection and it might be more appropriate to argue that the state kris was either assembled or modified in Bima, perhaps with the aid of foreign craftsmen. Balinese goldsmiths are known in Sumbawa and Balinese influence cannot be ruled out (cf. Ibbitson Jessup 1990: 262).

Another kind of sacred weapon, known as *La Nggunti Ranté*, is included among heirlooms of the royal family of Bima. The name means 'cutter of chains' (*guntung rantai* in Indonesian) and it may have been used as an execution knife (Ibbitson Jessup 1990: 240), though the Bimanese, like the Malays, usually stabbed condemned criminals to death with a kris. The knife is attributed magical properties and was carried around Sultanate council meetings on a plate; it allegedly rattled in the presence of traitors (Hitchcock 1987: 129). According to legend the knife intervened spectacularly in a battle in Manggarai when the Bimanese were trying to conquer West Flores. The knife flew between the opposing forces and so awed the Florenese that they surrendered, giving the Bimanese victory without loss of life (Ibbitson Jessup 1990: 240). Some Bimanese look back on the Sultanate's intervention in Flores as a *jihad*, or 'holy war' designed to expand the frontiers of Islam, and therefore hold the knife in high esteem. Myths link the knife to Bali where its first owner was said to have been the grandfather of Sang Bima (ibid.). Certainly, the motifs on the curve of the blade recall Balinese larva-forms, but the weapon seems to comprise components from a variety of sources and its provenance remains obscure. The iron and silver blade has foliage designs and a crouching beast that seems to be a *kirin*, a lion figure from Chinese mythology. The *kirin* appears on batik from North Java where Chinese influence is pronounced, but these designs date from the 19th century and *La Nggunti Ranté* is said to be much older. According to local sources the knife was the official weapon of the Sultan before the existence of the state kris and therefore belongs to the pre-Muslim era.

A pair of spears, which flanked the ruler during state ceremonies, are also included in the court *pusaka*. Spears like these were often displayed in specially made stands in the inner sanctums of Indonesian courts. The Bimanese pair date from the 17th century and have *pamor* heads decorated with raised gold lines. The diaporing on the gold shaft covers resembles Sulawesian workmanship, whereas the lower ends are encased in a silver-white metal, probably either zinc or a low silver alloy (Ibbitson Jessup 1990: 237). These Sulawesi-made spears are historically linked to Makassar's subjugation of Bima and conversion to Islam.

Although the state kris and associated *pusaka* may be linked to Sulawesi, the Bimanese probably absorbed a certain amount of kris lore from Java through contact with Majapahit. As can be seen on the relief carving at Candi Sukuh, Bima is associated with kris production in Java. The smith on the left of the Sukuh forge scene has been identified as the god Bima, whose great strength enabled him to be both a warrior and armourer (Frey 1986: 5). Despite this Javanese connection, the development of the kris tradition in Bima occurred under Muslim patronage, and the adoption of Islam and the veneration of sacred daggers are closely linked. The kris acquired an Islamic identity in eastern Indonesia and the Bimanese may be distinguished from their non-Muslim neighbours on account of their ceremonial daggers. Generally-speaking the distribution of kris in the archipelago coincides with the existence of centralized Muslim states - the opening up of Islamic trade routes facilitated the spread of kris technology. Indeed the only non-Muslim states with significant kris traditions were those of the Hindu-Balinese, the artistic heirs of Majapahit.

Status of kris makers

According to Raffles armourers were held in high esteem in old Java and were richly endowed with land (1965a: 172). Similar notions are encountered in Bima where members of the royal family are said to have been skilled kris makers in the past. But as Rassers has pointed out, though the kris maker might be honoured on account of his mystical abilities, his task is essentially a humble one (1940: 506). Despite the lowly nature of the work, kris makers were not held in low esteem in the Sultanate of Bima, and the possession of craft skills was an aid to social mobility. An able commoner could become the head of a task group and assume a noble title, the chief smith being known as the *Bumi Ndede.* Recruitment to the task groups was not invariably urban, and skilled artisans were drawn from the furthest reaches of the Sultanate. The highland communities of Wawo and Donggo were important in this respect, the former supplying silversmiths and the latter blacksmiths. The reputation of upcountry artisans remained intact until the 1980s and some residents of the ward of Paruga, the former goldsmiths' settlement, are proud of their highland ancestry.

The blacksmiths, precious metal smiths and carpenters were all involved in different aspects of kris production and, in common with other task groups, each *dari* was based in a separate ward. The location of the goldsmiths' ward is especially noteworthy, because it lay close to the southern entrance of the palace. These smiths provided the guards for the most discrete entrance in the perimeter wall, a responsibility that is said to have been derived from a kinship link with one of the Sultan's female forebears. This ancestress was semi-divine and possibly a kris maker, and the myth accords well with kris lore from elsewhere in Indonesia, notably Java (cf. Frey 1986: 13-16). Another occupation, which may have been linked to kris manufacture, was smelting. This task was conducted in a workshop on the main road leading east from the capital and came under the auspices of a military official known as the *Anan Guru Ova* (*ova*, to smelt). There were other links between kris makers and the military and, in troubled times, the war council met in the precious metal-smiths' meeting hall, *paruga suba*.

The maker of state kris was involved in producing something that was more exhalted than himself, and it was not customary to sign or otherwise place makers' marks on these sacred objects. Good craftsmen, however, received widespread recognition, and the names of highly regarded kris makers were passed on from generation to generation. Gifted artisans can, according to Bimanese tradition, be recognised by their grasp of both technical ability, *pandé* (skill), and their knowledge, *vitua*. Although the former word can easily be translated into English, the latter needs further clarification. *Vitua* literally means 'old knowledge' (*vi*, know; *tua*, old) and is an all-embracing term for both Muslim and locally-derived concepts, which can be divided into three categories.

In the first place the devotional aspects of Islam, *ibada* (Ar. '*ibāda*) are emphasized, prayers and fasting being used as meditative aids before commencing work. According to Bimanese tradition, work of high quality is produced by people who are spiritually attuned, and prayers are used to alter one's state of consciousness. The Bimanese usually hold a small festival, *doa*, which resembles the Javanese *selamatan* (cf. Geertz 1960), before commencing work on an important project. The use of prayer as an aid to meditation is a distinctive feature of Islamic mysticism and parallels can be found elsewhere in the Islamic world (Nicholson 1931: 214). The second aspect of *vitua*, known as *kébé* (Ar. *kabal*), concerns the magical ability to alter future events and cause an enemy harm. Because this magic may involve the failure of mechanical parts, it behoves the craftsman to be aware of this area of knowledge. The third element is called *firasa* (Ar. *firāsa*), the ability to discern a person's character from their appearance. Because kris are deemed to have personalities then the kris maker should ideally be a good judge of character and be able to match the temperament of the man to that of his weapon. To ensure harmony a man with a personality described as 'hot' (irascible) should be equipped with a 'cool' (phlegmatic) weapon and vice versa. Good armourers are said to be able to communicate with kris and ascertain their characters.

The link between knowledge and craftsmanship is reinforced at the popular level in a children's finger game in which the digits take on specific personae. During play the children call the index finger 'the craftsman' and when asked why, they show that this is the premier grasping digit and therefore the most important in handicraft. In the game the thumb is called 'the old man' and parents tell their children that should 'the craftsman' wish to work he must cooperate with the thumb, the point being illustrated by a gripping action in which the index finger is said to bow to age and seniority (Hitchcock 1985: 41).

Kris in society

Bimanese kris serve as items of inheritance, but in the past they were also used in warfare. According to Idrus Yahya, a skilled craftsman from Paruga, kris of different weights were used, the heaviest ones being reserved for war. This assertion is difficult to corroborate since most owners of heirloom kris maintain that their weapons were used in battle, whether light or heavy, and stories of past triumphs are an important ingredient in the appreciation of kris. Massir Q. Abdullah, for example, the Director of the Palace Museum, owns a kris that reputed to have been used in the 18th century campaigns in Flores. Likewise many other *pusaka* kris in Bima are associated with historical events. The fact that the kris is foremost a fighting weapon in the eyes of the Bimanese is recalled in male dances of the court, which involve the use of daggers and movements based on the martial arts. The Indonesian authorities still treat the weapon with some caution and in 1981 the Bimanese were banned from wearing real kris at an official reception for President Suharto: the welcoming committee went to the airport bearing kris made from silver foil.

Kris are symbols of wealth and status, and may be accumulated to boost the owner's spiritual power. Although daggers may be purchased, it is heirloom kris, inherited from one's male relatives, that are the greatest source of pride. In the Sultanate of Bima all males, with the exception of slaves, were allowed to wear kris, though in practice many could not afford them. Only the palace guards seem to have born kris on a daily basis, though Bimanese were expected to wear their daggers when going about state business or attending Sultanate ceremonials. When worn in public the kris is tucked into a sash or silver belt with the hilt placed close to the navel and the scabbard projecting outwards over the left hip. A small textile, usually pink in colour and embroidered or couched with silver ribbon, is often folded carefully around the hilt. Virtually all scabbards are equipped with a knob, *puki*, at the tip which, according to the local explanation, makes it difficult to slip the weapon under the sarong (cf. Skeat 1900: 33). The only people permitted to use knobless scabbards, known as *sarunggi*, were trusted officials and high ranking military personnel. These sheaths were worn tucked into the back of the waist cloth; similar scabbards were reserved for the royal family.

In the Sultanate of Bima social status was closely linked to the kris worn during state ceremonials. Commoners possessed wooden sheaths, the nobility silver and royalty gold, known as *cori-cori*, and the state kris could be identified by its loops, *bata gemala*. The head of customary law also owned a distinctive kris of the type characterised in the literature as a *kris majapahit* (cf. Gardner 1936: 24). Known as *na watu ka waja* (*na*, the part; *watu*, direction; *ka*, from; *waja*, tempered steel), this kris has a solid iron hilt in the shape of a grotesque figure and is closely associated with the Sang Bima story.

Aside from state ceremonials, and their modern day equivalents, kris are rarely seen by anybody other than the immediate family of the owner, the main exceptions being when they are cleaned or when they are shown to visitors. On the former occasions the blades, wrapped in rags soaked in citrus juice, are left outside in bamboo segments, after which they are rubbed vigorously with a cloth to remove rust and then are oiled with coconut juice (cf. Skeat 1900: 528 & Rassers 1940: 524). These activities may attract the attention and comments of passers-by. A degree of showmanship may be involved when kris are shown to guests with the owner bringing out his weapons one at a time from a chest in the interior of the home, heightening the atmosphere of anticipation. Despite the informality of these gatherings, kris etiquette is observed and the weapon is usually held respectfully with both hands. When drawn from the scabbard the blade is raised point upwards in a salute in

Fig. 25 Sultan Ibrahim (c. 1905) wearing the Bimanese royal kris.

Fig. 26 Iron and silver belt buckle on a glossy sarong.

front of the forehead to the accompaniment of a brief Muslim incantation. In conversation the owner may supply details of the kris' history, especially how it fared in campaigns, as well as some observations on its aesthetic qualities. Socially-accomplished visitors participate in these discussions demonstrating their knowledge of kris lore.

According to tradition the most esteemed feature of the kris is its damascene. Indeed there are straight-bladed kris, known as *sapupaka*, that are prized on account of their patterned blades alone, the waves, *nteko*, on a dagger being marginally less important. There are also kris blades with hollows, which are said to have been forged by Donggo highlanders using their bare hands, perhaps by coating their calloused fingers with oil (Gardner 1936: 45). With the exception of a few broad-bladed weapons, kris are usually slim and the blade only spreads out near the guard strip, *ganja*. Because of the off-centre grooves cut into both faces of the blade, the guard strip has a figure-of-eight appearance. The cutting edge closest to the groove usually has a decorative curl, an aesthetically prized feature which may originally have been a blade catching device (Gardner 1936: 8). The edge, *voi sempadi*, opposite the curl does not taper sharply, a characteristic that is especially marked on straight-bladed kris. Kris usually have odd numbers of undulations, from three to nine, though blades with twelve waves are greatly appreciated, especially when combined with intricate pattern welding. Parallels can be drawn with Java where twelve is esteemed as an expression of completeness (Rassers 1940: 518).

Kris may also be evaluated with reference to four colours - red, yellow, green or white. Generally-speaking the least esteemed kris are described as red, perhaps because lower grades of steel rust easily. Blades with a yellow or green sheen have equal status, whereas white ones are the most highly regarded, probably on account of the high content of the prized nickelous iron. Scabbards are slightly lower on the aesthetic register than blades and complex embellishments are not invariably accorded high status. A simple polished wooden handle and sheath may, for example, be greatly admired, especially when an interesting type of timber is used. Silver sheaths are usually intricately patterned with leaf and flower motifs, one of the most popular designs being based on the creeping stropanthius vine. In accordance with Muslim prohibitions on idolatry, figurative designs are uncommon, though some of the botanical patterns, *toho bungga*, are said to represent live animals - few Bimanese are able to identify them.

Kris may be evaluated not only in terms of specific details, but also on account of their overall appearance. In assessing kris in this manner, the daggers are ranked in accordance on an elusive scale into three hierarchical categories. This scale, which may also be applied to other important artefacts, is neither the subject of extensive critical debate nor defined with a fixed vocabulary. According to this notional system the degree of skill needed to produce the most basic kinds of goods is known as *lao pandé* (*lao*, know; *pandé*, skill). A greater degree of workmanship can be detected in objects belonging to the middle category, *caha ni* (*caha*, industrious; *ni*, good enough), whereas the expression *caha tingi* (*tingi*, clever) is reserved for the most aesthetically pleasing kris. Goods in the latter category would have been made by specialist task groups in the Sultanate and, according to AD Talu, a former minister, the term *caha ni* might be translated into Dutch as *kunst* (art). This nobleman also argued that the spirit in which a kris was made influenced its aesthetic value. For example, the process by which thought was turned into action at the most basic level could be described in simple terms: 1. *nggahi*, to speak 2. *ravi*, to make 3. *pa'u*, to use. The highest level of production, however, had to be described with recourse to a more elevated vocabulary: 1. *renta ba rera*, to utter with the tongue 2. *kapoda ba adé*, to use truth 3. *karavi ba veki*, to bring into operation.

Craftsmen may also refer to Islamic values when assessing the quality of their products. Idrus Yahya, for example, a skilled carpenter, claimed that he bore in mind the example of Muslim prophets when he went about his work. He admired Ibrahim (Abraham), for instance, on account of his honesty, piety and practical skill, the basic attributes of all good craftsmen. It was Daud (David), however, who stimulated the aesthetic sensibilities since it was recalled that he sang so sweetly that even the birds of the air were attracted. Parallels can be found elsewhere in Bimanese thought with regard to the link between music and beauty, especially when speaking Indonesian, the national language. The Bimanese, for example, seldom use the term *kesenian* (art) in its broadest sense, but use it in a more restricted way to refer to the arts of dance and music.

When viewed in its cultural context, the kris could be said to represent a paradigm of society. Kris like men are ranked and placed in order, and the division of society into three hierarchical classes is replicated in the aesthetic vocabulary. Rules-of-thumb link sheath types to social status and an elusive three part scale is used to compare and contrast ceremonial daggers. In practice, however, these models only serve as a rough guide since the art of kris appreciation is more complex and employs gestalt-like notions that appear to contradict these basic concepts. A kris with a wooden sheath, for example, is not necessarily confined to the lowest tier and may outrank more expensively embellished weapons if made in fine materials carved with exquisite care. As is the case in Java where the term *udawana* is used (Solyom & Solyom 1975: 15), the Bimanese place great value on the overall appearance of the kris and how the different parts relate to one another. Yet in spite of this flexibility the art of kris appreciation is founded on widely shared principles that have their roots in the Bimanese social system: order, though often ambiguous, is an essential ingredient in aesthetic appreciation.

VIII

Symbolic Cloth

Bimanese men are said to find the colour rose-pink irresistible, a predilection that is emphasized in a local tale. The story concerns a carpenter who, when distracted by a passing maiden in a sarong of this hue, fails to complete his scheduled task. As a consequence, numerous projects are delayed throughout the realm and eventually even the Sultan himself is inconvenienced. The monarch angrily demands to know the cause of the hindrance, and his dutiful courtiers trace the problem back through the system to the carpenter. When asked for an explanation the hapless artisan blames the young woman, who in turn blames the sarong. These excuses are received sympathetically by the Sultan and in the final outcome nobody is punished. The colour of the textile is held responsible for the hold up and everybody saves face.

What is interesting about this tale, aside from the fact that the carpenter is deemed blameless on account of a sarong, is the stress placed on colour. Although the Bimanese weave elaborately patterned textiles, it is the colour that is significant in this context. Despite the fact that colour is one of the most distinctive attributes of cloth, colour has received comparatively little attention from textile researchers on Indonesia, a notable exception being Rens Heringa's highly informative account of the symbolic value of cloth in the East Javanese villages of Kerek (1989: 107-129). As studies of textile designs have shown, there is much that can be learned about early trade patterns and the exchange of cultural values by careful analyses of patterns (cf. Maxwell 1990, Barnes 1989). The archipelago lies astride the trade routes between India and China, and Indonesian weavers have incorporated many elements from the design registers of these two civilizations.

One of the most important foreign influences has been that of *patola* from Gujarat on the west coast of India. The double-ikat silk cloths known as *patola* were traded in maritime South-East Asia from the 16th century onwards, though some scholars have suggested that they could have been introduced as early as the 14th century (cf. Bühler 1959). Muslim merchants played a key role in this trade, and eventually the Dutch became involved in the trans-shipment of *patola* (Bühler & Fischer 1979: 9). These cloths were held in high esteem in the Indonesian islands and were used as models for indigenous versions, though the way in which *patola* designs were incorporated varies considerably. Similar observations can be made with regard to the ubiquitous checked sarong, whose distribution around the Indian Ocean can be linked to Muslim trade.

Not only did the Indonesian islanders prize the designs on trade cloths, but they were also influenced by their colour. The process of imitation was probably assisted by the introduction of mordant techniques, which made dyes colourfast and enhanced the attractiveness of dyestuffs such as morinda (Turkey red). Although the botanical evidence suggests that morinda is indigenous to South-East Asia, mordant skills could have been acquired through trade from the Middle East via India (Bühler 1941: 1423-6; Maxwell 1990: 156). Coastal dwellers in Indonesia who share a Muslim trading history are known for their love of bright colours, as is especially the case with the Malays, Bugis and Makasars. The division between maritime and inland regions is particularly marked in Java, where the Central Javanese traditionally eschew bright colours in favour of more restrained batik dyes, in contrast to the peoples of the north coast who use a brighter palette. As is demonstrated by the story of the carpenter and the sarong, the Bimanese, like many maritime Muslims, are partial to bright colours. They associate rose-pink with young womanhood, and link red to vitality, and yellow (symbolic gold) to health, wealth and success. Similar notions are encountered in Malay culture where vivid hues are perceived as youthful.

Weaving and dyeing

Up until the mid 20th century Bimanese weavers and dyers relied primarily on local materials, though they had access to imported fabrics. The Island of Sumbawa was a source of dyes such as sappanwood and safflower, as well as heavy cotton (Crawfurd 1820: 461-463; Zollinger 1856: 265). Dyestuffs were prepared for export, particularly for Java's batik industry, a trade which flourished in the early 20th century (*Een Halve Eeuw Pakketvaart* 1941: 274). Following the introduction of industrially produced dyes and fibres, the export trade went into decline and by 1980 the Bimanese dyes industry had virtually disappeared, though untended indigo bushes could still be seen growing in the hedgerows. Cotton yarn continued to be woven in the hills and indigo dyeing persisted in the more remote areas; but most lowland weavers switched to pre-dyed synthetic yarns such as rayon, acrylic, acetate and polyester. Such was the abundance of unwanted indigo that dyers came from as far away as Flores to collect the dark blue leaves. Despite these changes the traditional knowledge was not lost entirely, and in the 1980s it was possible to compile a list of the main dyestuffs.

Traditional Bimanese dyes are used to colour handspun yarns. Cotton is obtained from the fibres surrounding the seeds of plants belonging to the genus *Gossypium*, the fibres from the hardy *Gossypium herbaceum* being popular. The latter cotton takes dyes well and, when woven, its fuzzy yarns produce a thick and slightly course cloth whose insulating properties are much appreciated in the cooler uplands. Cotton does well if it receives moisture as it grows, followed by a dry spell, and is often planted towards the end of the wet season. The cotton is picked and the remains of the outer layer removed, and then is dried for four to five days. A gin, comprising a pair of rollers turned by a handle, is used to remove the seeds. The cotton may be fluffed up with a bowstring, a method favoured by older women, or pounded with rattan beaters, often to the accompaniment of songs, the means preferred by younger women. The spinner twists the fibres into yarns with a hand-operated spinning wheel, using a spoked wheel to turn a belt-driven spindle. The spun yarn is looped around an H-shaped frame known as a hand reel or niddy noddy and the skeins are stored on a swift, an apparatus with revolving arms.

Bimanese	English	Botanical Name	Colour
cira	cudrania	*Cudrania javanensis*	yellow(with alum)/green (with indigo)
dau	indigo	*Indigofera tinctoria* *Indigofera hirsuta*	blue/black
jati	teak	*Tectona grandis*	red/brown
kasumba	safflower	*Carthamus tinctorius*	red/yellow
kunyit	turmeric	*Curcuma longa*	red (with lime)
nonu	Indian mulberry	*Morinda citrifolia*	red/purple/ brown
palawu	butterfly pea	*Clitoria ternatea* or *Sesbania grandiflora*	orange/ yellow
supa	sappanwood (bresilwood)	*Caesalpinia sappan*	red/brown
wako	boriti	*Rhizophora mucronata* or *Bruguiera conjugata*	yellow

What is significant about the Bimanese spinning technology is that it is more complex than that of the peoples further to the east. Individual pieces of equipment, such as hand reels, are encountered east of Sumbawa, but the Bimanese assemblage of swifts, beaters, bows, hand reels and spinning wheels is more complex and has much in common with the court cultures to the west and mainland Asia. The Bimanese, for example, use spinning wheels in contrast to many of their eastern neighbours who prepare yarn with a rotating spindle dropped from the hand. The Bimanese name for the spinning wheel, *jantal*, has Sanskritic roots, though this does not imply direct contact with India since similar terms are encountered in Malay and Javanese. A relief carving depicting a woman drawing thread from a weaver's swift on the

9th century temple of Borobudur demonstrates the antiquity of this material culture in Java. The Bimanese probably acquired textile skills through contact with Java before the arrival of Islam, though the adoption of the new religion and the establishment of a Muslim court undoubtedly speeded up the process of technological change.

There is also an Islamic connection with regard to the distribution of silk weaving in Indonesia, though the art of sericulture filtered south from China well before the Muslim era. Silk cloth was esteemed in Bima, but because sericulture was not practised locally, the yarn had to be imported from Muslim south Sulawesi, the nearest centre of silk production. Silk was sometimes woven with cotton to save money; alternatively the lustrous appearance of silk was imitated by ironing local cotton with cowries. Tamarind juice was pressed into the surface of the cloth by means of a bamboo pole wedged beneath the ceiling and inserted in the shell. Silk was often embellished with precious metal yarns which were either imported or made locally. Gold and silver wire was pulled through progressively smaller holes in perforated plates to make fine ribbon, which was then spun around a cotton or silk core. Precious metallic ribbons were also embroidered or couched directly on to cloth. Generally-speaking the art of weaving silk with metallic yarns is a Muslim preserve, a noteworthy exception being Hindu Bali. The contrast is especially marked in eastern Indonesia where the Bimanese can readily be distinguished from their non-Muslim neighbours by their colourful and shiny ceremonial fabrics.

Bima is also set apart from its eastern neighbours by its weaving technology. The Bimanese, like many other East Asians, use a body-tension loom in which the weaver leans back on a bar or strap to keep the warp threads in tension. These looms are made of relatively inexpensive materials and may be rolled up when not in use and therefore do not have to be kept in a purpose-built weaving shed. As is indicated by metal figures on a bronze container from Shizhaishan, looms of this type belong to the ancient toolkit of the Asia-Pacific region (Barnes 1989: 33). The site of Shizhaishan has been linked to a Bronze-Iron Age culture on the borders of the Han Empire (206 BC - AD 8) in south-west China. Various kinds of body-tension loom have been recorded throughout the Asia-Pacific region from the western fringes of Polynesia, to the Himalayas and northern Japan (cf. Ling Roth 1977). These looms may well have been introduced to maritime

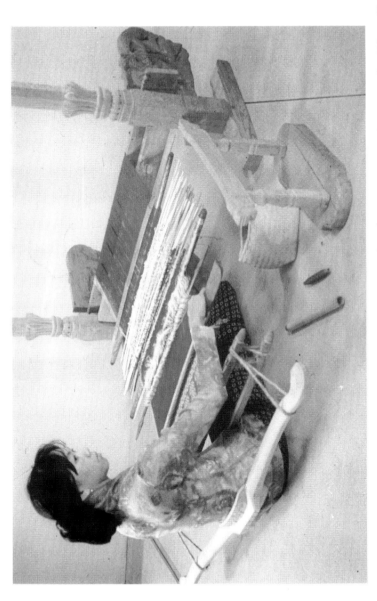

Fig. 27 The body tension loom was made on commission for the Pitt Rivers Museum by Idrus Yahya, Siti Samsia and Halimah M. Said. It has a discontinuous warp and is set up to weave a complex supplementary weft pattern. Mrs Diyan Leahe demonstrates the use of the sword in the museum. To her right are the shuttle case, sward rest and basket containing fresh yarn.

Fig. 28 A weaver in Ntobo beats in the weft with a hard wooden
sword. She weaves a *salampé* cloth using a body tension loom
with a discontinuous weft.

South-East Asia by the early Austronesians, though their distribution does not invariably coincide with that of Austronesian languages, especially in Polynesia.

The two main types of body-tension loom may be differentiated from one another by the arrangement of the warp (Hitchcock 1991: 55-68). On the first type the yarns pass under the beam nearest the weaver, breast-beam, and join up with those at the warp-beam to form a complete circle and are therefore described as continuous. On the second type the threads are attached to the warp-beam and the breast-beam and do not form a complete circle and are said to be discontinuous. As cloth is woven it is rolled around the breast-beam, while unwoven yarns are let out from the warp-beam as required. A heavy wooden frame, which may be elaborately carved, is used to keep the warp-beam in place on the discontinuous loom. Generally-speaking the first type of loom is found in small-scale communities in the Indonesian Archipelago, whereas the second kind is often associated with court-based societies that subscribe to a world religion, usually Islam. The latter kind of loom may also be furnished with a reed, a comb-like piece of equipment that helps to keep the warp threads in order. Although reeds are occasionally found on looms with continuous warps, they are commonly associated with the weaving of fine yarns, notably silver and silk brocades. In contrast to the peoples further east, who weave with continuous type looms, the Bimanese use looms with discontinuous warps, often furnished with splendid teak posts. The latter kind of loom has spread to the remote highland areas in eastern Sumbawa, though looms with continuous warps were used in the Donggo hills (Arndt 1952).

Longer lengths of cloth may be woven with a discontinuous as opposed to a continuous warp because the surplus yarn can be woven around the warp-beam. A great deal of space, however, may be needed for warping-up because the process involves stretching the yarn between poles placed some four to six metres apart. The weaver lays out the yarn before it is placed on the loom by walking back and forth between the poles, unwinding thread from a ball or spool in her hand. Bobbins may be stored on a rack in readiness for weaving. For greater convenience an apparatus known as a warping-frame may be used; the warp is zigzagged between pegs on the frame so that it is fully extended without taking up too much space. This kind of equipment is usually associated with western Indonesia, especially court-based cultures.

The Bimanese are able to weave complex brocade fabrics using inexpensive and locally-made tools. They are particularly skilled at weaving with what is known as the supplementary weft technique in which decorative yarns are inserted between the main yarns of the ground weave. Skilled weavers are able to ascertain the extent of each design element by eye, though they sometimes count along the warp. The pattern yarns are entered with a series of small shuttles and then are beaten in with the ground weave by means of a weaver's sword. This method is called *sungkit* in Indonesian and is usually employed to make fairly simple motifs. More complicated repeat designs can also be woven with the aid of seried ranks of pattern heddle rods, which are raised in sequence. The rods lift selected warp yarns and therefore determine the way the supplementary threads are woven in the cloth. Known as *songket*, this method may be used to weave highly complex motifs with between eighty and a hundred rows of heddles. The process of setting up a loom to weave *songket* requires both great expertise and patience. Sometimes a complex pattern is executed with the aid of heddles, while smaller details that are not repeated are added with a *sungkit* shuttle.

The production of *songket* is closely associated with the Malays and the sarongs woven by these widely dispersed peoples share common features. *Songket* cloth usually has a centre field, *kepala* (head), decorated with stars and botanical motifs, which is flanked by two rows of triangular, *tumpal*, patterns. The decorative borders of the centre field are known as *papan* (board, plank) and the rest of the sarong is called the *badan* (body). Bimanese *songket* textiles are usually woven in accordance with this basic pattern, though there is some local innovation, especially with regard to the *tumpal*. Non-Malays such as the Bugis and Makasars also produce this type of *songket* cloth and its distribution roughly corresponds with that of the maritime Muslim world.

Songket may also be woven on shaft looms, as is the case in the Malay peninsula and North Borneo. The South-East Asian shaft loom, which is sometimes referred to as the 'Malay loom', usually comprises a box-like wooden frame with a built-in weaver's bench. On this type of loom two pairs of shafts, which can be raised or lowered with treadles, are hung from a crossbar. The pairs of shafts are hung above and below the warp and have string heddles attached to odd or even warp threads. On the more traditional shaft looms the weft is woven with a hollow bamboo shuttle, though fly-shuttles are found in many small factories. Piles of discarded shaft loom parts and fly-shuttles are all that remain of a once vigorous textile industry in Bima. Since the 1960s most Bimanese *songket* has been woven on more easily maintained body tension looms.

The basic design of textiles woven on a body tension loom has changed little since the early 20th century. With the exception of one type of cloth, all the textiles noted by Jasper and Mas Pirngadie in their extensive survey of Indonesian material culture were still being woven in the 1980s (1912: 229-230). The most common textile is the sarong, *tembé*, a sewn tubular garment which the wearer secures around the waist.

The tubular sarong covers the wearer from the waist to the ankles and is closely associated with Muslim identity throughout the Indian Ocean. References to the distinction between sarong-wearing Muslims and differently garbed non-Muslims are often encountered in the Indonesian Archipelago. On Samosir Island in Lake Toba, for example, there is a carved headstone that commemorates a battle between Muslims whose movements were restricted by their sarongs and the unencumbered non-Muslim Batak. The Bimanese sarong may be either checked, *bali*, or decorated with supplementary weft, *salungka*, though a less common variety, known as *sanggar*, is made with light and dark blue bands. A shorter version, *weri*, which was reserved for courtiers, is worn during public festivals, but is no longer woven. These cloths have a glossy surface and are embellished with metallic yarns. During festivals the sarong is often worn with a sash or shoulder cloth known as the *salampé*. It usually has a brightly-coloured centre panel, though old varieties are often decorated with silver supplementary weft. Men wear checked headcloths, *sambolo*, decorated with couched and embroidered metallic yarns on festive occasions. Imported pink silk cloths may be embroidered with silver ribbon to make the kerchief known as the *pasapu*.

Cotton breeches, known as *deko*, are traditionally worn under the sarong, a custom which continued in Donggo until the 1980s (cf. Zollinger 1850: 51). In Wawo sashes may also be gathered around the waist and tucked between the legs to make shorts, *sarova*. The traditional woman's blouse comprises a piece of cloth folded in the middle, rather like a poncho, with a V-shaped hole for the head. The sides are sewn together leaving unstitched sections for the armholes. Lowland women commonly wear the Malay blouse, *kebaja*, though heavy cotton traditional blouses, *kebabu*, are worn in Donggo.

Colour symbolism

Bimanese weavers, while willing to experiment with a wide range of colours, tend to make use of hues that have enduring popularity. Chief among these is red, *kala*, a colour which is often included in the bands and stripes of local checked cloth. This colour is associated with good luck and during wedding receptions, when the newlyweds dress as a prince and princess for a day, the groom's costume is often red. The stuffed fabric linga that are sometimes displayed on the bridal couch are also usually coloured red. As the colour of blood, red is esteemed as a symbol of bravery, and early 20th century Bimanese troops wore short sarongs liberally decorated with this hue. According to the practitioners of traditional medicine red is the colour of one of the four humoral fluids found inside the body and is thought to bestow health and vitality.

One form of red that was especially prized in Bima was woven in a checked fabric known as *seri keta*. Red yarns, the colour of sirih (*seri*, betel), were combined with vermillion, *keta*, to make a gaudy check that was fashionable in the capital. This cloth caught the attention of Johannes Elbert, the German naturalist and explorer, when he visited the Sultanate (1912: 85); and, as many senior Bimanese recall, seri-keta remained popular until the mid 20th century. This colourful check served as a symbol of urban sophistication at a time when countryfolk had neither the skills nor resources to dye cotton bright red. In local eyes, bright and colourful garments are also associated with Islamic peoples, more sombre clothes being the lot of non-Muslim hill folk. Another esteemed variety of red is *bako*, the rose-pink colour mentioned in the story of the sarong and the carpenter. The colour is associated with youth and is worn for the last time by a woman on her wedding day. Thereafter she adopts *onggo* (brown-purple), the colour of restraint and sagacity, when wearing the traditional Bimanese woman's blouse. Rose-pink blouses are also worn by young female dancers belonging to the cultural organisations that keep alive the traditions of the Bimanese court.

Yellow, *monca*, is another colour that has favourable connotations, though this requires further qualification. While grooms often wear yellow - or better still gold- coloured costumes as symbols of health and success, it is the association with the precious metal that is of paramount importance. Gold is prized throughout the archipelago not only on account of its financial value, but also because of its alleged health-giving properties; yellow *per se* is not invariably regarded as a positive hue. In Bima, for example, yellow is the colour of a humoral fluid that is associated with destructive emotions such as anger.

Although the Bimanese esteem vivid colours, they also attach a great deal of significance to dark hues, as is especially the case with black, the humor of earth and death. Black is the colour of the countryside and, in particular, the lords of the land of the Sultanate of Bima. High-ranking courtiers also wore light and dark blue checked textiles embellished with silver supplementary wefts. Known as *me'e ova* (*me'e*, black; *ova*, blue), this cloth symbolized loyalty, a virtue associated with rural people.

White also has positive connotations and is worn by both Mecca pilgrims and the *imam* as a symbol of purity. During the state ceremonials that used to be held in accordance with the Muslim calendar, the Sultan also dressed in white to show that he was ritually pure. For similar reasons the life cycle is opened and closed with white cloths known as *malanta* (*lanta*, white): new born babes, as yet unsullied by life, are placed on white textiles and the dead are wrapped in white shrouds once the soul has departed to a purer existence. Although the use of white in these contexts is seen locally as a Muslim tradition, alternative perspectives can also be considered. The fact that white is both the colour of the humoral fluid linked to conception, and the colour of the shaman-herbalists known as *sando*, strongly suggests a pre-Islamic derivation. White is also generally associated with purity in Indonesia, most notably among the non-Muslim Balinese, and it seems likely that these attitudes to colour were easily accommodated within the Muslim faith because they did not differ greatly from Islamic concepts.

Textile design

The most striking feature of Bimanese textile design is the use of checked cloth. Generally-speaking these textiles are associated with maritime societies, though subtle differences in colour and the arrangement of the checks may indicate the island of origin (cf. Raffles 1817: 87). Sulawesian influences have been detected in the fabrics of Sumbawa, a legacy of the years of Makasar domination, though this requires some qualification (Gittinger 1979: 53; Jasper & Pirngadie 1912: 142 & 229). Although the Bimanese acknowledge a debt to Sulawesi, they also identify strongly with their own distinctive checks. They weave, for example, checks with broad bands of pink and mushroom, often arranged symmetrically, which is referred to as Bugis cloth. Much of the cloth, however, that is woven in Bima has narrow asymmetrical bands with pink used sparingly. The latter kind of check may be regarded as a local variant of the general maritime pattern.

Although the appearance of Bimanese checks varies, they usually conform to identifiable rules. Innovation is permitted within certain parameters and the different parts of the design are named. The bands and stripes are known as *bali*, while the small squares they enclose are called *lopa*. The finest checks are said to have squares the size of small blocks of gambier (a plant extract used in tanning), which are pressed into a standard size for sale in local markets. Weavers identify the narrow stripes along the selvage as the *penta* and *nganto*, and refer to the panel worn at the back as the *tinti*. The latter has fewer bands and the squares of colour may differ from those on the rest of the cloth - similar panels can be seen on Malay, Bugis and Javanese checks. The location and balance of the colours can be altered to suit the taste of the customer, and before commencing work the weaver may wind samples of yarn around a strip of lontar-palm leaf. By adding and subtracting threads the weaver and the purchaser are able to modify the design because each section of the strip corresponds to a different part of the check.

Another distinctive feature of Bimanese weaving is the use of tapestry techniques to make large hexagonal motifs on fringed textiles, *salampé*, which are worn around the waist or, less commonly, over the shoulder. The Bimanese use interlocking weaves around a brightly-coloured centre field, a style reminiscent of the *kain kembangan* of Java. It is possible that early contact between Sumbawa and Java gave rise to this kind of design, though alternative explanations also deserve consideration (cf. Gittinger 1979: 154-155; Jasper & Pirngadie 1912: 229). Robyn Maxwell, for example, has described a sacred heirloom cloth from South Sumatra which originated in the Coromandel region of India. This 17th or 18th century trade cloth is made of cotton decorated with block printing and mordant painting (Maxwell 1991: 211). The textile has a circular centre field ringed with spikes and is not unlike certain Javanese cloths, *cemukiran*, that have a central lozenge licked by flames (ibid.).

The border of the hexagon on the Bimanese *salampé* is also spikey, suggestive of an interplay between local and foreign designs, and an Islamic trade connection.

Tapestry-woven and checked cloth may also be decorated with embroidery, couching, appliqué and supplementary weft. Coloured thread and metallic yarns or ribbons are used to execute a wide range of geometrical and botanical designs, some of which may be derived from Indian sources. Although the term *patola* is not encountered in Bima, South Asian trade cloths were widely distributed in the archipelago and copies were made close of hand in Sulawesi (Bühler and Fischer 1979: 159). The star-patterned *patola*, for example, was one of the most popular of all Indian fabrics imported to South-East Asia, inspiring local weavers to produce their own varieties (Maxwell 1991: 25). The Bimanese eight-pointed star, *nggusu waru* (*nggusu*, point; *wasu*, eight) has much in common with motifs found throughout the archipelago, indicative, perhaps, of trade cloth origins. Likewise the form of the Bimanese triangular designs, known as *kakando* (bamboo shoot), could also have been influenced by *patola*. These motifs are often used to border or enclose central patterns, especially on the back panel of a sarong, as is also the case with many Malay textiles. The style and arrangement of this group of designs on Bimanese textiles strongly resembles that of Malay songket, and is locally associated with a Muslim identity. These designs resemble the familiar Indonesian *tumpal*, and though triangular motifs have probably long been used in South-East Asia, the more elaborate varieties have an Indian appearance (Maxwell 1991: 219). The arrangement of the stars and triangular patterns closely conforms to the Malay *songket* style, though other motifs, notably birds and chickens, are sometimes added in Bima. The treatment of the border stripes in Bimanese sashes may also be linked to *patola*.

Rosettes and flower motifs are also popular in Bima and may be based on illustrations in commercially-produced pattern books. Old cloths with interesting designs may be kept for future reference, as are sheets of graph paper showing the structure of patterns. Motifs may also be based on natural observation, as is the case with the four-petalled *samado*, a flower that blossoms in the rice fields. Of particular interest are the creeping vine designs, known as *bungga satako*, which may have become stylized in response to Muslim prohibitions on idolatry. They are said to have represented humans and animals in the past, but the skill in interpreting them has fallen into abeyance. Although deer and birds can be seen on some royal textiles, a striking feature of Bimanese textile design is the paucity of figurative representation (cf. Ahmad Amin 1971: 46). Ships and onthropomorphic designs can, for example, be seen on textiles from neighbouring Semawa, a Muslim domain with a similar material culture, but they are absent in Bima. The fact that some realistic designs are encountered in Bima suggests that this transformation from figurative to non-figurative design is part of the ongoing process of Islamization. Although ordinary weavers may not be conversant with the precise Muslim teachings on idolatry, they are aware that realistic depictions of living creatures are frowned upon in Islam.

Although Muslims abhor idolatry, the prohibitions on figurative images have never been enforced with equal vigour in all Muslim societies and were often not applied to secular arts. Nevertheless, these restrictions appear early in Islamic history, the first references being in the moral and legal commentaries known as the *Hadith* (Rice 1965: 17-18). While court arts flourished under Islam, realistic portrayals of living creatures were tolerated providing they remained in the secular domain. Figurative images were shunned in the mosques where decorative arts such as calligraphy rose to prominence. Similar observations can be made with regard to Indonesia, though scholarly opinion is divided concerning the influence exerted by Islam on indigenous art forms. The debate has primarily concerned the Javanese shadow puppet which, when placed alongside counterparts from Hindu Bali, appears to be highly stylized (cf. Prawirohardjo & van Ness 1980: 10). But whether these distortions arose in response to Muslim prohibitions or were simply the consequence of the Javanese tendency to increasing refinement remains debatable (Wagner, 1959: 127). The shadow theatre deals with the divine world and perhaps Islamic influences should not be ruled out, though reliefs showing *wayang* figures on the 14th century temple of Panatasam indicate that the trend towards stylization pre-dates the Muslim era (Ibbitson Jessup 1990: 175).

With regard to textiles, however, a different picture emerges. The trade in *patola* cloth led not only to Indian-influenced designs, but also to Islamic Indian inspired motifs (Maxwell 1991: 396). By means of trade the influence of these Indian cloths spread far beyond the confines of the maritime courts into the hinterlands and the

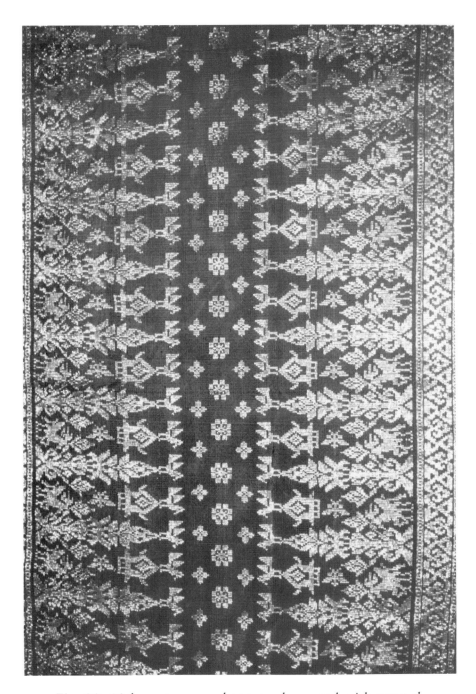

Fig. 29 19th century royal sarong decorated with *tumpal*, star, house, bird and deer designs. Red silk and cotton with a gold supplementary weft.

Fig. 30 19th century royal sarong decorated with *tumpal*, house, bird, star and deer designs. Red silk, cotton and gold supplementary weft.

remote corners of this region. Moreover, the trade flourished as India became increasingly influenced by the Islamic courts of the Moghul emperors, and though the export wares bound for South-East Asia were not necessarily based on court arts, they originated in an Islamic dominated world (Maxwell 1991: 154). As the evidence from Bima shows, local weavers not only based designs on Islamic trade goods, but also adhered to Islamic teachings on art: ideas, as well as material culture, travelled along the trade routes to Indonesia.

Sacred cloth

Cloth is attributed with many magico-religious qualities and may be used in Bima to ward off evil, especially during transitional periods when the individual is thought to be particularly vulnerable to malevolent forces. As is the case in many Indonesian societies, the Bimanese exchange or display textiles at the ceremonies that mark salient points in the life cycle, and in eastern Sumbawa this commences shortly after birth. The new born babe is usually wrapped in white cloth, a symbol of its purity, until its hair is shaved off some seven days after birth. Even if a child is still born or dies shortly afterwards, it is still wrapped in a white cloth because the soul is believed to enter the body four months before birth. The child, therefore, is thought to be fully human, whether dead or alive, since the soul is said to bring the various parts of the body together. More elaborate textiles, often decorated with supplementary weft and embroidery, are used during circumcision, the next important rite of passage. The circumcision bench is covered with cloth, as is the bed that is used afterwards. The latter may be festooned with drapes and embroidered hangings.

Cloth is associated with liminality and uncertainty in other contexts, most notably in the division between upper and lower worlds. According to Zollinger, for example, the Bimanese thought that the mountain known as Soro (Doro) Mandi was spanned by an invisible cloth of woven gold that could not be stepped over. In the opinion of Zollinger's lowland informants, it was only people who delivered up two pure virgins who could cross the magic barrier (Zollinger 1856: 256). To these coastal dwellers the mountain probably seemed to be a remote and forbidding place, the abode of spirits. Although the lowland Bimanese do not symbolically orientate themselves in relation to the mountains, as do many other Indonesian peoples (cf. Teljeur 1990: 42-43), they do strongly differentiate the mountain and coastal environments.

Textiles are also identified with women, and weaving and dyeing are predominantly female occupations. As symbols of womenhood, therefore, textiles feature prominently in the ceremonies that precede marriage. Upon mastering the art of weaving a Bimanese woman was traditionally judged to be ready for marriage, and looms are associated with the rituals of courtship. Young women were expected to demonstrate their skills to potential husbands, but in Muslim Bima it was deemed unseemly for a girl to work alone in full public view. Bimanese women, therefore, were often secluded in an upstairs room and were obliged to advertise their weaving abilities by attaching noise-makers to their looms. There are tales of suitors reciting quatrains beneath the windows where young women worked; the level of rattling was linked to the degree of affection. The sound made by the rattler and clappers not only indicated that the young woman was hard at work, but also helped to ward off evil spirits. The noise of cotton being beaten to the accompaniment of songs is also said to have attracted the attention of young men. Likewise, when young women gathered together to spin cotton by firelight, they would be regaled from the shadows with love poetry.

Textiles are also used in the gift exchanges that precede marriage, and only when the requirements are met does the wedding take place. The bride's family are traditionally expected to provide goods made by women (e.g. cloth, basketry) and receive in return items made by men (e.g. jewellery). The families set a date by which the exchanges should be completed, and the conclusion is marked by a ceremony, known as *sinto*, which is held some four to six months later in the bride's home. On this occasion the young woman sits on a couch covered with a brocaded cloth in front of a textile hanging. When the groom's family arrives, they are served with refreshments such as glutinous rice, coconut cakes and coffee. Representatives of both families then formally announce the end of the presentations and list the goods that have been exchanged, including cash payments. Up until the mid 20th century, women were expected to weave a specified number of brocade textiles for their future in-laws. Cloth is still given as a symbol of womanhood and, though it may be woven by the bride-to-be if she is a skilled weaver, it may also be purchased for the occasion. A small number of heirloom textiles also circulate round the community through the medium of ceremonial gift exchanges.

Sacred and royal canopies were modified under Islam to provide decorative backdrops for ceremonial occasions, though the cloths used for these purposes may retain pre-Islamic names. These textiles are prominently displayed during the wedding celebrations when the newlyweds, dressed as a prince and princess, receive the guests while either standing or sitting on a raised platform. The family of an aristocratic bride may hang up a sacred brocade cloth known as *ndidi langi* (*ndidi*, complete; *langi*, sky), the name of which recalls, perhaps, the heavenly world of the pre-Islamic belief system. In an alternative explanation, Robyn Maxwell describes this cloth as the 'wall of heaven' (*dindi*, wall; *langi*, heaven, sky), though this may also be a reference to the beam at the top of the platform, *langi dindi* (Maxwell 1991: 305; Abdul Karim Sahidu 1978: 54). Although the symbolic value of this cloth has become obscured by Islam, parallels can be found elsewhere in Indonesia, notably in the link between the sky world and death. In Lombok, for example, the deceased are covered with fabrics referred to as *langit* (heaven, ceiling), despite the dominance of Islam on that island. Islam has managed to accommodate customs that belong to an older pre-Islamic world, and textiles remain some of the most culturally significant of all artefacts in maritime South-East Asia.

IX

Houses and Palaces

The house is the central feature of many South-East Asian societies and is closely associated with identity. Many different styles of building are encountered in the archipelago, though strong underlying principles can be detected, suggestive of a common cultural heritage (Waterson 1991: 1). Throughout the region houses are erected according to traditional practices which vary between different societies, but share common features. Buildings are rarely set directly on the ground and are usually constructed on a raised platform supported by rows of wooden posts. Java, Bali and Lombok are notable exceptions, though relief carvings on the 9th century temple of Borobudur indicate that wooden platform-style buildings may have been the norm in earlier periods (Waterson 1990: 2-3). There are also a few surviving examples of old houses set on low posts in West Java and in Lombok the dwellings built on clay platforms eventually give way to raised port structures in the east of the island. The raised platform provides a number of distinct advantages in a tropical island: the house is cooled by the flow of air under the floor and is protected from floodwater by the high posts. The underfloor space serves as an airy workspace by day and at night the family retires to the security of the platform, drawing up the ladder in times of duress.

The South-East Asian house, though technologically ingenious, is not simply a practical structure and is usually designed by paying close attention to the householder's social and spiritual needs. The house often serves as a microcosm of society and is built in accordance with a kind of ritual topography in which the structure and layout of the building have meaning (Izikowitz 1982: 4). The building's shape, size, location and decoration may reveal much about the owner's ancestry, status and religious orientation - his attitudes, and those of the society in which he lives, may be conveyed by the design of the building and its contents. The building may express personal preferences, but also tells us much about the values of the wider society, especially with regard to ethnicity and gender. Thus the study of the ordinary house provides as much a key to understanding a given society as research on grander buildings such as palaces and mosques. The more conspicuous public buildings are often the starting point of analysis because they tend to be more ornate and, from the aesthetic point of view, more striking (Izikowitz 1982: 5). Public buildings tell us much about the values of the macro-society, especially its political aspirations, but it is through an appreciation of the significance of more humble abodes that we learn about the identities and world views of ordinary peoples.

The Bimanese house

Bima's central market is bounded by the box-like homes and stores of Chinese and Arab traders. Made of brick and concrete, these buildings are limewashed regularly, though they may be streaked with mould and grime in the wet season. The offices and hotels that lie between the commercial and residential districts are also made of brick rendered with cement, though many have substantial pantiled roofs with overhanging eaves. The buildings that lie outside the town centre are more varied and range from bungalows on stone platforms to gaily-painted wooden houses raised high above the ground on posts. The majority of these dwellings are also roofed with tiles, though some are protected from the elements with sheets of corrugated iron. Thatch is uncommon in urban areas because of the risk of fire, but small shelters and outhouses are often thatched with straw or palm leaves.

The Bimanese reserve the term *uma*, home, for dwellings inhabited by families, thereby excluding all public buildings such as meeting halls, government offices and mosques. By the same token a field shelter with a thatched roof and bare earthen floor would not be regarded as a home because it is only used as an overnight resting place. These shelters are erected near swidden sites and usually comprise a single pitched roof supported with four corner posts. They have no walls and are roofed with branches, leaves and other debris from the cleared fields. More substantial shelters, known as *salaja*, with gabled roofs resting directly on wooden platforms are also built near swiddens, but are too crude to be regarded as homes. Larger varieties of *salaja*, however, may be regarded as homes, especially when they have plaited bamboo walls and roofs thatched with *alang* grass. The thatch is tied over battens and is taken ready-made to outlying fields, along with the bamboo screens. There is usually a sleeping platform supported by six trimmed branches, under which tools and cooking pots are stored. Another three poles support the roof over a packed earth floor which serves as a workplace and kitchen. Mosquitoes are driven off at night with the aid of smoke from fires lit under the platform.

When planting begins at the start of the wet monsoon in western Sumbawa, whole families may reside temporarily in the field shelters (Goethals 1961: 27). This is less common in lowland Bima where agricultural workers usually prefer to return home after a day's work. A field shelter provides protection from the sun and rain during the day, but cannot compete with the comfort of a permanent home; only boys and young men are usually left overnight to protect the crops. Thirsty farmers consume a lot of water and during the dry season supplies have to be replenished daily; if more people were to camp out, then the guards' provisions would rapidly become depleted. Villages are located close to rivers and springs where there is sufficient water for washing and drinking. Gardens are kept clear of weeds and rubbish, and streets are swept regularly to reduce the number of pests, especially mosquitoes. The Bimanese also feel secure in their permanent dwellings which are solidly built and are surrounded by the homes of friends and relatives. For many it is not only comfort factors which draw them home, but also the fear of evil spirits which are thought to roam the fields and forests after nightfall.

The Bimanese are justly proud of their wooden houses, designed as they are to withstand the ravages of storms, floods and earth tremors. The *uma* comprises a raised platform dwelling, typical

Fig.31 Farmers use the *salaja* as a temporary shelter when clearing swidden fields on the hills above Bima.

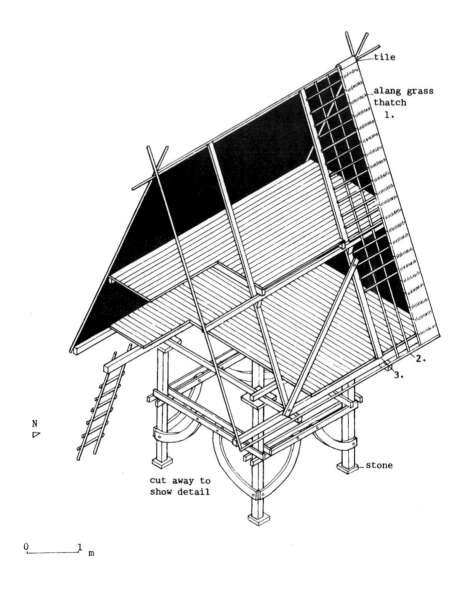

tile

alang grass
thatch
1.

2.

3.

N

stone

cut away to
show detail

0   1 m

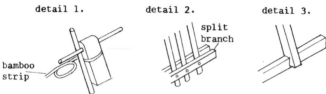

detail 1.

detail 2.

detail 3.

bamboo
strip

split
branch

Fig. 32 Drawing of an A-frame house.

of a kind of house that is found throughout maritime South-East Asia, especially in the Malay world. The Bimanese house has much in common with a style of building that is encountered in central Sulawesi, though it more closely resembles homes of the Bugis and Makasar type (cf. Kaudern 1925: 82). Similar dwellings are common in west Sumbawa and Manggarai, and doubtless certain building techniques were introduced during the period of Makasar overlordship (Goethals 1961: 24; van Bekkum 1946: II & III). The *uma* does not, however, resemble the Bugis and Makasar house in every respect, and incorporates features that appear to be of local derivation. Although some Bimanese acknowledge the debt to south Sulawesi, many regard another type of house, the *uma lenggé*, as being the island's traditional home (cf. Abdul Karim Sahidu 1978: 55). Makasar and Bugis methods have not entirely supplanted indigenous techniques; *uma lenggé* construction techniques can be detected in the lowland *uma* .

The Bimanese *uma* typically consists of three rows of teak house posts set approximately two metres apart. The twelve posts stand on stone footings to prevent rotting and are held together by four tie beams. These beams are morticed on to the top of the house posts and are secured with sappan wood pegs. Each tie beam comprises two lengths of timber fastened together with a diagonal joint that resembles the scarf joint. The three rows of posts are linked by long beams that lie on the projecting edges of the tie beams; this arrangement provides the frame of the building. A central row of posts set into wooden shoes on the tie beams is used to support the ridge pole. From the ends of the tie beams blades are laid below the ridge pole to form a series of roof trusses. Each truss is strengthened with struts and is used to support the rafters and purlins that carry the roof (Hitchcock 1983: 244-247). The roof projects the side of the house to throw rainwater clear of the wooden walls and tiled canopies are used to shield the gable ends (cf. Kaudern 1925: 60). This house is closely associated with Islam and the lowland Bimanese identity, though the *uma lenggé* is regarded as the island's autochthonous dwelling.

The floor beams rest on spurs carved approximately 1.35 metres above ground level on the sides of the house posts. The floor beams support the joists that bear the floor and are securely braced to the house posts. Although the floor boards are laid closely side by side, gaps eventually appear as the wood warps and the building ages. These holes are seldom plugged since they provide convenient outlets for dust when the house is swept. The floor is enclosed by panels set into frames that rest on the projecting edges of the joists and are secured with pegs to the tie beams. The house posts bear the roof and floor, but are not incorporated into the outer walls as is the case with 'box-frame' buildings in Europe; the manner of construction is distinctively South-East Asian.

The doors are usually set into the wall panels in the eastern half of each gable end and are linked by a corridor running north and south. This arrangement differs from that described in the west of the island by Goethals (1961: 24). The Bimanese claim that their layout provides security because the householder has a clear view of both entrances from the main living area. The front door opens directly on to the reception room and the sleeping quarters branch off the corridor on the western side of the building. Doors are usually hung with brass hinges and are furnished with strong wooden bolts for protection. A substantial wooden staircase may be built outside the front door, whereas the back entrance is often equipped with a simple bamboo ladder. There are windows on all sides of the building, the largest being in the gable ends; all are fitted with shutters.

The main floor is usually divided into three rooms - a living room and two bedrooms - which are partitioned by wooden panels. The interiors of the homes of poor householders may be partitioned with bamboo screens, though this may be a temporary measure in the case of newlyweds who are saving up to buy the timber for the walls. Planks are often laid across the tie beams to make an attic that serves as an additional workplace and store. An open door is a sign of good relations with one's neighbours and guests are usually entertained on the verandah at the front of the house. The verandah may be nothing more than a beaten earth floor covered with a thatched roof, but may also comprise a solid wooden platform enclosed by panelled walls and a thatched roof.

The kitchen is usually located to the rear of the dwelling in a thatched outhouse with bamboo walls. Food is cooked over a small wood fire in a large earth-filled terracotta dish. The cooking pots are supported over the heat on three round stones and the smoke escapes through chinks in the screens. If food has to be cooked indoors, then the terracotta dish prevents the floorboards from becoming scorched. Rice barns are also erected at the back of the house, but are kept well away from kitchens because of the fire hazard. The construction of the lowland rice barn resembles that of the highland house, especially with regard to the use of rat baffles on the piles. The barn may have a tiled roof and panelled walls and is set on posts approximately 1.5 metres above ground level.

In common with many other peoples in maritime South-East Asia, the Bimanese adhere to a strict protocol concerning access to granaries (cf. Barnes 1974: 65; Cunningham 1964: 45; Waterson 1991: 185-191). Only the wife of the householder - who is not necessarily the oldest woman residing in the home - is permitted to enter the barn, *jompa*. Seeds may be taken out of the barn at the start of the agricultural cycle and sheaves may be brought in after the harvest, but it is always the householder's wife who officiates and has unrestricted access to the granary. This etiquette is observed on all occasions, the only exception being during menstruation. If the householder's wife is menstruating, then her place is taken by her eldest daughter to prevent rice, the staff of life, from becoming contaminated with blood. According to Brewer, granaries are not only built in the same style and with the same methods as houses, but are also seen as the residences of rice (1979: 57).

The lowland rice barn and the highland traditional house have much in common and this suggests that the Bimanese may at one time have had granaries in their homes (cf. Barnes 1974: 65). The use of panelled walls on barns seems to be a relatively recent innovation since up until the early 20th century lowland rice barns closely resembled highland houses (Elbert 1912: 62-65). The older style of barn survived in the Wawo foothills until the mid 20th century (Heberer & Lehmann 1950: 173) and in the early 1980s old-style barns could still be seen in a fenced enclosure close to Maria village. Although the highland traditional house serves as a granary, it is also lived in and is therefore a more substantial structure than the lowland rice barn. The highland house serves as a general symbol of ethnic identity throughout the region, though its distribution is largely restricted to Wawo and Donggo. The Wawo version, also known as *uma lengeé*, only differs from the Donggo type, *uma lemé*, with regard to the location of the doors: the former is entered via a trapdoor in the floor, whereas the latter has a side entrance. Models of the highland house may be displayed during festivals and are placed above the podium where the Koran is read in public (Hitchcock 1983: 239).

The highland house is supported by four thick teak piles standing on stone footings. The piles are capped with rat baffles and carry joists which project over the sides to form a cantilever. Planks are laid across the joists to make a floor, on to which four poles are halved to carry an 'A' frame. The poles are braced and support a ridge pole approximately 2.8 metres above the floor. Alang grass thatch is tied over battens with rattan and is secured to bamboo frames fixed to the 'A' frame. Poles which cross over one another at the apex of the roof are laid over the thatch at each gable; the gable ends are also enclosed with thatch covered frames. There is another floor, approximately 2 metres above ground level, which is protected by the eaves. This floor is supported by joists pegged to the piles and strengthened with wooden braces. A bamboo lattice is laid across the joists and the floor serves as a reception area and workplace.

Visitors to the main living area have to climb a long ladder from ground level and pass through a hole in the floor which may be sealed with a bamboo hatch. The main floor has a hearth with a packed earth base and stone tripod, over which trays are hung to dry wet sheaves of rice. The other side is divided with two screens to make a sleeping area, furnished with lonthar palm mats, and two storage compartments contain water pots and other household goods. A small ladder from the main floor leads to a loft where sheaves of rice are stored. The granary is supported by joists resting on spurs on the 'A' frame of the roof.

The palaces

The 'A' framed house is held in high regard as a *rumah asli* (*rumah*, house; *asli*, original), though the most esteemed dwellings are the palaces, *asi*. The eastern palace, *asi bicara*, belonged to the prime minister and closely resembles the wooden *uma* in terms of construction. It comprises two *uma* built beside one another and covered with a double gabled roof. Unfortunately, the double roof collapsed in the 1950s and was replaced by a somewhat insecure corrugated iron roof. This palace does, however differ from the *uma* with regard to the floor: the beams are set into mortices cut through the house posts.

In the 1930s the Sultan and his family moved into the colonial-style brick palace, though some of his retinue continued to reside in the older wooden residence, *asi bou*, next door. Part of the original wooden palace complex was dismantled to make way for the new building, but the main section has survived virtually intact. Nobody can remember precisely how old it is, though some sections may date back to the 19th century if not earlier.

At first glance the *asi bou* appears to consist of two long buildings placed side by side, which are protected from the elements with a double gabled roof. But on close inspection the true nature of the building is revealed: it comprises two houses beside one another on a north-south axis, with a third running east to west. The outer wall panels on the third structure are different, suggesting that it was added later. Because the roofs extend the full length of the building, the palace appears to be structurally coherent. The palace was conceivably built piecemeal, with new sections being added as funds permitted.

There is a five metre wide extension at the back of the palace which serves as a kitchen, while at the front (the north) there is an open verandah. The floor of the verandah is lower than the main floor and comprises a dressed stone platform surfaced with glazed tiles. The building is entered by two wooden staircases on the east, and by stone steps on the northern face. Visitors passing through the verandah reach the main palace by means of the stone staircase and imposing double doors. An attic, which is reached by wooden stairways, runs the whole length of the building. It is not only a sacred, but also a functional building and the underfloor space is used for storing tools, just like an ordinary *uma*.

The Dutch-designed brick palace was completed in the early 1930s with the aid of cooperative work parties drawn from throughout the kingdom. It follows the traditional layout of the *uma* with a verandah at the front and the kitchens at the back. The palace is built on a raised stone platform and thus there is no storage area below the main floors. It has a massive timber box frame, jointed in the traditional manner and braced at the corners. The walls are filled with brick nogging and are rendered outside with cement, and inside with plaster. A noteworthy feature is the first floor, which is so skilfully made that many local people think that it was laid by shipwrights. The floor boards are tightly fitted together, expertly butt-joined and are securely fastened with pegs. The roof looks more elegant than the pantiled *uma*, and is covered with light wood or bark tiles, *sira haju*, which are hung from battens with pegs.

The carpenter's art

Carpentry is considered to be as important for men as weaving is for women and all Bimanese males are expected to have a knowledge of woodworking. The rural Bimanese traditionally regard carpentry as a skill, *pandé haju* (*pandé*, skill; *haju*, wood), rather than a separate profession and there is no indigenous term for carpenter. There were, however, professional carpenters attached to the court who belonged to the woodworking task group, *Dari Ncavu*. With increasing professionalisation since independence, partly through the introduction of government-sponsored training courses, the use of the Indonesian term *tukang kaju* (carpenter) has become widespread. In the early 1980s headmen began to record occupation statistics on village notice boards at the behest of the Department of Industry, though this only provided a rough guide to full-time professional activities since many Bimanese possessed more than one source of income. Generally-speaking, the number of people who declare carpentry to be their main occupation is higher in urban than rural areas.

Despite the fact that a wide range of tools is imported, especially from China and Japan, Bimanese carpenters purchase much of their equipment from local suppliers or make it themselves. The traditional toolkit includes both wooden mallets made from elbows of wood and steel-headed hammers, though the latter are reserved for splitting logs with steel wedges and are primarily regarded as blacksmiths' tools. Carpenters rarely resort to nails when building houses, though they are not averse to using them to hold together fences. Trees are felled with axes and hardwood wedges and the brushwood is cleared with curved-bladed knives (cf. Raffles 1817: 112). The wood is trimmed and cut to shape with machetes and short-handled adzes; the fine work is carried out with the aid of short-bladed cleavers, knives and steel chisels (cf. Raffles 1817: 174). A long-bladed knife with a serrated edge, similar to those found in Java, is used for reaming out the corners of mortices. Saws are not

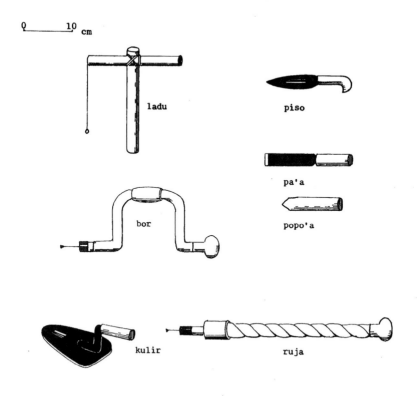

0 ___10___ cm

ladu

piso

pa'a

popo'a

bor

kulir

ruja

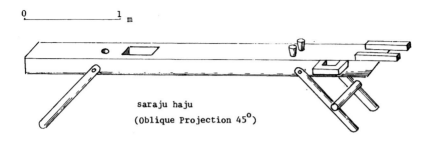

0 _____1 m

saraju haju
(Oblique Projection 45°)

Fig. 33 Carpentry tools.

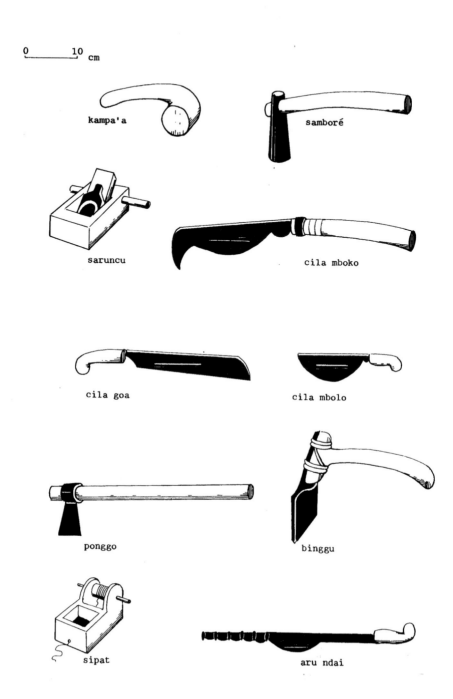

0   10 cm

kampa'a

samboré

saruncu

cila mboko

cila goa

cila mbolo

ponggo

binggu

sipat

aru ndai

Fig. 34 Carpentry tools.

made locally, though they may have been in the past, and the Bimanese name for this tool, *garagaji*, has affinities with the Javanese term *graji* (Raffles 1817: 174). Portable work benches furnished with convenient slots and pegs are used to hold the wood while it is being sawed (Hitchcock 1983: 213).

The Bimanese braced drill has parallels on the Asian mainland (Pinto 1969: 380) and closely resembles the type recorded in Java by Raffles (1817: 174). Holes can also be bored by means of a locally-made pump drill of a type that was known in Asia long before it appeared in Europe (Goodman 1964: 181; Pinto 1969: 380; Raffles 1817: 174). The Bimanese drill is carved from local hardwood and is furnished with a cylinder that is pumped to turn a grooved shaft, thereby converting linear into circular motion to turn the steel drill bit. Mainland Asian influences can also be detected in the two-handled plane, which comes in a variety of sizes and resembles the type used in China (Goodman 1964: 86-87). Another pan-Asian tool is used to mark timber with the aid of string drawn through a wooden box containing pigment. The container is known as a *sipat*, a Malay word of Arabic origin meaning 'measured line' (Wilkinson *et al* 1963: 264), though similar tools have long been known in China and Japan (Pinto 1969: 381). A lead weight hung from a T-shaped frame is also used as a plumb line.

Skilled carpenters possess a good knowledge of local forest products and their properties, and as many as nineteen different species of plant may be employed in house construction. Teak is the most sought after wood because carpenters find it relatively easy to work, though it is durable. The wood does not splinter when carved and has an attractive grain if sanded. This wood is held in high regard, despite the fact that it is less resistant to rot and insect damage than is often claimed (Burkill 1966: 2165). There are even stories concerning teak trees, including one called *jati kasi* which grew alone in the hills of Wera. The Sultan's foresters heard it crying and they decided to chop it down and take it to the capital where it would have plenty of company. Being tall, the tree was used as a royal flagpole and was thought to be magical because of its ability to bleed (Hitchcock 1983: 218). Sappanwood is another important variety of timber; it is used for pegs in joints and is believed to ward off misfortune. The following list of Bimanese construction materials was compiled with the help of Idrus Yahya and the local Department of Forestry:

Bimanese	English	Botanical	Use
acang	ebony	Diosyros	carving, cabinet making, joists
bintangur		Calophyllum	keels, house posts
bumbu	bamboo	Bambusa	floors, screens, roofing, scaffolding
fanda	pandanus	Goona sureni	matting, screens, roofing
indalo	alang grass	Imperata	thatch
jati	teak	Tectona	house posts, wall panels
kalanggo		Duabangga moluccana	house panels, crates
kedongdong		Canaria	resin, glue
kemiri	candlenut	Aleurites moluccana	lighting
luhu		Shoutenir ovata	tool handles, ladder rungs
manggé	tamarind	Tamarindus indica	tool handles, ladder rungs
monggo		Eugenia grandis	carving
miro	rattan	various	cordage, furniture
nara		Pterocarpus indica	carving, cabinet making
ridi			carving
sambi		Antidesma; Canarium	house posts
sonokiling		Dalbergia latifolia	carving
supa	sappanwood	Caesalpina sappan	pegs
ta'i	lonthar	Borassus	screens, mats, house posts

The island's vernacular architecture is in a constant state of change: in the hills 'A'-framed houses are being replaced by lowland-style wooden houses; in the valleys brick buildings are becoming common. The layout of the latter often resembles that of the wooden house, especially with regard to the location of verandah and kitchen. The internal plan of a brick house, however, is usually more varied than a wooden one and there may be additional bed- and store-rooms. A brick house is protected from floods by a stone foundation of dressed stone, approximately half a metre of which rises above ground level. This kind of house often has a hipped roof supported by concrete pillars, a precaution against earthquakes. The concrete is tipped between wooden shutters and is packed with wooden rammers, though it may be poorly bonded because it is not poured in one session and therefore dries at different rates. Local blacksmiths recycle scrap iron to reinforce the concrete columns. The bricks serve as infill and are laid in single rows of stretcher bond between wooden profiles, a technique introduced by the Dutch. The walls are rendered on the outside with cement and plastered on the inside. Palm leaf mats may be laid on hard cement floors for greater comfort. Windows have wooden shutters, though glass, imported from Java, is becoming popular.

Mortar - a mixture of lime, sand and water - is used throughout Indonesia as a binding agent from brick and stone, though it is often used sparingly. The builders of the region's Hindu-Buddhist temples often did without mortar and simply piled highly polished building blocks on top of one another (Pigeaud 1962: 510). In 9th century Java the proportions were usually two parts of lime for three parts of sand, though this was sometimes reduced to two parts. A binding agent, probably a mixture of plant sap and sugar, was used from the 13th century (Dumarcay 1986: 99). With the arrival of the Europeans the use of mortar became widespread: the Portuguese strengthened their fortress at Malacca with the aid of mortar; Dutch merchants built elegant town houses in bricks and mortar alongside the canals of Batavia. Muslim traders were also responsible for introducing masonry techniques since many, especially the Arabs, came from countries with well-established architectural traditions (Briggs 1931: 155-179). In eastern Indonesia in particular there are many fine brick, stone and mortar buildings that date back to the period of Islamic conversions. There is, for example, a royal vaulted tomb at Dantaraha that bears witness to the skill of early Muslim masons in Bima.

Lime, the active ingredient in cement and mortar, is made locally, though supplies are sometimes imported from Surabaya. Chunks of limestone are broken into smaller pieces with hammers and then are fired in stone kilns lined with clay. The firing reduces the limestone to a powder, which may be mixed with coconut juice to make plaster. The purer the lime, the better the building material, though this requires a higher temperature of calcination, which is difficult to achieve with local techniques (Hamilton 1958: 447-499). Reefs are increasingly being stripped of coral to keep up with the demand for lime in the building trade, though the long term environmental consequences have yet to be fully appreciated. Locally-made bricks are fired with brush wood in damp kilns, but are often soft and porous because high temperatures are not achieved easily with traditional methods. The mortar is spread with metal trowels, whereas wooden ones are used to smooth the cement rendering. Tiles are made by men in villages where women make traditional pots with paddle and anvil techniques. The clay tiles are cut to shape with wire on a wooden form, and then are stacked with coconut husks between them to assist the circulation of air during firing.

All manner of construction activities, ranging from roofing to bricklaying, are carried out by Bimanese carpenters. The term *tukang batu*, bricklayer, is used for official purposes, but very few builders describe themselves as such since bricklaying is often perceived as a low skilled occupation in Bima. Similar notions are encountered with regard to tiling. The carpenters who erect house frames and construct shuttering are held in high esteem, but not the labourers who build walls of brick infill. Specialist bricklayers are seldom brought in to complete domestic projects since the carpenters are well able to supervise the construction of brick walls and, if necessary, to build them themselves. Carving stone, however, is regarded as a different order activity and the masons who carve gravestones and repair religious buildings have high status. Wood and stone-carving are seen as being closely-related activities, as was especially the case in the Sultanate of Bima where masons belonged to the woodworking task group.

Known as *Dari Ncavu*, the woodworkers' task group was charged with erecting and maintaining government buildings. This task group comprised both carpenters and masons, as well as foresters and an assortment of other functionaries. They are credited with building the Sultan's palace and the central mosque, along with a wide range of other state buildings, including meeting halls and tombs. Like the other task groups, the woodworkers were administered by skilled practitioners who were awarded official titles and access to governmental lands. It is widely agreed in Bima that the most senior official was known as the *Bumi Jero*, though there are discrepancies regarding the titles and responsibilities of the other postholders. It is possible, however, to appreciate the diversity and complexity of this task group by combining the accounts provided by Ahmad Amin and A.D. Talu (Ahmad Amin 1971: 66; Hitchcock 1983: 60).

Each official had a separate area of expertise, one of the most important divisions having been that of masonry and joinery. There were specialists in morticing joints, tool-making, bricklaying, as well as decorative carving in both wood and stone. Since the task group had to supply its members with materials, occupations such as brick-making, storage and forestry came under its auspices. One of the most important officials in this respect was the head of the royal timber yards, *Bumi Jawé*, whose title may be linked to his occupation. Before the introduction of the pit saw in the early 20th century, baulks of hard wood had to be split (*jawé*, split) along the grain with the aid of wedges, a laborious but highly skilled process. Responsibility for stocking the yards was devolved to another official, the *Bumi Lumba*, whose name implies that he was brave enough (*lumba*, brave) to venture into the forests. The Bimanese dislike dense woodland and will seldom venture into a forest alone, and therefore the *Bumi Lumba* was held in high esteem.

The Bimanese fear of forests stems from their traditional belief system, elements of which have not been entirely supplanted by Islam. The woodlands were believed to be inhabited by tutelary spirits, *rafu*, who congregated around water pools, huge boulders and large trees. Since the royal forester's duties included felling trees, he was assisted by a forester-priest, a lord of the land, who knew the correct rituals to exorcize the spirits. The priest, known as the *Bumi Sari Haju Naé* (*bumi*, earth; *sari*, festival; *haju*, wood; *naé*, big), had to persuade the spirits to vacate trees that he selected for the royal lumber yards. Because the timber would later be used in ships and houses, the intervention of the forester-priest helped to reduce the risk of haunting. On the night before a tree was felled, the woodsmen gathered at its base to eat glutinous rice, some of which was offered to the spirits. The foresters recited Muslim prayers to protect them from harm and the priest banished the spirits with the aid of sacred verses. So thoroughly has lowland Sumbawa been Islamized that few people could be described as traditional believers and yet the fear of forests lingers on. Although the rituals associated with tree felling are no longer performed in their entirety, no Bimanese would be prepared to chop down a living tree without first offering up a Muslim incantation.

Many of the ceremonies associated with tree felling have fallen into disuse, but houses are rarely erected unless the correct rituals have been observed. There is usually a *doa* for the workmen and the householder's family on the eve before the house frame is raised to ensure the success of the venture. The host is expected to sacrifice a goat and provide his guests with glutinous rice and saté, followed by coffee and clove cigarettes. The ceremony usually ends with the recitation of Muslim prayers, but can also lead on to further traditional rituals. The guests may be taken by a senior carpenter, who is familiar with the appropriate ceremonies, to the site of the new home. Under the supervision of the carpenter, parcels containing rice, gold, cloth and seeds are deposited in the postholes; they symbolize health, wealth, security and fertility. Sacred earth is also placed in the holes to protect the family from misfortune and prevent the house from becoming haunted. The earth is dug from the site beforehand and is blessed by the priest-carpenter at the start of the ceremony (cf. Skeat 1967: 143). A white textile, which is likened to a sail, may be tied to the central beam and is not removed until work on the house has ceased.

The joints are marked with numbers made by cuts in the wood so that the timbers can be assembled correctly. The numbers are not erased after construction in case the householder wants to dismantle the house and move it at a later date. Bimanese carpenters have access to metric tape measures, but may use measurements based on the body. Like weavers they use finger lengths, hand spans, arm spans and cubits to calculate distance; standard lengths of building components may be recorded on sticks. Symbolic parallels are sometimes drawn between the life of a house and a living human being; the design of a dwelling may be based on the personal body measurements of the householder, so that a house will be in proportion to its owner (cf. Just 1984: 41).

Cooperative work groups

The artisans who belonged to the task groups resided in the capital and were full-time professionals. In contrast, rural craftsmen tended to be semi-professional and were often involved in seasonal

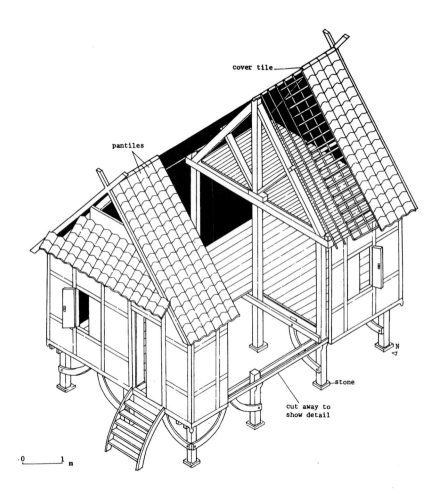

cover tile

pantiles

stone

cut away to
show detail

N

·0   1 m

Fig. 35 Drawing of a lowland house.

Fig. 36 The raised floor of this lowland house, *uma*, provides security and protection from flooding. Bugis-style houses have replaced the A-frame indigenous houses in the lowlands.

agricultural work. The task groups, however, were not completely divorced from the countryside and were expected to help out with the harvest, especially on land allocated to them by the Sultan. Both urban and rural settlements made use of similar means of mobilising labour, all of which conform to the general Indonesian pattern. Known in the national language as *gotong royong*, cooperative work was still a feature of urban life in the 1980s, though it was becoming less common. The Bimanese use the term *gotang royang* for official purposes, but distinguish three varieties of cooperative work in their own language.

The smallest unit of labour, *ndecé*, is organised on an informal basis and the work party usually comprises friends and family. Women may gather together to warp up a loom on this basis, whereas men may be involved in adding an extension on to a house. Although nobody is expected to be in charge, the group usually works under the guidance of the most senior member. The tasks they undertake do not require a great deal of advance planning and the group is held together by ties of reciprocity. More organisational skills are required to bring together a larger work party, known as *weherima*, which may occupy as many as fifty people for a whole day. Houses, for example, are moved with this kind of mutual assistance; according to a local rule-of-thumb, it takes forty men seven hours to dismantle and transport a wooden building. No payment is expected, though the householder is obliged to provide a substantial meal of rice, meat and vegetables. The Bimanese, like other Indonesians, like to make light of work and the atmosphere is usually festive. First all the furniture is removed from the house and then the tiles are stripped from the roof and are set aside. Next, the wall panels are lowered with ropes and finally the assembled company joist the frame on to their shoulders and march to the new site to the accompaniment of songs. Sometimes the frame is not carried, but is eased on to planks and is pushed to the new location on bamboo rollers (Hitchcock 1983: 265-266).

The participation of the headman and village council is usually required to organise the largest work parties, which are known as *ka jobu*. These work groups may be engaged on a project that lasts several days, sometimes scattered over two to three weeks. The project is normally supervised by the headman - or somebody delegated by him - and it is his responsibility to ensure that each household provides workers, tools, food and money for the materials. There is usually an informal sliding scale of taxation with wealthier members of the community making larger contributions than poorer ones. Roads and irrigation channels are built by these work parties, as well as dams, weirs and bridges. The Bimanese take pride in the fact that not only were the mosques built in this manner, but so were the palaces. Older people recall serving in the work group that built the brick palace with materials drawn from throughout the realm. The project lasted approximately three years and each district head was responsible for coordinating work parties supplied by the village headmen (Hitchcock 1983: 76-77).

Decorative features

The Bimanese adorn both houses and palaces with decorative features, many of which have symbolic and talismanic properties. The carvings are usually located on the gables, the lower wall panels and the door frames, though the palaces are furnished with decorative screens. Carpenters usually rough out blocks of wood with adzes and cleavers, and then work on the details with knives and chisels. Carvings on the exteriors of buildings are left slightly rough; but interior features are usually sanded with pumice, fine grit and abrasive leaves. The patterns are either engraved or carved in relief; but when a detail is designed to be seen from both sides, the incisions are cut through the wood. Fine lines are also engraved on bamboo - the pattern emerges when soot is rubbed into the cuts. The designs found on both palaces and houses resemble one another, though there are certain motifs which are reserved exclusively for royal buildings.

Decorative gable boards in the form of crossed horns are a repeatedly recurring feature of South-East Asian architecture, both on the mainland and in the islands (Waterson 1991: 7). Virtually all wooden houses in Bima are adorned with horns, either plain or richly carved, and the local Department of Education and Culture periodically runs campaigns to persuade the owners of brick houses to retain this custom. Some of the most elaborate gable decorations can be seen on the Sultan's palaces: the wooden section has buffalo heads made from entwined botanical designs, whereas the brick palace has sharply angled plain horns above three tiers of canopies. The number of canopies in the gable end also indicates status, a custom which may have been introduced from South Sulawesi. Gables are also commonly furnished with single horns, often decorated with flower patterns, that are strapped to the ends of ridge poles. These features are said to represent buffalo horns, though some householders claim that the single horn represents a stylised horse. Wooden houses, richly adorned with botanical and abstract designs, are closely associated with an Islamic identity in lowland Bima.

The choice of horns reflects the importance of the buffalo in many South-East Asian societies as a sacrificial animal and a source of riches (Waterson 1991: 8). As Muslims the Bimanese do not hold feasts of merit or honour the dead or the spirit world by slaughtering buffalo and therefore horns usually symbolise wealth. A house with twelve or more house posts usually has a single horn to show that the owner possesses livestock; wealthier members of society have double-horned gables. The single horn may also represent a horse because this animal, like the buffalo, symbolises prosperity in Bimanese society. The householder may also be likened to buffalo and therefore the horns serve as both symbols of welcome and warning. They show that although the host is usually shy and polite, he could become aggressive if annoyed. Houses in the Wawo hills are sometimes furnished with single horns shaped like roosters which possibly indicate not only wealth, but also serve as symbols of the dawn and the sun (van der Hoop 1949). There is usually a tail at the gable end opposite the cockerel's head and the ridge pole acts as a spine in the same manner as the back of the naga in the prime-minister's palace.

Throughout much of South-East Asia the house posts, as well as the gable horns, are symbolically significant. A common South-East Asian rule is that the house post must be 'planted' with the root end at the bottom in the same way that the tree, from which it was made, originally grew (Waterson 1991: 124). This custom is not adhered to in Bima, though it may have been in the past since tree imagery is encountered in buildings. For example, the house posts in the Sultan's wooden palace are encased with fretwork panels decorated with leaves; the botanical patterns are repeated on the joists of the floor above, suggestive of branches. The tops and bottoms of the spiral-shaped posts that hold up the naga's spine in the prime-minister's palace are also embellished with botanical patterns. Tree symbolism can also be detected in the foliage patterned cloths that are used to decorate the posts of marital beds during wedding receptions. Likewise, the upright posts on looms are topped with fruit and foliage designs.

Gable boards and house posts, as well as door frames and wall panels, are embellished with a wide range of motifs, many of which are inspired by natural phenomena. Generally-speaking, the Bimanese favour botanical and geometric designs in accordance with Muslim teachings on idolatry, and figurative motifs are rare. Botanical designs are popular because they are not only visually attractive, but also celebrate the local people's prowess as farmers. The designs range from simple leaf patterns to the more complex chilli with its fruit full of seeds. There are round and oval dots; the former represents seeds in general, the latter, cucumber seeds in particular. Like the chilli, the breadfruit has a shape that appeals to carvers and is also much appreciated as a source of starch when rice is scarce. The lonthar palm provides sugar and toddy; its curved trunk and crown of leaves lend themselves to visual representation in the hands of skilled craftsmen. Highly-stylised figures are sometimes included in the twisting tendrils and leaves of a design based on *Stropanthius*, an ornamental vine and source of poison (Burkill 1966: 2127-2128). This vine is depicted on the walls of the Sultan's wooden palace alongside the rhombus, an elemental pattern that is widely dispersed in South-East Asia and was encountered in the Dong-son excavations (Coomaramaswamy 1927: 156; Wagner 1959: 29). There is also a fan or propeller-shaped design which may have been inspired by the flying boats of the 1930s, but is probably much older since it appears on the wooden panels of the Sultan's palace.

The carved designs are sometimes painted; but, before the advent of imported paint, the choice of colour was restricted to what could be produced locally. White was obtained from lime, red from iron-rich soil and black from either soot or charcoal; the islanders welcomed the introduction of industrially-produced paint. Once these paints became available many householders began to brighten up the exteriors of their homes with multi-hued designs and particularly with red and yellow, the colours of health and wealth. Sometimes flamboyant touches were added, including logos borrowed from commercial products and even airlines (Hitchcock 1983: 280-281). In contrast, some home owners prefer the appearance of natural wood, especially teak, and leave their houses un-painted, whereas others simply apply a protective coat of limewash. Interiors may be painted in a medley of colours, ranging from light blue to green, though the choice may depend on the owner's financial circumstances and the availability of paint rather than aesthetics. Some houses, however, have brown or purple interiors, perhaps because of the association of these colours with married women. Framed photographs, red prayer mats and souvenirs from Mecca (if the householder has made the pilgrimage) may enliven the inside walls, as well as cuttings from magazines, paper wrappers and old calendars. The latter may serve no useful purpose save to brighten up the living quarters and exude a feeling of well-being.

X

Tourism and Identity

Indonesia is officially a republic, but it is also a country held together by a series of interlinked courts representing different regional and ethnic interests. Like the members of many smaller court societies, the Bimanese acknowledge the superiority of Yogyakarta and are quick to remind visitors of their historical ties with Java. As the premier Indonesian court, Yogyakarta often serves as a role model for lesser courts, as is especially the case with cultural tourism. The Sultan's palace in Yogyakarta was a tourist destination long before the advent of republican Indonesia, though the continuity of performances was disrupted in the early independence years. It was not until 1973 that palace performances were re-introduced into the palace itself from the annex to which it had been assigned while the Sultan was busy as a government minister and vice-president of Jakarta (Hughes-Freeland 1993: 143).

The smaller courts eventually followed Yogyakarta's example, but it was not until the late 1970s that the Bimanese succeeded in cleaning up their palace and using it once again as a venue for the performing arts. Unlike Yogyakarta, however, Bima became a court without a king since the restoration of the palace was not accompanied with the reinstitution of the monarchy, though the royal family continued to play an active role behind the scenes. There are Bimanese who oppose the restitution of the Sultanate, regarding it as a backward step to 'feudalism', but the pro-monarchy faction has strong roots. Pro-monarchists steer clear of overtly political discussions and instead draw attention to what they see as the potential benefits of reestablishing the Sultanate. Arguments are often couched in terms of local pride and regional identity, and especially cultural tourism.

The Komodo National Park

Bima's fortunes are closely linked to those of the nearby Komodo National Park, the internationally renowned wildlife reserve. Ecological tourism plays an important part in regional development in eastern Indonesia, not least because its distinctive flora and fauna is especially attractive to visitors with strong currencies, such as the Japanese. The Komodo National Park lies between Sumbawa and Flores, and forms part of the province of Nusa Tenggara Timur (NTT), though it was formerly part of the Sultanate of Bima. The park comprises the islands of Komodo, Padar and Rinca and has a unique ecosystem of scientific interest (Hitchcock 1993: 304).

The park is best known as the home of the giant lizard, *Varanus komodoensis*, the world's largest terrestrial reptile. The 'Komodo dragon' has powerful jaws, a long tail and can grow to around three metres in length. It has been suggested that some of the dragon mythology of the Far East was inspired by seafarers' accounts of this giant lizard with its long, flickering (fire-breathing) tongue, though the documentary evidence is lacking (Broughton 1936: 321). The international scientific community first became aware of the existence of the 'dragon' through the work of P.A. Ouwens, the curator of the Zoological Museum in Bogos. Ouwens learned about the lizard from a Dutch East Indies army officer, J.K.H. van Steyn van Hensbroek, and a description based on collected specimens was published by the curator in the *Bulletin du Jardin Botanique de Buitenzorg* (1912).

On realising that the lizard's habitat was largely restricted to Komodo and neighbouring islands, the Netherlands Indies Society for the Protection of Nature attempted to introduce appropriate conservation measures. The society, which was founded in 1912, approached the Sultan of Bima, who eventually issued a decree prohibiting the hunting and capture of the giant lizard, though it could only be enforced within the Sultanate's borders. The authorities in Manggarai issued another decree in 1926, but this did not become effective until Manggarai and Komodo were removed from Bimanese control in 1930 by the colonial regime. As a result of the transfer of sovereignty, Komodo and West Flores came under the jurisdiction of the Resident of Timor. The Resident later ratified the second decree and it became applicable throughout the Dutch East Indies (Blower *et al.* 1977: 6).

Scientists only learned of the existence of the giant lizard in the early twentieth century, but the 'dragon' was already well known to local people. The Komodo islanders call the lizards *ora*, whereas the Bimanese refer to them as *mbou*, though they may switch to 'Komodo' when talking to tourists. It is not surprising, in view of their dramatic appearance, that the 'dragons' have given rise to a certain amount of local folklore. The lizards are said, for example, to be the siblings of the Komodo islanders and that, if one of the animals is harmed, then its relatives, who have taken human form, will also fall ill (Bagus 1987: 175). The myths of origin of the Bimanese kingdom also contain dragon mythology, though the story of the prince and the naga princess belongs to the wider Asian tradition and need not necessarily be directly linked to Komodo. According to the Bimanese, the giant lizards used to live in east Sumbawa, until they were driven off by a local hero known as La Hami.

The legend of La Hami, which comes from Dompu, begins when the child of a rajah is swapped by a minister and is left for dead in the forest. Brought up by local people, the prince becomes an accomplished warrior and hunter, though he is unaware of his royal blood. One day the rajah meets the young man in the forest and, impressed by La Hami's prowess, asks who he is. La Hami's fortunes change when he slays a giant serpent that is terrorising the district of Sanggar. The young man gives the animal's head to the lord of Sanggar, who then takes it to the rajah, falsely claiming credit for the deed. La Hami refuses to be duped and when he appears, he is identified as the rightful slayer of the serpent. In recognition of his services, La Hami is offered the hand of a princess in marriage. La Hami's heroic deeds continue and he does not rest until all the 'dragons' have been driven out of Sumbawa.

The park is closely associated with the 'dragon' in terms of tourism, thought it contains many other distinctive species belonging to both the Australian and Asian environmental zones. Despite the diversity of wildlife, the human population is sparse, largely because of the scarcity of water. The local villages are located close to the few reasonably reliable sources of fresh water, and the two main settlements are Kampung Komodo and Kampung Rinca. The villages hug the shoreline and comprise wooden framed houses with bamboo walls and thatched or corrugated iron roofs.

Little is known about the earliest inhabitants of Komodo, though some grave sites and artefacts have been discovered. I Gusti Bagus has suggested that the current population does not have a long history of settlement, and that Komodo may have been used on only an occasional basis in the past when water supplies were more abundant than today (Bagus 1987: 175). Komodo lies strategically between Bima and its former territories in Manggarai and, though the islanders were technically subjects of the Sultan, they do not appear to have been closely integrated into the kingdom. The island's population was probably always quite small and Bimanese rule appears to have amounted to little more than periodic demands for tribute. So remote was Komodo, in the eyes of the Bimanese court, that it was regarded as a place of exile, though it remains unclear how many people were actually banished there. Isolation, however, did not prevent Komodo from being drawn into the Sultanate's trading networks, but attacks by pirates forced the inhabitants to seek sanctuary in Bima (Zollinger 1856: 243).

Like the Bimanese, the majority of the islanders profess Islam, though they live in the Christian-dominated province of NTT. However, not all the inhabitants of the national park are indigenous islanders, since seafarers from other Indonesian regions make use of the seas around Komodo. I Gusti Bagus has published a breakdown of the ethnic groups within the reserve, though it is unclear how these statistics were compiled because the figures are only expressed in terms of percentages. According to Bagus the indigenous inhabitants comprise a mere 18.4 per cent of the population and are outnumbered by maritime peoples such as the Bajau (33.3 per cent) and Bugis (27.6 per cent). It also remains uncertain whether the latter groups comprise temporary or permanent residents (Bagus 1987: 175).

The development of tourism

Komodo was established as a national park to help conserve its environment for scientific purposes. In order to implement the initiative, a management plan was drawn up under the auspices of the UNDP and FAO. The main objective was to ensure the '... survival in perpetuity of the Komodo dragon', a unique species occurring nowhere else and for which Indonesia had '... a special responsibility' (Blower *et al.* 1977: vii). A team of European and Indonesian consultants conducted field research in the reserve, and were involved in lengthy discussions with the Indonesian authorities. The scientific consultants realised that the reserve's agricultural potential was limited and that it would be unsuitable for transmigrants from elsewhere in Indonesia (Blower *et al.* 1977: 30). The consultants appreciated that in order to survive the park had to bring in revenue, not least because it was located in one of Indonesia's least developed regions. Tourism, it was argued, would not only protect the reserve from environmentally destructive forms of commercial exploitation, but would also provide a boost to the local economy.

The consultants provided a detailed account of the equipment and personnel that would be needed to maintain the park, and also made a series of proposals concerning the development of visitor services. The consultants did not want to impose too many restrictions on the tourists, but suggested that visitors should be encouraged to follow signposted nature trails to reduce their impact on the environment. It was envisaged that tourists travelling further afield would be accompanied by guides. Many of the recommendations were ecologically sensitive, such as the need to build a 'tourist village' with local materials and the imposition of a ceiling of forty visitors at any one time, rising to eighty as the facilities improved (Blower *et al.* 1977: 44).

Komodo had become a tourist destination long before it became a national park, though visitor numbers remained limited until the improvement of local communications in the 1980s. *National Geographic*, for example, included features on Komodo in the 1920s (Burden 1927) and the 1930s (Broughton 1936), and in the 1950s the reserve was brought to the attention of a wider readership through the work of Ton Schilling (1957) and David Attenborough (1959). Komodo appeared for a third time in *National Geographic* in an account of a journey through eastern Indonesia with an amphibious vehicle (Schreider & Schreider 1962). By the 1970s Komodo was being mentioned in popular guidebooks, such as the *Indonesia Handbook* (Dalton 1978: 242-244), though the tourist facilities in the reserve were still very basic.

Few of the tourist developments envisaged by the authors of the Komodo management plan had taken place by the end of the 1970s, but the situation began to change rapidly during the next decade. Nusa Tenggara, hitherto one of Indonesia's more inaccessible regions, became more closely integrated into the national mainstream. By 1980, for example, a telephone system had been installed in Bima, which provided a long-distance service of somewhat variable quality via a series of microwave relays (Just 1986: 37). The following year the overland route to Komodo was improved by the completion of the east-west highway across Sumbawa. The Indonesian Directorate General of Tourism also began to investigate the possibility of upgrading the existing, though infrequent, ferry service from Bali to Komodo by the introduction of special cruise ships.

Initially, however, it was thought that a sea voyage would prove unattractive to tourists on package holidays of limited duration and, therefore, the authorities concentrated on improving the air services. The authors of the Komodo management plan had proposed building an airstrip within the park so that it could be connected directly to Bali, the main regional tourist area (Blower *et al.* 1977: 41). A piece of land was cleared so that helicopters could land on Komodo, but the introduction of a scheduled air service to Denpasar remained optimistic. Most airborne visitors continued to make use of local ferries after landing in either Bima or western Flores.

Because of the time factor the tourism authorities also showed little enthusiasm for the overland route to Komodo, though this was later promoted as being suitable for young travellers with limited means and a sense of adventure. Eventually the potential of cruise ships was recognised by the tourism authorities and by the mid 1980s the sea route via Bima harbour was becoming a popular alternative. A new ferry service, which greatly reduced the travelling time between Sapé harbour and Komodo, was also introduced and the national park authorities acquired a launch to take visitors to Padar and Rinca. Eventually, all three principal routes were in use by visitors to the national park, integrating Bima more closely into the 'Komodo run'.

Much of the park's infrastructure was also upgraded in the 1980s and, in accordance with the management plan, these developments were located as far away as possible from Kampung Komodo to minimise the disruption. This socially-sensitive decision, however, proved to be quite expensive because of the shortage of water, and many metres of new pipes had to be installed to supply the tourist enclave. Two small hostels - each divided into nine compartments - were built, along with a cafeteria and information centre; but the number of visitors began to rise steadily, exceeding the quota recommended by the planners and placing a strain on the already overstretched resources (Hitchcock 1993: 312).

Tourism in Bima

By the late 1970s, tourism had begun to make a significant contribution to the economy of Bima through the provision of hospitality and the sale of local goods, such as handicrafts. Initially the rise in visitor numbers was modest, but, despite a somewhat negative portrayal in Bill Dalton's *Indonesia Handbook* (1978: 249-251), Bima's share of tourism began to increase steadily. The development of an exclusive resort on the nearby island of Moyo, comprising air-conditioned tents, also enhanced Sumbawa's image as a tourist destination, leaving aside the question of whether or not these facilities were appropriate for a nature reserve.

Surfers who wanted to get away from Bali's overcrowded beaches also began to explore the extensive coastline of southern Sumbawa, leading to the development of a small-scale aquasports industry. The promotion of neighbouring Lombok in the 1990s as the 'new Bali' also has implications for Sumbawa. As visitor levels rise, it seems likely that tourists will increasingly be drawn to the relative tranquillity of less densely-populated Sumbawa. In the long term, however, Sumbawa should expect to face competition from the islands further east offering similar attractions, especially if too much reliance is placed on beaches as the principal tourist attractions.

In view of its significance, tourism increasingly needs to be taken into account in any discussion of boundary maintenance and identity in eastern Indonesia. Commonplace assumptions about the positive and negative impacts of tourism need to be treated with care, not least because tourism alone cannot account for social change. Robert Wood has characterised this view as the billiard ball model, in which a static sphere (culture) is struck by a moving projectile (tourism) (Hitchcock *et al.* 1993: 8-9). On one hand tourism is praised as the preserver of tradition, while on the other it is reviled as the harbinger of commercialisation and the dreaded 'commodisation of culture'. A resolution is not readily achieved because tourism cannot easily be isolated from other social forces, as is especially the case in Bima. But before moving on to consider how tourism has become interwoven into local formulations of identity, it is worthwhile considering how tourists are perceived on the island.

Terms such as 'hosts' and 'guests' are idiomatic, not least because not all the people that tourists encounter during the course of their vacations are economically engaged in tourism. In theory, a host is a person who entertains another as his or her guest, and this does not apply to everybody with whom tourists interact. The situation is further complicated in a place like Bima because many local people do not use 'tourist' as a general category that transcends ethnic boundaries. European-looking visitors are often referred to by the Bimanese as *Dou Turi*, though Japanese and other Asian tourists are named after their country of origin (e.g. *Dou Nipo*, Japanese). The term *Dou Turi* is used locally like an ethnonym, and thus no distinction is made between tourists and expatriot Europeans, Americans and Australians living and working in the province of NTB. As is the case in Yogyakarta in Java, Caucasian visitors are more likely than other visitors to be categorised as tourists, regardless of whether they are there for business or pleasure (Hughes-Freeland 1993: 140).

In popular Bimanese formulations the *Dou Turi* are regarded as 'rich' and 'clever', though somewhat stupid on account of their ignorance of local prices and their lack of familiarity with bargaining. The 'red hair', size and hairiness of Western tourists fascinates the local youths who often egg each other on to shout "Hello Mister", an activity that promotes fits of giggles among the children. The situation closely resembles that in Java where the term *turis* has come to replace *londo* as something to shout at Caucasian-looking foreigners (Hughes-Freeland 1993: 140). The islanders sometimes talk disapprovingly of visitors they regard as 'hippies', a term that is often applied to people who wear shorts in public places. Short trousers on adults are widely seen as disrespectful in Indonesia unless worn for sport or relaxation at home.

The islanders also look on the activities of tourists with mild amusement, though they recognise the economic importance of the visitors. The Bimanese welcome the busy periods associated with the arrival of tourists, because they provide a respite from boredom, as well as opportunities to sell handicrafts and snacks. Parallels can be drawn with Singapadu in Bali where the villagers not only appreciate the revenue derived from tourists, but also miss coming together during quiet periods in the tourist cycle (Sanger 1988: 89-96).

Tourism provides a modest but welcome boost for Bima's craft industries, many of which are located in the capital, close to the main centres of tourism. Visitors are taken from cruise ships to the palace where they may be entertained with local music and dance. Women are encouraged to try the Bimanese headdress, *rimpi*, and hopefully purchase the sarong from which it is made. A clear distinction cannot be made in Graburn's sense of those artefacts that are made for local consumption (inwardly directed) and those made for tourists (outwardly directed) (Graburn 1976). Robert Cooper has argued that Hmong crossbows made for tourists are of questionable quality since they will never be fired. Productivity is high and the input modest, but because so many shops sell similar products, profit margins are low (Cooper 1984: 119). The Bimanese who make goods for tourists are usually traditional artisans who have simply adapted their products to suit an additional tourist market. Attitudes to material culture may change over time, but it would be wrong to assume that goods made for tourists are invariably shoddy.

Tourist activities are largely concentrated around the Sultan's palace, which serves as a museum and venue for the performing arts. The impression gained from the locally-produced tourist literature is that it is the court that is the most significant local feature. The Indonesian authorities, however, regard Bima's identity as a sultanate as a resource that contributes not only to the implementation of tourism, but also to the development of national pride. Similar observations have been made in relation to Bali, where the island's culture is perceived as one of the 'cultural peaks' of international tourism and Indonesian national identity (Picard 1993: 94). The revival of the *sirih puan* festival in Bima in the early 1980s, which celebrates the Prophet's birthday, occurred partly in response to tourism, but proved difficult to hold regularly because of the expense involved.

Parallels may be drawn with Yogyakarta where the dances that are performed for the court have been simply adapted for tourism. Court performances are usually accompanied by a reception of some kind, during which food is served. The custom continues, albeit

Fig. 37 Designed by a Dutch architect, the Sultan's palace has many local features such as tiers of canopies and wooden buffalo horns.

Fig. 38   Wooden house painted to resemble the fuselage of an aeroplane.

transformed into an occasion when the guests are tourists who pay to attend (Hughes-Freeland 1993: 143). Court performances were initially taken up by the national academies as representatives of national culture, and were gradually made available for tourists. Court as opposed to village performances have tended to be packaged for tourists because they are staged regularly in accessible urban centres. Bima's dance traditions were never static and it would be misleading to regard the performance for tourists as simply examples of 'staged authenticity', divorced from the 'real life' backstage.

The rediscovery of Bima's royal past, dormant since the early post-colonial era, was inspired by a combination of tourism and the search for local identity within the context of multi-ethnic Indonesia. Especially significant in the latter context appear to have been the ideas of Dewantara, who actively supported the development of many regional cultures that would eventually contribute to the emerging national culture. Together these cultural peaks, *puncak-puncak dan sari-sari kebudayaan*, would lay the foundations of a rich and unique national culture (Nugroho-Heins 1995: 16-17). It is, however, not invariably seen this way in the foreign travel literature, where emphasis may be placed on other kinds of identity.

The wide-ranging cultural motifs that are used to promote tourism are often decontextualised and dehistoricised so that they conform to an easily identifiable formula that can readily be understood by potential customers. The ill-informed representation of peoples within a tourist destination can have consequences (presumably unintended) at the local level, which have unexpected ramifications. Brochures and guidebooks, for example, often refer to the people of Maria, whose village is passed by tourists bound for Sapé harbour and Komodo, as a distinct 'hill tribe'. Unlike their neighbours the *Dou Wawo*, the people of Maria are regarded by lowlanders as ethnically Bimanese, though they are thought to have some knowledge of the Wawo language. The villagers of Maria have long been baffled by the interest shown in them by passing tourists and it remains unclear what they make of their 'hill tribe' status. It is just possible that tourism has unintentionally unleashed a latent local identity that had been submerged by the Sultanate of Bima.

It is reasonable to argue that the rediscovery of Bima's royal heritage occurred in response to a combination of tourism and national integration. Bima's court culture was seen as a cultural peak within a regional context that would eventually enrich the Indonesian nation as a whole. Court culture appears to have been the focus of these developments because it is comparatively accessible, not only to Indonesian national leaders, but also to tourists. What is significant is that the identity mediated by the local tourism authorities is not necessarily the one that the tour operators respond to. The local authorities have little control over how the area is marketed, and it remains unclear whether or not this has resulted in the downplaying of the negative Islamic identity portrayed in such publications as the *Indonesia Handbook*.

What is significant is that it is difficult to analyse encounters between the different Bimanese ethnic groups and tourists in terms of standard theories of ethnicity such as primordial and situational perspectives. These approaches are largely concerned with identity and boundary maintenance at the local level, and not with the global-local articulations that occur within touristic encounters. The differences between self-representation and representation by tourists raises methodological and theoretical issues. The concept of pluralism appears to have analytical value when applied to the interaction between tourists and local people in the marketplace, though the revival of court culture may be interpreted in situational terms. What is clear is that tourism and national integration have become part of the process by which cultural difference is communicated in Indonesia, and are thus an integral part of a discussion of inter-ethnic relations.

XI

Conclusions

Given the vast extent of the Indonesian Archipelago and the number and variety of its cultures, the term 'Indonesian' remains problematic in terms of human geography (de Josselin de Jong 1984: vii). The archipelago has long been a transitional zone between Asia and Oceania, and, before the polar ice caps melted, served as a land bridge to Australia, leaving only a short sea crossing. The sea levels rose, but did not completely isolate the ancestors of the Indonesian peoples from one another. Seafarers exploited the monsoon winds and learned how to ride out tropical storms at anchor in the shallows of the South China Sea. Austronesian settlers mingled with and sometimes supplanted the indigenous people, further enriching Indonesia's cultural foundations. Today, the Austronesian family comprises 500-700 languages spoken in a huge geographical area ranging from Madagascar to Easter Island, and from Taiwan to New Zealand. Uncertainty regarding the precise number of languages arises from the difficulty of deciding whether some varieties are separate languages or simply dialects of the same language. As a result of trade contacts there are also many mixed languages (Crystal 1992: 34).

The Austronesian family may be sub-divided into Formosan (one or more of the subgroups in Taiwan) and Malayo-Polynesian, all the Austronesian languages outside Taiwan. Linguists commonly use the family tree model to display splits inferred from exclusively shared innovations, though this is to some extent an idealized view of the real processes of linguistic variation. Each branch represents a subgroup of the larger collection of languages, and thus Malayo-

Polynesian may be divided into western, central and eastern groupings, with the split between the first two occurring at a higher level in the structure. The division between the western and central subgroups occurs in the middle of Sumbawa, and therefore Bimanese is the westernmost representative of the central group (Blust 1984: 29). The split between the western and central groups is thought to have occurred earlier than the division between the central and eastern groups, and thus Bimanese is genetically closer to Fijian and the Polynesian languages than it is to Sumbawanese with which it shares a border (Blust 1984: 30). This linguistic division was of particular interest to P.E. de Josselin de Jong who suggested that FAS researchers should use it as a basis for conducting comparative work within either the Western Malayo-Polynesian or the Central-Eastern Malayo-Polynesian areas (de Josselin de Jong 1984: 257).

Bima not only occupies a linguistic border, but also belongs to a transitional zone in terms of cultural ecology. There is sufficient rain to support dense woodlands, especially around Tambora, though the eastern coastline is parched by arid monsoon winds. The forests have been greatly reduced by a combination of over-grazing, swidden farming and, more recently, logging. On the one hand the area is known for its intensive rice agriculture, while on the other it is famed for its horse breeding. A visitor passing through the island is simultaneously reminded of the verdant paddy fields of Java and the open grasslands of eastern Indonesia. The coastal economy has much in common with Sulawesi and the Malay world.

The picture is further complicated by the fact that Indonesia lies along the trade routes from India to China, and has absorbed much from the cultural registers of those two great regions. For roughly fifteen centuries the western portion of the archipelago was exposed to Indic culture, an influence that eventually permeated as far east as Bima. Such was the extent of Indic influence in Java that we are justified in talking of Hindu-Javanese art and society, and Hindu-Javanese religion. The great monuments of the heyday of Central Java in the 8th and 9th centuries bear witness to the vitality of Indic influence. By the 10th century in East Java, the monumental art had become decidedly Javanese in character, much of the Indic material having been incorporated into the indigenous cosmology (de Josselin de Jong 1977: 175). It was an extensively Javanized version of Indic culture that finally reached Bima, the formative influence being the expansionist East Javanese kingdom of Majapahit.

Indonesia's cultural debt to India is widely appreciated, but China's contribution is often overlooked, not least because of the absence of stone monuments on the scale associated with Indic influence (Maxwell 1991: 239). Chinese influence, though perhaps less dramatic than that of India's, is nonetheless pervasive, especially with regard to material culture. Successive Chinese dynasties maintained active trading links with the kingdoms of the archipelago, and the presence of Chinese goods, particularly porcelain, in Indonesian grave sites serves as a reminder of the strength and longevity of this relationship. The Chinese also exerted an influence that was probably not easily apparent to Dutch scholars steeped in the traditions of Indian scholarship. Chinese social life, even in the countryside, was centred on the town and it seems likely that this image of the city was introduced to the archipelago by southern Chinese migrants. Walled cities of the type encountered in China were not built in Malaysia and Indonesia, but the concept of dense urban living in a clearly defined space was used as a kind of mental map for Chinese urbanism in South-East Asia (Evers 1984: 147). Like other Indonesian trading emporia, Bima has a distinct Chinese quarter, the only truly urban part of the capital.

The Indonesians of the western archipelago exhibited a considerable receptivity to Indian forms over many centuries while remaining loyal to local identities. This is particularly true of Java where, despite the adoption of numerous Sanskrit words, the language lost nothing of its indigenous character and remained thoroughly Indonesian (de Josselin de Jong 1977: 178). The longlasting exposure to Indic culture was eventually superseded by a new religion, Islam, that exerted a markedly different influence on the indigenous cultures. Islam did not find the same points of contact as Indic culture, and one cannot think in terms of a close relationship between the teachings of Islam and the essence of Hindu-Buddhism. Islam's success may be due to the comparative weakness of the caste system and the willingness of the Indonesian courts to adopt it as their state religions. The marriage between Islam and indigenous culture occurred in the field of ritual and popular culture, in which ancient elements deviated from strict doctrines. Thus the popular religion continued to exist alongside the official religion, without the Indonesians being any less Muslim than Muslims elsewhere (de Josselin de Jong 1977: 179). Islam probably owes much of its success in the Indonesian Archipelago to its tolerance of indigenous customs, not in theory but in the practical experience of everyday life. The religion came to fulfil indigenous intellectual needs with its systematic methods of instruction, and thus we can talk about the ongoing process of Islamization. In Bima, which was converted to Islam much later than Java, this process has continued unabated since the early 17th century.

It was Bima's transitional appearance that discouraged systematic investigation on the part of FAS researchers, though the situation was exacerbated by the premature death of the Dutch scholar, G.J. Held. Sumbawa's linguistic division was associated with a cultural boundary, albeit complicated by a long history of Islam, and thus Bima has a recognizable affinity with van Wouden's 'Groote Oost'. Despite the Sanskrit sounding name, Bima's Indic heritage was a veneer, and it is more appropriate to think in terms of Javanization, especially of the court culture. The Islamization of the island for more than three centuries has extensively modified the underlying culture, all but obscuring its eastern Indonesian roots. Islam may have flourished because of its tolerance of old indigenous customs, but rarely left them completely unchanged. Lying at the extreme periphery of the Islamic world, where expressions of identity were intensified by vulnerability, this process was especially marked. Hemmed in by the resurgent Hindu-Balinese to the west and the defiantly non-Muslim headhunters of the east, the Bimanese looked north to Makassar for guidance. The House of Islam provided security in times of crisis, and thus became the bedrock of Bimanese culture in a seemingly hostile world.

Despite the intensity of the Islamic experience in Bima, eastern Indonesian themes can be detected, especially with regard to socio-political organization. Thus one encounters the division of the realm into spiritual and more worldly authorities, with a priest king at the Centre. Before the Dutch upset the indigenous order and invested overall authority in the Sultan, the *Ruma Sangaji* was a somewhat Frazerian character. Claiming divine descent, he was linked to the natural world, and to the land, the sea and the sky. The Sultan was expected to remain tranquil and never become angry or excited, and on ceremonial occasions he wore white to symbolize his purity. The interval between the death of the Sultan and the accession of the next was regarded as dangerous, and was obscured in various ways (cf. van Wouden 1977: 191). As was the case elsewhere in eastern

Indonesia, the concentration of power in the hands of the divine ruler undermined alternative sources of authority.

Islam became the dominant force in Bima, but did not completely obliterate the indigenous religion. Islamic judges and teachers exercised considerable authority, though the local people continued to be guided by *adat* and to respect traditional leaders. In the staunchly Muslim capital references to the *parafu* (cf. Sumba, *marapa*), the revered ancestors, are occasionally overheard. The forests were believed to be inhabited by tutelary spirits who congregated around large trees, boulders and water pools. When wishing to replenish the royal lumber yards, the Sultan's forester would not venture into the woods without the forester-priest who knew how to exorcise the spirits. Before a house could be erected, a priest carpenter was required to bless some earth dug from the site beforehand, a custom that persisted well into the 20th century. Until the early 1980s, white cloths, likened to sails, were attached to the tie beams of newly erected houses.

The idea that the builder of a house, *uma*, may later be venerated as an ancestral spirit by his patrilineal descendants has been weakened, but not entirely supplanted by Islam. For the Bimanese the house is not simply a physical structure, but the material embodiment of the people that live there. By building a house, the most tangible expression of well-being, a man is assured high prestige. Sons are encouraged to live virilocally and the ideal wedding is celebrated in a house built next door to the father's. The association between the house and the ancestors lingers on, but in a Javanized form with sacred kris and ceremonial cloths being stored in the interiors.

Elements of the socio-cosmic dualism that J.P.B. de Josselin de Jong postulated as being one of the core elements of his Indonesian FAS are also observable in Bima. The textile, for example, represents the bride and her family, as opposed to the knife or kris that symbolizes the groom and his family (cf. Niessen 1984: 68). Textile processing is carried out exclusively by women, and occasionally by men who adopt female roles short of marrying. The work is time-consuming and demands a high level of skill. Young girls learn by helping their mothers and grandmothers, and are expected to be expert weavers by the time they marry. A rattling sound indicates that the young woman is hard at work, and thus looms are widely associated with courtship. It was Jager Gerlings who interpreted the life-generating attribute of cloth in Indonesia as a female element, and similar notions are encountered in Bima. The bride's family bestow spiritual and life providing 'female gifts' upon the wife-takers, who reciprocate in the form of worldly support, gifts of livestock, money, tools, etc. Textiles serve as mediators, linking wife givers to wife takers, and bridging the human and supernatural worlds. A textile that links the sky world with death may be displayed during a wedding, and the passage from the cradle to the grave is marked by rituals involving cloth.

Bima shares much in common with its eastern neighbours, but at some stage in its history it began to diverge markedly from them. The critical factor appears to have been the absorption into Majapahit's sphere of influence and the accompanying Javanization. The kingdom dates from the period of contact with Majapahit, though it remains unclear what level of state formation existed before the intervention of the legendary prince known as Sang Bima. Local myths recall the presence of chiefs, *ncuhi*, and it is possible that the region was divided into domains based on patrilineal groupings like elsewhere in eastern Indonesia. According to Peter Just the highland Dou Donggo belong to exogamous, totemic, patrilineal clans, *rafu*, and it is possible that the lowlanders had such clans in the distant past (Just 1986: 84). The lowlanders are also divided from the highlanders by their elaborate class system which recognizes several levels of titled nobility. It remains undecided precisely what insulated the Dou Donggo from the cultural changes taking place in the valleys, though geographic isolation combined with a fierce independence were doubtless critical factors.

Bima's court culture owes much to Javanese inspiration, though the kingdom was later substantially modified through contact with Makassar and the Malay world. Relief carvings and inscriptions associated with Java's Indic culture bear witness to contact with East Java, as do the dynastic myths. The presence of wavy-bladed daggers with solid iron hilts suggests that the kris, but not necessarily the art of kris-making, was introduced by the Javanese. The parades and court rituals favoured by the Bimanese may be derived in part from Java, as well as the ceremonial canopies and royal parasols. Specialist artisans began to settle around the court to satisfy the demand for ceremonial weapons and regalia. These newly emergent professionals flourished under royal patronage and, as their numbers grew, they became organized in trade-based wards. Craftsmen from elsewhere in the archipelago, either displaced by political strife or simply attracted by the opportunities offered by the new kingdom, introduced new ideas and techniques. Exposure to Java's high culture doubtless enhanced the local sense of aesthetics, leading eventually to a critical artistic tradition.

The fact that some kind of emergent political entity existed at the time of Majapahit, and was able to maintain a relationship with East Java, is confirmed by Bima's entry in the *Negarakertagama*. The process of state formation was doubtless a protracted affair and it remains unclear what kind of political structure existed in Bima at this stage. Certain noble titles (*aji, rato, bumi*) suggest Javanese linkages, as does the division of the realm into districts and village wards. The existence of task groups, *dari*, to carry out specialist duties on behalf of the state is reminiscent of Java, though it may be more appropriate to think in terms of the general western Indonesian pattern. Many of these features could easily have been introduced at a later date through the medium of Malay and Makasar culture. The developments initiated by Majapahit appear to have come to fruition under overlordship of Makassar.

So pervasive is the Makasar influence, coupled with that of Islam, that the modern visitor could be forgiven for thinking that s-he had arrived in southern Sulawesi by mistake and was not in Nusa Tenggara at all. Visual clues with Sulawesian themes abound: *perahus* at anchor in the bay, Bugis style stilt houses, filigree jewellery worn with fine clothes, animated conversation in the streets, and the ubiquitous fish markets. The image is compounded on Muslim holy days when the whole population steps out in checked sarongs, fez, turbans and veils. Only the distinctively eastern character of the local language, faintly reminiscent of Polynesia, serves to remind one that we are on the fringes of the Islamic world. Despite their adoption of a world religion and many associated cultural elements, the local people are both self-confessedly Muslim and patriotic to their local identity.

The name Bima has endured many upheavals - the rise of Islam, and the collapse of the Sultanate - since the 14th century. Its boundaries are marked not only by a language but by a complex material culture, the apex of which comprises court art. 'Bima' is not strictly an ethnonym, though it is often used as one, and is instead the name of a state named after a prince. Minorities who recognized the state, but did not share the majority 'Mbojo' identity, also identify with the name. Thus people of Malay or Makasar descent can easily refer to themselves as people of Bima. Sometimes the use of the term 'Bima' is highly situational, and is used to transcend barriers, especially when invoked in connection with Islam. The Islamization of the island links its inhabitants to the Malays and Makasars, and the wider Muslim world. House styles, forms of dress and jewellery and weaponry reinforce these associations. The term can, however, be used situationally without recourse to Islam, particularly in association with the non-Muslim highlanders who played a key role in the foundation of the kingdom. The state relied on invented traditions, but appeals to the non-Muslim periphery did not rely on the mere manipulation of signs, but on enduring symbols of local identity. Some of these symbols were constructed on an impressive scale, such as the naga spine that held up the entranceway to the prime minister's palace. Through dynastic myths and royal marriages, the people of Bima claim kinship with modern Indonesia's most powerful culture, the Javanese. Intermarriage between the ruling dynasties reinforces bonds and ties within a rapidly developing modern nation.

The founders of what became known as the Dutch School paid little attention to Sumbawa and it seems likely that this was because van Wouden failed to include the island in his delimitation of the 'Groote Oost'. According to van Wouden the different societies of these islands were characterized by the '... possession of clan systems, still fairly intact, coupled with an explicit preference for cross-cousin marriage in its restricted form' (1935: 1). From what was known of Tau Semawa or Bimanese society at the time, there would have been little to stimulate his interest. It is puzzling that van Wouden was not drawn to the reports of the Dou Donggo (Zollinger 1850; Jasper 1908; Elbert 1912) that existed at the time, that mentioned patrilineal clans, but it is possible that he found them inadequate for his analysis (Just 1986: 23). One of the goals of Just's research was to investigate whether Bima faced east and the Tau Semawa west, and better to determine the nature of this transitional zone (Just 1986: 524). His preliminary assessment was that, although the Dou Donggo possessed patrilineages, they did not practice cousin marriage. Just's initial conclusions were that the Dou Donggo were indeed transitional, representing neither east nor west, and that van Wouden was perhaps right to exclude Bima from the 'Groote Oost' (Just 1986: 524).

The Dutch structural anthropologists shared a distrust of any 'grand theory' that was not based on the meticulous study of the relevant ethnographic data (de Josselin de Jong 1977: 9). With hindsight it would appear that the exclusion of Bima from the 'Groote Oost' was not an oversight, and to the contrary was a reflection of van Wouden's attention to detail, the exemplary application of a sound methodology. Van Wouden's comparative research was based on well-conceived generalizations, though one needs to bear in mind Levi-Strauss's statement that in '... anthropology as in linguistics generalization is not based on comparison, but vice versa'. Comparisons do not lead directly to generalizations, but for the development of the latter the former are a prerequisite: to think is to compare (Marschall 1984: 84). Bearing this in mind we are led to conclude that van Wouden's exclusion of Bima was entirely consistent within the terms of reference identified by the Dutch Schools. But are there other ways of looking at the issue?

According to Wolfgang Marschall, J.P.B. de Josselin de Jong's error in his quest for an Indonesian anthropological *studieveld* was to focus on behaviour and beliefs that were not common traits. So convinced was he that he had identified the common cultural core that he was happy to advance the hypothesis without a thorough consideration of material that might have been relevant from the vast islands of Borneo and Sulawesi. By applying generalizations that were not truly pan-Indonesian to a concept that purported to be precisely that, he risked undermining the general applicability of his FAS scheme (Marschall 1984: 85). As long as the concept of Indonesia as a Field of Anthropological Study remains rooted in the notion that asymmetric connubian is a major component then no research based on this notion will ever be completely successful (Marschall 1984: 86). In the light of these observations it would appear that anthropologists either have to find a way out of this dilemma or drop the concept in its entirety.

In attempting to salvage what he perceives as the strengths of the Dutch School, Marschall makes three helpful suggestions regarding the future of FAS type research. These are summarized as follows:

1. If the core elements in FAS are to be used in further studies, then the area selected for comparative research should be consistent with the distribution of the core elements. The term 'Indonesia' should be dropped from de Josselin de Jong's notion to enable

us to take a more relaxed stance and to avoid feeling obliged to look for hints and survivals of the cultural core.

2.   Studies should concentrate on what appear to be pan-Indonesian elements: the construction of language, dualistic concepts of the cosmos, textiles, houses, etc. This is especially appropriate with regard to Java where one encounters many negative correspondences with the core concept: no connubian, no long genealogies (with the exception of rulers), no examples of the Nias-Batak-Toraja type house construction, no special ikat weaving.

3.   Other major features such as slash and burn cultivation and wet rice agriculture might be added to the cultural core. The cognatic systems of Kalimantan, Sulawesi, Java and the Northern Moluccas, as well as the systems analysed by de Josselin de Jong, might be seen as transformations or adaptations, which together might form an element in the cultural core. Research might focus on the adhesion of genealogical patterns on textiles, and the links between weaving and *fuya* making.

If this preliminary study of Bima has not adopted Marschall's suggestions in their entirety, it has in spirit, and thus endeavours to view this society with reference to a wider concept of a cultural core. By examining Bima with regard to the general ethnography of eastern Indonesia, rather than van Wouden's somewhat restricted definition, we can see how it conforms to certain general patterns. It is the contention that the linguistic division of Sumbawa represented a real cultural barrier at some stage in history, but this has been obscured over time. Bima became the dominant kingdom on the island, but it did not begin as such. If one bears in mind Renfrew's concept of 'peer-polity interaction', then we might see this cultural exchange as a two and not one way process. It might be worth enquiring whether or not any distinctly eastern Indonesian elements have filtered eastwards over this border? One is reminded of a genealogical fault line where the plates rub over one another, one ascendant, the other submerged. Thus we can see how an eastern Indonesian people like the Bimanese have been Javanized and Islamized over time, becoming more thoroughly western Indonesian; nowhere is this more apparent than in their material culture.

The commonplace assumption is that art communicates, but establishing what a particular visual form has to tell us about a given society is not an easy matter. Teasing out the meaning of art objects is fraught with difficulty, not least because the people that make them often show little concern with, or indeed aptitude for, translating what they do into ordinary speech (Bowden 1992: 67). The lack of interest, or perhaps ability, on the part of the creator poses particular problems for the anthropologist. The situation is compounded when the artist makes something that is more exhalted than him or herself, as is especially the case with the spiritually and politically charged artworks of the Indonesian Archipelago. The reluctance of Indonesian artists to either sign or place makers' marks on the items they create is indicative of the artist's status in relation to what s-he creates. As the Bimanese material shows it may be the recipient of the goods whose personality is included in the transaction: houses are built to the owner's specifications, the kris must suit the person who wields it. There may be good reasons (magical, structural, personal) why the maker should maintain a discrete wall of silence when faced with a persistent questioner. The problem is not, however, insurmountable, since when one observes how these objects are used and engages in discourses with those who are permitted or empowered to reveal their significance, their *raison d'être* gradually becomes apparent.

Throughout this book I have been concerned to illustrate some of the ways in which the arts of the Bimanese express certain ideas and values which may hold in relation to themselves and the wider society. Textiles, houses and krisses constitute some of the most outstanding art forms that are encountered in the Indonesian Archipelago. Much of this art has yet to be documented and this analysis provides a preliminary account of a poorly understood region. It explores the way in which these artefacts communicate information about the society that makes and uses them, and moreover shows how these messages have been transformed over time. Through their art we can see how the Bimanese have defined and re-defined their identity, and how they have long been involved in a process of culture change that has gradually taken them away from their eastern Indonesian origins. The visual form is one of the dominant modes of communication, and thus the study of material culture in the processes of boundary maintenance and renewal deserves our full attention. The meanings attributed to works of art are not necessarily static, and thus we might regard the process of interpretation as potentially situational, dependent on motive and context. Tourism has created new markets, though goods designed for internal consumption cannot readily be distinguished from those sold to visitors. Artefacts are themselves 'plastic' and thus may be modified physically in response to new needs, new influences and new power relations. Nowhere is this more evident than in the regalia of the Sultan of Bima, which simultaneously communicates solidity and continuity, adaptability and change.

The Indonesian Archipelago has been exposed to an exceptionally wide variety of cultural influences, and in order to make sense of this complexity, analysts often resort to metaphorical models. In their search for appropriate levels of abstraction, anthropologists and historians often approach the question as they would an onion. They peel off the cultural accretions of many centuries like imaginary vegetable skins, gradually laying bare the underlying cultural core. They proceed rather in the manner of archaeologists dealing with stratification, with each layer of skin representing a distinct era in history. This rough and ready analytical framework provides us with an overview of the ebb and flow of cultural forces that have shaped maritime South-East Asia. In many respects this represents an idealized view of the true process of cultural integration, not least because it is usually impossible to separate all the elements that comprise contemporary culture into discrete categories. Despite its limitations, however, the adoption of the onion analogue does enable us to impose some order on these apparently disparate cultural elements. Bimanese history cannot readily be divided into distinct epochs bounded by fixed dates and events, though it is possible to think of identifiable, and often overlapping, influences that have occurred at different times.

East Sumbawa's destiny has been shaped by three major forces that have shaped Bima's identity in the following chronological order. First, there was the settlement of speakers of Central Malayo-Polynesian languages and the division of the region into domains on the East Indonesian pattern. Second, there was the Javanization of local elites, probably brought about by trade, and the foundation of the kingdom. Third, there was the Islamization of the island, the rise of the Sultanate and the selective adoption of Malay and Makasar cultural elements. Islam may be regarded as a cultural phenomenon and Islamization as a process of widespread social change and adaptation. If Bimanese culture were to be located in one individual, we might say that s-he was born in East Indonesia, crowned in Java, married in Makassar and educated in Cairo. These remain the prominent cultural components, though one should not lose sight of the other detectable features, Chinese, Arab and European. Of course, there is a fourth major element, Indonesian nationalism and the associated phenomena of development and tourism, and, though relatively recent introductions, they already exert a powerful influence.

Appendix

Material Culture and Ethnographic Research

Sir Edward B. Tylor took particular interest and delight in the ethnological collections of the Pitt Rivers Museum (Haddon 1946: viii), but he perceived the study of material culture as merely one of many departments in the wider subject of anthropology (Tylor 1946: xii). During the first two decades of the twentieth century British scholars interested in material culture, who were known as ethnologists, '. . . tended to be more preoccupied with things than with people'; nevertheless, behind the study of objects there remained an interest in the people who made them (Lienhardt 1979: 5). It was clear that while ethnological specimens might be objects of intrinsic interest worthy of study in their own right, they might also reveal much about the societies whence they came. Sturtevant was later to emphasize the role of ethnological specimens as an important primary source and indeed argued that '... artefacts also have advantages over written records of behaviour and belief in being concrete, objective, difficult to distort, and little subject to personal or ethnocentric bias' (Sturtevant 1977: 2).

If ethnological collections are to be worthy of scholarly attention above the level of mere curiosities and possibly, as was suggested by Sturtevant, as an undistorted source of information, then their manner of acquisition must be open to investigation. If they are to be used as a source, then the scholar needs to know in what way the specimen records the ethnography and whether it is representative; and, since Sturtevant's claims of objectivity for the material record need to be qualified, whether personal prejudice on the part of the collector influenced the selection of specimens.

Field collecting is one of the methods by which anthropological museums and departments acquire ethnological artefacts, and yet it is a subject that has been sparsely mentioned in the specialized literature. In his Guide to Field Collecting of Ethnographic Specimens, Sturtevant argued that the best collections were usually those made during the course of fieldwork by anthropologists interested in both artefacts and the local ethnography; but he did not give many specific examples (Sturtevant 1977: 2). This chapter provides an account of how a field collection was recently made for the Pitt Rivers Museum, in the hope that this may be of assistance to other ethnographers. The chapter aims to show how the ethnographical record is illuminated by collections and what considerations influenced the selection of artefacts. The collection represents the culmination of an interactive process that reflects not only the researcher's interests, but also records an important aspect of Bimanese identity. Material culture comprises tangible phenomena that are the products of learned patterns within human society. Material culture is also not a synonym for either technology or museum artefacts since its scope is much wider (Reynolds 1983:213).

The purpose of the collection was to establish a record of a variety of Bimanese craft industries, tracing aspects of their history and recording their adaptation to the contemporary social and economic environment. I was at the time a research student at the Pitt Rivers Museum, which has a policy of asking students to collect for it. I agreed to purchase Bimanese materials gathered during the course of my research, and was advanced funds for the purpose.

With this project I aimed to explore how the collection and documentation of material culture could be integrated into research in the social sciences. In this respect I was partly influenced by studies in the related field of visual anthropology, and in particular the work of Bateson and Mead in Bali between 1936 and 1939, which led to the publication of *Balinese Character* (1942). Bateson and Mead were the first to try to investigate the implications of using film and photography as an integral part of anthropological research (Heider 1976). Thus, the collection was designed to complement the other elements of ethnographic reportage (photography, drawings, field notes, etc.) and provide a more holistic picture of Bimanese identity in relation to material culture. I was also concerned with the process of selection and how this might distort the record in order to support particular hypotheses.

The Museum was interested in acquiring artefacts from a range of Bimanese crafts, though since an important part of the research was concerned with the manufacture of textiles, both the curator (B.A.L. Cranstone) and I were particularly enthusiastic to collect examples of textile technology and the completed fabrics. This emphasis upon textiles and their technology was also influenced by the Museum's tradition of collecting examples of craft processes and the fact that we knew from Dutch colonial sources that Bima had been historically a significant textile-producing region; but since the regency had hardly been documented by anthropologists we had no information about the conditions of the industry in the 1980s.

Before commencing research in Indonesia I had several meetings with the curator to discuss methods of collecting and he provided many useful suggestions based on his own experience in Papua New Guinea. I had undertaken both library and museum research in Britain and Holland prior to leaving for Indonesia, which further enabled me to assess Bima's collecting potential from the academic perspective: as has been pointed out by Sturtevant, a collector informed in this manner is better able to fill the gaps in existing museum collections (Sturtevant 1977: 6).

The initial research in Indonesia revealed that while some of Bima's craft industries had declined, many, such as textiles, were still important. The latter had managed to stay in business, despite competition from mass-produced goods, by exploiting the regional ethnic and custom-made markets, which had not been penetrated by larger competitors. Textiles remained powerful symbols of ethnic and religious identity in a multi-ethnic state. I thus had the good fortune of being able to collect specimens from a contemporary domestic textile industry, and it is worth examining four aspects of the technology which were of significant research interest.

The first of these concerns the manufacture of thread in the Indonesian archipelago, which is recorded in publications and represented in a number of British museum collections. Despite the acknowledged skill of some of the authors on the subject (e.g. Haddon & Start 1982: 5-9), there remain vague areas and it is unclear whether museum collections illustrating the process are complete. In this context Bima is of academic importance because its cotton industry was still operating, though in decline, and the thread-manufacturing equipment was still available.

Secondly, the method of transferring the thread to a loom (warping-up) has been poorly recorded. In Bima this task can be undertaken with or without the use of specialized equipment, the former method being quicker and easier. The latter method is generally well understood (Jasper & Pirngadie 1912: 98), and information from Bima was likely to provide only further evidence of regional variation. However, while the technology of the first method is well represented in British and Dutch museum collections, its use has been only partially described.

A third potential area of interest both to researchers and possibly to the craft-oriented general public (such as the Weavers' Guild) was one of the Bimanese methods of patterning textiles. While the techniques of batik and ikat were widely known in Britain at the time, some of Indonesia's great textile traditions have received scant attention. This technique, called supplementary weft, is one of the foremost in Bima, and therefore a collection in this area was likely to have wider scholarly and craft implications.

Fourth, it was clear from museum collections in Britain and Holland that the material culture of the Bimanese differed sharply from that of neighbouring peoples to the east, despite their linguistic affiliation. Not only could Bimanese textiles be readily distinguished from those of other eastern Indonesians in terms of design, but they were also made with different methods and materials. The material culture appeared to mark ethno-religious and political boundaries not only in terms of product, but also with regard to process. One of the best, and perhaps only, ways to document this empirically was to make a collection of the material evidence with the supporting ethnographic data: drawings and photographs alone would not have sufficed.

Following this outline of the technical significance of Bimanese textile methods it is worth considering two aspects of the technology which have wider social and economic implications. First, one of the reasons for the persistence of the Bimanese textile industry, in spite of the factory-based competition, lies in its reliance on simple domestic technology. The main apparatus, the body-tension loom, is flexible because it can be swiftly brought into operation and easily stored when not in use. This allows women, who are the weavers in Bimanese society, to manufacture cloth at odd moments in the working day. Since they are not totally dependent on weaving for an income, and as the equipment is not capital-intensive, they are able to take advantage of local market changes with low financial risk. The latter point can be compared with the garment trade of southern India, where Swallow has argued that the domestic industry has maintained its competitiveness by low overheads and market adaptability (Swallow 1982: 151).

In the second place, until the 1950s Bimanese unmarried women were largely confined to their homes in accordance with local Muslim practice. Men appreciated the economic advantages of having wives who were good weavers, and young women were expected to advertise their industriousness to potential husbands. However, since they were unable to demonstrate these skills in public, the unmarried women broadcasted their abilities by means of rattles attached to or built into their looms, which clattered as they worked. Examples of similar devices from Indonesia can be found in British museums, such as the model of the Bugis loom in the Skeat Collection, in the University Museum of Archaeology and Anthropology at Cambridge; yet there is insufficient documentation to explain the technical features. Therefore an example from Bima with accompanying background information was likely to provide useful comparative material.

While the textile technology was interesting and worth collecting, the fabrics themselves were also noteworthy from the perspectives both of social anthropology and of the general public. An example of this is the manner in which textiles had been used as indicators of social position during the period when Bima was ruled by a Sultan. The region had been governed through a complex bureaucracy in which people of high social status had worn sarongs woven of expensive materials and occupation was indicated by the colour of the clothing. Though this use of textiles declined when Bima came under republican government in 1950, another social aspect of textile is still of contemporary significance. In common with many other Indonesian peoples, the Bimanese exchange elaborate fabrics at festivals held at salient points in the life cycle, and this tradition has not diminished in importance. With their Biman aesthetic and symbolic value, these textiles indicate vividly the modern relevance of the festivals, and are therefore of interest to social scientists. When the cultural revivals of the 1980s began in eastern Indonesia, partly in response to improved economic circumstances and the advent of tourism, it was to the court traditions that the people turned in their quest for identity.

As indicated above, the selection of artefacts was undertaken with reference both to museum and literary records, and to what was available and noteworthy in the contemporary society. It is, however, worth considering two aspects of European and North American ways of perceiving artefacts which would have been ethnocentric and possibly socially irresponsible in the Bimanese context. Anthropologists such as Paul Henley have drawn our attention to the ethnocentrism inherent in ascribing worth to objects of antiquity in societies without such values (Henley 1979: 640). Furthermore, he has indicated the limited usefulness of praising certain materials because they appear to be traditional, as these often may not have been indigenous. As will be examined below, both these observations and an attention to collecting ethics were pertinent to the Bimanese situation.

It is very difficult to define what might be a traditional material in a society such as that of Bima, where imported thread has been available since at least the turn of the century (Jasper 1908: 100). By the 1980s the handloom industry mainly used synthetic thread made on the island of Java, which is preferred by the Bimanese to locally-spun cotton for practical and aesthetic reasons. In the first place, synthetic thread is easier to weave because it does not break as often as does the local cotton, and garments made with it are both lighter and cooler than those made of heavier homespun. Secondly, though the Bimanese were able to obtain a range of bright colours with vegetable dyestuffs, these were difficult to fix and tended to fade. Since local aesthetics demanded colour definition, especially when they were combined in checks, fading was particularly undesirable and therefore the vivid, long-lasting aniline dyes of the imported thread were easily incorporated into Bimanese society. A textile made of synthetic thread, in the eyes of the people, is no less Bimanese than one woven from home-grown products; and as the collection was intended to reflect contemporary reality, examples of both types were acquired.

In the art-dealer markets of Europe and North America antiquity is associated with value, yet these preoccupations are not relevant in the Bimanese context where objects are not revered on account of their age. In the Bimanese markets an old item is not necessarily more expensive than its modern counterpart. Nevertheless old objects, such as textiles, are important in Bimanese society, not because they fetch a better price, but because they are often used as a design resource. When weavers design a new high-quality textile they sometimes employ old cloths as a reference from which successful motifs and combinations of colour can be copied. The local market price does not reflect this value possibly because the resource does not usually leave the area, nor is the local economy sufficiently wealthy to support prices like those of the antique markets of the industrialized nations.

Old Bimanese textiles are of academic interest because they were employed as indicators of social status, and since they were available on favourable purchase terms they would have made a valuable addition to the Museum's collections, but this would have been at the risk of depleting a local resource. For similar reasons it would, for example, have been difficult to collect kris. Many of the kris in use in Indonesia are of pre-independence vintage and their popularity with foreign collectors has led to the removal of cultural property. The solution to these ethical considerations was to focus the collection on the contemporary industry, recording the use of established designs in the modern fabrics and tracing their history with photographs of some of the older textiles.

While the varying academic, ethnographic and ethical demands influenced the selection of items, the process of collecting itself was not straightforward. Textiles, for instance, were available in the markets or could easily be bought from pedlars in the villages, but had the collection consisted only of objects acquired by outright purchase it would have been devoid of examples from the important custom-made trade. A further problem was that, while the Museum wished to collect some of the textile manufacturing equipment, these items were not usually for sale. Bimanese weavers normally inherit their tools or they have them specially made by their male kinsmen, in which case they hardly ever appear in the market-place; also, since they are not items of common trade, it was difficult to put a price on them. The tools themselves are also important markers of identity both in terms of ethnicity and gender. These artefacts therefore had to be acquired by a variety of often complex transactions which it would be tedious to list here. In summary, however, the items were secured for the Museum either by direct purchase or by being made to order. It is the latter method I propose to discuss here, with reference to the largest apparatus brought back, which was the body tension loom.

During my research I had regular contact with a local cultural organization comprising a group of enthusiasts who were interested in regional history and the performing arts. After I had told them I was interested in purchasing a loom they introduced me to one of their members, a well-known carpenter called Idrus Yahya, who agreed to build one for me. As Idrus had to buy special materials and equipment I arranged to pay him in advance; and to protect the investment we drew up an official contract, written in the national language, which was in accordance with Indonesian law.

Idrus commenced work in May 1981 and a deadline was set at the end of September the same year. As the component parts of a loom are subject to dissimilar stress when in operation, they are made from different timbers selected for their appropriate qualities, and it took longer to gather the materials than was anticipated. Had I not embarked on making the collection, I could easily have overlooked this important area of traditional knowledge. Furthermore, a completely new Biman loom is seldom made, the new parts usually being added to an existing apparatus as old sections wear out. Therefore it was beyond anybody's experience to be able to predict exactly how long it would take to build it. As it happened we were not able to start entering the thread (warping-up) into the loom until February the following year, and so were fortunate to have commenced the project fairly early in my fieldwork.

In order to keep the project running I had to keep calling on Idrus to provide encouragement and monitor his progress. Despite the irritation of having to make constant visits, which increased in intensity as we went beyond the deadline, I did have the rare opportunity of observing at first hand many aspects of local carpentry; and the data gained through this kind of participant observation later formed an invaluable part of the doctoral thesis and subsequent publications (e.g. Hitchcock 1991). What was interesting was that the design for the carvings which were to embellish the loom were, like the designs for the textiles, quite eclectic. Some motifs were traced from wall panels in the Sultan's palace, while others were copied from old looms, which in turn were combined with yet further ideas from the carpenter's imagination. It is also significant that the loom was designed to present a particular face of Bimanese society to the outside world and was therefore built in the court style. Usually the customer is expected to participate in the design process by adding suggestions or even helping the craftsman though, being a novice in local terms, my role seldom progressed beyond holding steady pieces of wood. We both agreed, however, that the loom would be more complete if fitted with a rattle of the type once used by unmarried women, although this mechanism is seldom employed today.

The loom built for the Pitt Rivers Museum has a discontinuous warp and a heavy wooden frame which is used to hold the warp-beam in place. These frames, which are often decorated with carvings, vary from region to region. In Bali, Lombok, Java and the Wawo area of Sumbawa, for example, the holder usually comprises two short upright posts with vertical slots cut for the warp-beam. These posts are set into long horizontal planks, which lie on either side of the weaver. A similar kind of holder is used by weavers in coastal Borneo, Sumatra and southern Sulawesi, and the Malay peninsula. The Bimanese version does not have long horizontal bars and therefore the base has to be strapped to the floorboards. The Bimanese also make use of tall posts, which can be tied to the rafters, to hold the warp-beam in place.

This kind of body-tension loom is usually associated with the more densely populated lowland and coastal regions where the majority of inhabitants have long professed a world religion and recognised some form of central authority. Until the mid-twentieth century these looms were not only found in rural villages but were also used in palaces for weaving prestige fabrics. Generally speaking the continuous warp is used by peoples in the more remote eastern islands and the upriver and highland areas of the north and west, while the discontinuous warp is characteristic of court-based societies. There are, however, some exceptions. In Tenganan in Bali, for example, both the continuous and discontinuous warp looms are known, though the continuous warp is reserved for weaving the sacred double-ikat *geringsing* (also written *gringsing*) cloth where the warp is finally cut during a special ritual (cf. Bolland 1971). Similar reasons seem to lie behind the retention of both types of loom in north Lombok. It would appear that both kinds are known in southern Sulawesi, since there is a model of a Bugis loom with a continuous warp in the Skeat collection in Cambridge; but it is unclear whether or not this type of loom is used for weaving ritual fabrics.

The Bimanese loom is furnished with a sword-rest, which is placed to the right of her loom so that she does not have to pick up the sword from the ground after changing sheds. This labour-saving device usually comprises a bar which is supported, at roughly the same height as the warp, by two posts set into a solid base. The sword-rest may be elaborately carved. Sometimes the bar of the rest is made from a tube of bamboo with a slit in it and this makes a 'whooshing' sound as the sword is pulled over it. Noise-making devices can also be found in other parts of the loom, as is the case in southern Sulawesi and western Sumbawa where warp-beams are often fitted with clappers. (In Sumbawa bamboo rattles and bells are also attached to the frame that holds the warp-beam.) These sound-producing items not only advertise the industriousness of the craftswoman but are said to scare off the evil spirits that can annoy solitary weavers.

The weaver usually keeps a range of items within easy reach, such as spools with fresh yarn, extra shuttles, records of patterns and, perhaps, a betel-chewing kit. (Betel, a mild narcotic made from the areca palm, *areca catechu*, is sometimes chewed by weavers as they work.)

Although a loom may be attributed with certain mystical qualities, it must satisfy practical criteria before it can be used, as is especially the case with the materials used in its manufacture. Because the different parts of a loom are subject to varying stresses, they are made from different materials. The backbar on the Pitt Rivers loom is made from an unidentified timber, known locally as *luhu*, which does not have a slippery surface and is easy to grip. Slivers of hard bamboo were used for the teeth of the reed, which are held in place with a coconut-wood frame. Although the Bimanese usually carve beaters from black ebony, this loom is furnished with a red ebony sword. The hard, heavy wood has a smoothly sanded surface that does not snag the warp yarns. The heddle rod is made from durable areca wood (tamarind is also sometimes used) and the laze-rods from bamboo. The rod that is used to fasten the warp to the loom is secured with smooth buffalo-horn pegs which will not become entangled in the threads. Because the warp-beam and its holders help to keep the warp in tension, they have to be fairly immovable and are, therefore, made from heavy teak.

The Pitt Rivers loom, as it is based on the Bimanese court style, is decorated with high-relief carvings. The bar worn behind the weaver's back is embellished with botanical patterns and cockatoo heads, while the ends of the sword-rest are shaped like foliage. Carved lontar palms can be seen on the warp-beam holders, as well as carved pineapples and leaf designs. The incised motifs on the shed-stick are darkened with soot, as is also the case with one of the laze-rods. Many carved details can be seen on other parts of the apparatus. Looms from other Indonesian regions may also be furnished with various decorative features, particularly those used in the old royal capitals.

Indonesian shuttles, like the looms in which they are used, are varied in appearance, though they belong to several distinct types. One of the most basic kinds is the stick shuttle, which comprises a plain straight stick around which the weft is wound. This shuttle can be found among the Iban, Bugis and Rotinese. A shuttle that closely resembles a 'carpet shuttle' is also known in Borneo and consists of a narrow wooden board with notched ends on to which the yarn is wound lengthwise. Another shuttle, which has much in common with the 'carpet' type, is also used by the Iban: both ends of the shuttle are tapered so that it can be passed easily through the shed. The weft is wound lengthwise in a groove around the outer edge of the shuttle. Generally speaking the 'stick' and 'carpet' kinds of shuttle are used for weaving the ground weave on the body-tension loom with a continuous weft, though there are some exceptions.

Since the loom was required to be in an operational condition to provide an example of the supplementary weft technique, it was necessary to set it up and weave a portion of the fabric (because the component parts of a back-strap loom are mainly held in place by the warp threads, some degree of weaving was of course a basic requirement). Two women from a nearby village, Halimah M. Said and Siti Samsia, arranged to take on the task, and between us we selected the materials and the designs. By this time many people had become interested in the project, a number of whom (including the eldest daughter of the last Sultan of Bima) provided drawings of motifs or old textiles for reference purposes. The choice of the designs, the colour of the yarn, the weaving methods used and the type of loom on which the cloth was woven reflect Bima's identity as a Muslim court in eastern Indonesia. The work progressed swiftly and the only problem occurred when, on reaching the half-way point, there was general agreement that part of the design did not suit the remainder of the textile. The weavers decided to unpick approximately eight inches of fairly finely-woven cloth and try another series of motifs which, fortunately, were successful. This reworking delayed the textile's progress and the women were still weaving it on the morning of my departure from the field. Even then they were slightly reluctant to part with it as it was incomplete.

While there were immense difficulties in arranging the complete manufacture of complicated specimens for the Museum, there were, in addition to its usefulness for research, two advantages. First, it involved the Museum in some minor patronage of craftsmen in a poor country, which may not have been possible had the modest funds been diverted by dealers and other middle-men. In the second place, since the Indonesian government is concerned about the removal of items of local significance, there might have been difficulties in obtaining shipping permits for older specimens. Because the specimens were new they came under the commercial category of handicrafts, the export of which the government is keen to encourage.

For museum artefacts to be of value, either to the scholar or to the general public, they need to be well documented. In the case of this collection the documentation was likely to be greatly increased by the information contained in the thesis. In addition to my thesis field notes, I kept a collection notebook in which I entered as many details about each specimen as could be gathered. Where possible, I recorded the local names of the objects and their components, and in what circumstances they had been used. The source of each item was included and in some cases whether it had been moved since its original manufacture. The names of the people involved in making, owning or selling the object were also noted, and occasionally it was possible to record their (or other people's) opinion about it. Also of importance was the price paid for each specimen, whether in money or in kind and the date of the transaction, because these might be of interest to future researchers. I added sketches of the specimens in the notebook to aid identification in Britain and attempted to provide labels for each item, though both of these tasks proved difficult to achieve in the final rush at the close of the fieldwork.

The process of making a collection also raises questions concerning intellectual property rights, especially with regard to ethno-botanical knowledge, an issue that has begun to be addressed by ethnographic museums. Designs and patterns are often closely linked to identity and their use may be highly restricted in traditional contexts. Does the unauthorised use of these art forms by researchers and designers, particularly fashion designers, who have access to ethnographic displays, infringe the intellectual property rights of traditional peoples?

Since the collection was to be shipped across three islands along sometimes extremely rough roads by assorted means of transport, the packaging had to be secure. The large specimens were dismantled, and we made extensive use of cigarette cartons for padding and plastic bags for protection from damp and dust. There was an abundance of locally-grown wood for use in packing cases and it was both cheap and straightforward to arrange the construction of purpose-built crates. The collection was finally air-freighted from Bali, which is an important commercial centre for the export of handicrafts. In this case it would have been more expensive to take the collection to a major Javanese port or to Singapore for shipment, as this would have involved long and costly overland journeys and possibly delays in various harbours with extra hotel bills as a consequence.

The ethnographic collector may and should do all within his power to recognize and overcome subjectivity and ethnocentric bias in an attempt to approach Sturtevant's ideal for obtaining ethnological specimens, and I have shown some of the ways I tried to achieve this while collecting in Bima. Yet however informed and careful one may be, it must not be forgotten that each field situation imposes its own host of problems beyond practical control: droughts or floods may affect accessibility; transport may not operate; sickness may cause delays; items may be lost or damaged in transit. In order to overcome a wide range of practical problems the collector has to be selective and the final results are by definition interpretive. The ethnographic collection is undoubtedly highly informative, but should not be regarded as completely objective. Academic ideals and field realities always conjoin in the resulting collection.

Bibliography

Abdul Karim Sahidu, *Kamus Bahasa Daerah Bima - Indonesia* (Nusa Tenggara Barat: Kantor Pendidikan dan Kebudayaan, 1978).

Adams, M.J., Structural aspects of a village art. *American Anthropologist* 75: 1, (1973), 265-79.

Adams, M.J., Style in Southeast Asian materials processing: some implications for ritual and art. In *Material Culture, Styles, Organisation and Dynamics of Technology* (eds.) H. Lechtman & R.S. Merrill. St Paul: West Publishing Company. Proceedings of the American Ethnological Society, 1975.

Ahmad Amin, *Sedjarah Bima* (Bima: Kantor Pendidikan dan Kebudayaan, 1971).

Akbar S. Ahmed, *Millenium and Charisma among Pathans* (London: Routledge & Kegan Paul, 1976).

Akbar S. Ahmed., *Postmodernism and Islam* (New York: Routledge, 1992).

Arndt, P., Zur religion der Donggo auf Sumbawa. *Anthropos* 67 (1952), 483-500.

Attenborough, D., *Zoo Quest for a Dragon,* 2nd edition. (London: Companion Book Club, 1957).

Bagus, I Gusti Ngurah., Komodo national park: its role in tourism development in Indonesia. *Man and Culture in Oceania* 3 (special issue) (1987), 169-76.

Barnes, R., *The Ikat Textiles of Lamalera: A Study of an Eastern Indonesian Weaving Tradition* (Leiden: E.J. Brill, 1989).

Barnes, R.H., *Kedang: A Study of the Collective Thought of an East Indonesian People* (Oxford: Clarendon Press, 1974).

Barnes, R.H., The Leiden version of the comparative method in Southeast Asia. *Journal of the Anthropological Society of Oxford* 16 (1985), 87-110.

Barth, F., Introduction. In *Ethnic Groups and Boundaries* (ed.) F. Barth (Oslo: Norwegian University Press, 1969).

Bateson, G. & Mead, M., *Balinese Character: A Photographic Analysis* (New York: Academy of Sciences, 1942).

Bellwood, P., *Prehistory of the Indo-Malaysian Archipelago* (Sydney: Academic Press, 1985).

Bickmore, A.S., *Travels in the East Indian Archipelago* (London: John Murray, 1868).

Bird, B. *Langkawi From Mahsuri to Mahathir: Tourism for Whom?* (Kuala Lumpur: Insan, 1989).

Blower, J.H., van der Zon, A.P.M. & Yaya Mulyana, *Proposed National Park Komodo, Management Plan 1978/79-1982/83*, (mimeographed) (Bogor: National Conservation and Wildlife Project of the Food and Agricultural Organisation of the United Nations, Directorate General of Forestry, 1977).

Blust, R., Indonesia as a 'Field of Linguistic Study'. In *Unity in Diversity: Indonesia as a Field of Anthropological Study.* P.E. de Josselin de Jong (ed.) Verhandeligen van het Koninklijk Instituut voor Taal-, Land en Volkenkunde 103 (Dordrecht/Cinnaminson: Foris Publications, 1984).

Bolland, R., A comparison between the looms used in Bali and Lombok for weaving sacred cloths. *Tropical Man* 4 (1971), 171-82.

Bowden, R., Art, architecture, and collective representations in a New Guinea society. In *Anthropology, Art and Aesthetics* (eds.) J. Cooke & A. Shelton (Oxford: Clarendon Press, 1992).

Brewer, J.D., Bimanese kinship terminology: true or false? unpublished paper, 77th Annual Meeting of the American Anthropological Association, Los Angeles (1978).

Brewer, J.D., Agricultural knowledge and cultural practice in two Indonesian villages (Ph.D. thesis, University of California, Los Angeles, 1979).

Brewer, J.D., Agriculture, ideology and sex in an Indonesian village, unpublished paper, 78th Annual Meeting of the American Anthropological Association, Washington D.C. (1979b)

Bridge, D., Latter, J.H., McClelland, L., Newhall, C., Siebert, L. & Simkin, T., *Volcanoes of the World* (Washington D.C.: Smithsonian Institution, 1981).

Briggs, M.S., Building construction. In *A History of Technology*. Vol. 3. (Oxford: Clarendon Press, 1957).

Broughton, Lady, A modern dragon hunt on Komodo: an English yachting party traps and photographs the huge and carniverous dragon lizard of the Lesser Sundas *National Geographic* (September, 1936), 321-31.

Bühler, A., Turkey red dyeing in South and Southeast Asia, *Ciba Review* 390 (1941), 1423-6.

Bühler, A., Patola influences in Southeast Asia, *Journal of Indian Textile History* 4 (1959), 4-46.

Bühler, A. & Fischer, E., *The Patola of Gujarat: Double Ikat in India*, 2 vols (Basle: Krebs, 1979).

Burden, W.D., Stalking the dragon lizard on the island of Komodo. *National Geographic* (August, 1927), 216-30.

Burkill, I.H., *A Dictionary of the Economic Products of the Malay Peninsula*, 2 vols (Kuala Lumpur: Ministry of Agriculture and Cooperatives, 1966).

Cederroth, S., *The Spell of the Ancestors and the Power of Mekkah: A Sasak Community on Lombok*. Gothenburg Studies in Social Anthropology 3 (Goteborg: Acta Universitatis Gothoburgensis, 1981).

Chabot, H.T., Bontorama: a village of Goa, south Sulawesi. In *Villages in Indonesia* (ed.) R.M. Koentdjaraningrat (Ithaca: Cornell University Press, 1967).

Chambert-Loir, H., *Syair Kerajaan Bima* (Jakarta/Bandung: Ecole Française d'Extème-Orient, 1982).

Chambert-Loir, H., (ed.)., *Cerita Asal Bangsa Jin dan Segala Dewa-Dewa* (Bandung: Angkasa & Ecole Française d'Extème-Orient, 1985).

Clamagirand, B., The social organization of the Ema of Timor. In *The Flow of Life: Essays on Eastern Indonesia* (ed.) J.J. Fox (Cambridge: Harvard University Press, 1980).

Coomasamaswamy, A.K., *History of Indian and Indonesian Art* (New York: Dover, 1965).

Cooper, R., *Resource Scarcity and the Hmong Response: Patterns of Settlement and Economy* (Singapore: Singapore University Press, 1984).

Couvreur, A., Aanteekeningen nopens de samestelling van het zelfsbestuur van Bima. *Tijdschrift voor het Binnenlandsch Bestuur* (1917) 52, 1-18.

Cragg, K., *The House of Islam*. 2nd ed. (Encino (Calif.): Dickenson, 1972).

Crawfurd, J., Report on Djogdjokarta. MS India Office Records, Commonwealth Relations Office (London, 1812).

Crawfurd, J., *History of the Indian Archipelago*, 3 vols (Edinburgh: Archibald Constable and Company, 1820).

Crawfurd, J., *Journal of an Embassy from the Governor-General of India to the Courts of Siam and Cochin China* 2nd ed. (London: Colburn and Bentley, 1830).

Crystal, D., *The Encyclopedic Dictionary of Language and Languages* (Oxford: Blackwell, 1992).

Cunningham, C.E., Order in the Atoni house. *Bijdragen tot de Taal-, Land- en Volkenkunde* (1964) 120, 34-68.

Dalton, B., *Indonesia Handbook.* 2nd edition (Vermont: Moon Publications, 1978).

Damsté, H.T., Islam en Siripoean te Bima (Soembawa) - Atjèhsche invloeden? *Bijdragen tot de Taal-, Land en Volkenkunde van Nederlandsch Indië* (1941) C, 55-70.

De Josselin de Jong, P.E., (ed.), *Structural Anthropology in the Netherlands: A Reader*, Koninklijk Instituut voor Taal-, Land- en Volkenkunde 193 (Dordrecht/Cinnaminson: Foris Publications, 1977).

De Josselin de Jong, P.E., (ed.), *Unity in Diversity: Indonesia as a Field of Anthropological Study.* Verhandelingen van het Koninklijk Instituut voor Taal-, Land- en Volkenkunde 103 (Dordrecht/Providence: Foris Publications, 1984).

De Josselin de Jong, P.E., The comparative method in Southeast Asia: ideal and practice. *Journal of the Anthropological Society of Oxford* (1985) 16, 197-208.

Derks, W., 'Sumbang': incest in de Indonesische mythologie (Ph.D. thesis, University of Nijmegen, 1983).

Du Bois, C., *The People of Alor* (New York: Harper Brothers 1961) (1st publ. 1944 University of Minnesota Press).

Duff-Cooper, A., The family as an aspect of the totality of the Balinese form of life in western Lombok. *Bijdragen tot de Taal-, Land- en Volkenkunde* (1985) 141, 230-252.

Dumarcay, Jacques, *The House in South-East Asia.* (Singapore: Oxford University Press, 1987).

Durrans, B., Introduction. In *Natural Man: A Record From Borneo.* C. Hose (Kuala Lumpur/Singapore: Oxford University Press, 1988).

Een Halve Eeuw Pakketvaart (Amsterdam: J.H. de Bussy, 1941).

Eidheim, H., *Aspects of the Lappish Minority Situation* (Oslo: Norwegian University Press, 1971).

Elbert, J., *Die Sunda-Expedition des Vereins für Geographie und Statistik zu Frankfurt a.m.* 2 vols (Frankfurt: Minjon,1912).

Eriksen, T.H., The cultural contexts of ethnic differences. *Man* (1991) 26: 1, 127-144.

Evers, H.D., Cities as a 'Field of Anthropological Studies in South-East Asia'. In *University in Diversity: Indonesia as a Field of Anthropological Study.* (ed.) P.E. de Josselin de Jong. Verhandelingen van het Koninklijk Instituut voor Taal-, Land- en Volkenkunde 103 (Dordrecht/ Cinnaminson: Foris Publications, 1984).

Forth, G., *Rindi: An Ethnographic Study of a Traditional Domain in eastern Sumba.* Verhandelingen van het Koninklijk Instituut voor Taal-, Land- en Volkenkunde 93 (The Hague: Martinus Nijhoff, 1981).

Fox, J.J., Introduction. In *The Flow of Life: Essays on Eastern Indonesia.* J.J. Fox (ed.) (Cambridge: Harvard University Press, 1980).

Frey, E., *The Kris: Mystic Weapon of the Malay World* (Singapore: Oxford University Press, 1986).

Furnivall, J.S., *Colonial Policy and Practice* (Cambridge: Cambridge University Press, 1968).

Gardner, G.B., *Keris and Other Malay Weapons* (Singapore: Progressive Publishing Co, 1936).

Geertz, C., Form and variation in Balinese village structure. *American Anthropologist* 61 (1959), 991-1012.

Geertz, C., *The Religion of Java* (Glencoe (Ill.): Free Press, 1960).

Geertz, C., *Agricultural Involution: The Process of Ecological Change in Indonesia* (Berkeley (Calif.): Univesity of California Press 1963).

Geertz, C., *Negara: The Theatre State in Nineteenth Century Bali* (Princeton (N.J.): Princeton University Press, 1980).

Gittinger, M., *Splendid Symbols: Textiles and Tradition in Indonesia* (Washington (DC): Textile Museum, 1979).

Goethals, P.R., Aspects of local government in a Sumbawan village (eastern Indonesia) Cornell University Southeast Asia Programme, Modern Indonesia Project Monograph Series (Ithaca: Cornell University Press, 1961).

Goethals, P. R., Rarak: a swidden village in West Sumbawa. In *Villages in Indonesia,* Koentjaraningrat (ed.) (Ithica: Cornell University Press, 1967).

Goodman, W.L., *The History of Woodworking Tools* (London: G. Bell & Sons, 1964).

Graburn, N.H.H., (ed.) *Ethnic and Tourist Arts: Cultural Expressions from the Fourth World* (Berkeley: University of California Press, 1976).

Guillaume, A., *Islam*. 2nd ed. (Harmondsworth: Penguin, 1956).

Haddon, A.C., Introduction. In *Anthropology* volume 1, E.B. Tylor (London: Watts & Co., 1881).

Haddon, A.C. & Start, L.G., *Iban or Sea Dayak Fabrics and their Patterns* (Carlton: Ruth Bean,1982) (First publ. 1936).

Hall, D.G.E., *A History of South-East Asia* (London: The Macmillan Press, 1976) (1st ed. 1955).

Haneef, S., 1979. *What Everyone Should Know About Islam and Muslims* (Lahore: Kazi Publications, 1979).

Hamilton, S.B., Building and civil engineering construction. In *A History of Technology*, vol. 4 (Oxford: Clarendon Press, 1958).

Heberer, G. & Lehman, W., *Die Inland-Malaien von Lombok und Sumbawa* (Göttingen: Muster-Schmidt KG, 1950).

Heider, K., Ethnographic Film (Austin London: University of Texas Press, 1976).

Henley, P., The economic and aesthetic value of ethnic art. *New Society* (1979), 641.

Heringa, R., Dye process and life sequence: the colouring of textiles in an east Javanese village. In *To Speak with Cloth: Studies in Indonesian Textiles* (ed.) M. Gittinger (Los Angeles: Museum of Cultural History, University of California , 1989).

Hitchcock, M., Technology and society in Bima, Sumbawa, with special reference to house building and textile manufacture (D.Phil thesis, University of Oxford, 1983).

Hitchcock, M., Basket makers of the highlands: the Dou Wawo of Bima, Sumbawa. *Expedition* (1986) 28: 1, 22-28.

Hitchcock, M., Islamic influences on Indonesian design. In *The Diversity of the Muslim Community: Anthropological Essays in Memory of Peter Lienhardt* (ed.) A. Al-Shahi (London: Ithaca Press, 1987).

Hitchcock, M., Colour symbolism in Bimanese textiles. *Indonesia Circle* 49 (June, 1989), 19-30.

Hitchcock, M.,*Indonesian Textiles* (London: British Museum Press, 1991).

Hitchcock, M., Dragon tourism in Komodo, eastern Indonesia. In *Tourism in South-East Asia* (eds.) M. Hitchcock *et al.* (London: Routledge, 1993).

Hitchcock, M., Woodward, Mark R. Islam in Java (book review). *Man* (1991) 26: 3, 582.

Hitchcock, M., Inter-ethnic relations and tourism in Bima, Sumbawa. *Sojourn* (1995) 10:2, 233-58.

Hobsbawm, E.J.E. & Ranger, T.O. (eds.) *The Invention of Tradition* (Cambridge: Cambridge University Press, 1983).

Hodgson, M., *The Venture of Islam: Conscience and History in a World Civilization.* 3 vols (Chicago: University of Chicago Press, 1974).

Horridge, G.A.,*The Prahu: Traditional Sailing Boat of Indonesia* (Kuala Lumpur: Oxford University Press, 1981).

Hose, C., *Natural Man: A Record from Borneo.* introd. by B. Durrans (Singapore: Oxford University Press, 1988) (orig. London: Macmillan, 1926).

Hussin Mutalib, *Islam and Ethnicity in Malay Politics* (Singapore: Oxford University Press, 1990).

Hughes-Freeland, F., Packaging dreams: Javanese perceptions of tourism and performance. In *Tourism in South-East Asia* (ed.) M. Hitchcock *et al* (London: Routledge, 1993).

Izikowitz, K.G. & Sorensen, P., (eds.), *The House and Southeast Asia: Anthropological and Architectural Aspects.* Scandinavian Institute of Asian Studies Monograph Series 30 (London: Curzon, 1982).

Jager Gerlings, J.H., *Sprekende Weefsels: Studie over Onstaan en Beteekenis van Weefsels van Enige Indonischen Eilanden* (Amsterdam: Scheltens en Giltay, 1952).

Jasper, J.E., Het eiland Soembawa en zijn bevolking. *Tijdschrift voor het Binnenlansch Bestuur* (1908) 34: 60-147.

Jasper, J.E. & Mas Pirngadie, *De Inlandsche Kunstnijverheid in Nederlands Indië Vol. 2 De Weefkunst* (The Hague: Mouton & Co, 1912).

Jessup, H. Ibbitson, *Court Arts of Indonesia* (New York: Asia Society Galleries in Association with Abrams, 1990).

Just, P., Houses and house-building in Donggo. *Expedition* (1984) 26: 4, 30-46.

Just, P., Dou Donggo social organization: ideology, structure, and action in an Indonesian society (Ph.D. thesis University of Pennsylvania, 1986).

Just, P., Let the evidence fit the crime: evidence, law, and 'sociological truth' among the Dou Donggo *American Ethnologist* (1986) 13, 43-61.

Just, P., Going through the emotions: passion, violence, and 'other control' among the Dou Donggo *Ethos* (1991) 19: 3, 288-312.

200   *Islam and Identity in Eastern Indonesia*

Kana, N.L., Order and significance in the Savunese house. In *The Flow of Life: Essays on Eastern Indonesia* (ed.) J.J. Fox (Cambridge: Harvard University Press, 1980).

Kaudern, W., *Structures and Settlements in Central Celebes* (Elanders Boktryckeri Akteibolag, 1925).

King, V.T., Introduction. In *Essays on Borneo Societies* (ed.) V.T. King, Hull Monographs on South-East Asia 7 (Hull: Hull University Press, 1978).

Kruyt, A.C., De Soembaneezen. *Bijdragen tot de Taal-, Land- en Volkenkunde* (1922) 78, 466-608.

Leach, L.R., *Political Systems of Highland Burma: A Study of Kachin Social Structure* (London: Athlone Press, 1977).

Le Bar, F.M., (ed.), *Ethnic Groups of Insular Southeast Asia*. Volume 1: Indonesia, Andaman Islands and Madagascar (New Haven: Human Relations Area Files Press, 1972).

Lienhardt, G., *Social Anthropology*. (Oxford: Oxford University Press, 1964).

Ling Roth, H., *Studies in Primitive Looms* (Carlton, Bedford: Ruth Bean, 1977) (1918 Halifax, Bankfield Museum).

Ligtvoet, A., Aanteokeningen betreffende den economischen toestand en de ethnographie van het rijk van Sumbawa. *Tijdschrift voor Indische Taal-, Land- en Volkenkunde* (1876) 23, 555-92.

Marschall, W., Comments on Sandra Niessen's paper. In *Unity in Diversity: Indonesia as a Field of Anthropological Study*. P.E. de Josselin de Jong (ed.) Verhandeligen van het Koninklijk Instituut voor Taal-, Land en Volkenkunde 103 (Dordrecht/Cinnaminson: Foris Publications, 1984).

Maryan, H., Pattern welding and damascening of sword blades. *Studies in Conservation* (1960) 5, 25-50.

Mauss, M. & Durkheim, E., *Primitive Classification* (trans. from French and edited with an Introduction by R. Needham) (London: Cohen & West, 1969).

Mauss, M., *The Gift: The Form and Reason for Exchange in Archaic Societies* (London: Routledge, 1990). Foreword by M. Douglas. (1950 Presses Universitaires de France).

Maxwell, R., *Textiles of Southeast Asia: Tradition, Trade and Transformation* (Melbourne: Oxford University Press/Australian National Gallery, 1991).

Millar, S.B., *Bugis Weddings: Rituals of Social Location in Modern Indonesia*. Center for South and Southeast Asia Studies Monograph 29 (Berkeley: University of California, 1989).

Miller, D., *Artefacts as Categories: A Study of Ceramic Variability in Central India* (Cambridge: Cambridge University Press, 1989).

Moebirman, *Keris and Other Weapons of Indonesia* 2nd English ed. (Jakarta: Yayasan Pelita Wisata, 1973).

Nas, P.J.M., Settlements as symbols: the Indonesian town as a Field of Anthropological Study. In *University in Diversity: Indonesia as a Field of Anthropological Study* (ed.) P.E. de Josselin de Jong. Verhandeligen van het Koninklijk Instituut voor Taal-, Land en Volkenkunde 103 (Dordrecht/Cinnaminson: Foris Publications, 1984).

Needham, R., Principles and variations in the structure of Sumbanese society. In *The Flow of Life: Essays on Eastern Indonesia* (ed.) J.J. Fox (Cambridge: Harvard University Press, 1980).

Needham, R., *Mamboru: History and Structure in a Domain of Northwestern Sumba* (Oxford: Clarendon Press, 1987).

Nicholson, R. A., Mysticism. In *The Legacy of Islam* (ed.) A. Guillaume (Oxford: Clarendon Press, 1931).

Niessen, S.A., *Motifs of Life in Toba Batak Texts and Textiles*. Verhandelingen van het Koninklijk Instituut voor Taal-, Land- en Volkenkunde 110 (Dordrecht/Providence: Foris Publications, 1985).

Noorduyn, J., Makasar and the Islamization of Bima. *Bijdragen tot de Taal-, Land- en Volkenkunde* (1987) 143, 312-42.

Noorduyn, J., *Bima en Sumbawa: Bijdragen tot de Geschiedenis van de Sultanaten Bima en Sumbawa door A. Ligtvoet en G.P. Rouffaer* (Dordrecht-Holland/ Providence, USA: Foris Publications, 1987).

Nugroho-Heins, M.I., Regional culture and national identity: Javanese influence on the development of a national Indonesian culture (unpublished conference paper, European Association for South-East Asian Studies 1, Leiden, 1995).

Peacock, J.L., *Muslim Puritans: Reformist Psychology in Southeast Asian Islam* (Berkeley: University of California Press, 1978).

Picard, M., Cultural tourism in Bali: national integration and regional differentiation. In *Tourism in South-East Asia* (eds.) M. Hitchcock *et al* (London: Routledge, 1993).

Pigeaud, T.C. Th., *Java in the Fourteenth Century: A Study in Cultural History* (The Hague: Martinus Nijhoff, 1962).

Pinto, E.H., *Treen and Other Wooden Bygones* (London: G. Bell & Sons, 1969).

Pires, T., *The Suma Oriental of Tomé Pires: An Account of the East, From the Red Sea to Japan ... and the Book of Franscesco Rodrigues* (trans. & ed. A. Cortesao) (London: Hakluyt Society, 1944).

Prawirohardjo, S. & van Ness., *Javanese Wayang Kulit: An Introduction* (Kuala Lumpur: Oxford University Press, 1980).

Raffles, S. (Lady). *Memoir of the Life and Public Services of Sir Thomas Stamford Raffles, F.R.S.* (London: John Murray, 1830).

Raffles, T.S., *The History of Java*, 2 vols (London: Black, Parbury and Allen, Booksellers to the Hon. East India Company, and John Murray, 1817). (Kuala Lumpur: Oxford University Press, 1965).

Rassers, W.H., On the Javanese kris. *Bijdragen tot de Taal-, Land- en Volkenkunde van Nederlansch-Indie* (1940) 99, 501-82.

Rauf, M.A., *A Brief History of Islam, with Special Reference to Malaya* (Kuala Lumpur: Oxford University Press, 1964).

Reid, A., *Southeast Asia in the Age of Commerce 1450-1680*. Vol. 1, The Lands Below the Winds (New Haven: Yale University Press, 1988).

Renfrew, C., *Archaeology and Language: The Puzzle of Indo-European Origins* (London: Penguin, 1989).

Reynolds, B.,The relevance of material culture to anthropology. *JASO* (Trinity, 1983) 14: 2, 209-17.

Rex, J.A. Arderne & Moore, R., *Race Community and Conflict: A Study of Sparkbrook* (London: Oxford University Press, 1967).

Rex, J.A., *Race and Ethnicity* (Milton Keynes: Open University Press, 1986).

Rice, T.B., *Islamic Art* (London: Thames & Hudson, 1965).

Rickleffs, M.C., *A History of Modern Indonesia, c.1300 to the Present* (London: Macmillan, 1981).

Rouffaer, G.P., Oud-Javaansche inscriptie in Soembawa. *N.B.G.* (1910) 48, 110-13.

Sanger, A., Blessing or blight? The effects of touristic dance-drama on village life in Singapadu, Bali. In *The Impact of Tourism of Traditional Music* (Kingston: Jamaica Memory Bank, 1988).

Schilling, T., *Tigermen of Anai* (London: Allen & Unwin, 1957).

Schreider, H. & Schreider, F., East from Bali by seagoing jeep to Timor. *National Geographic* (August 1962), 237-79.

Schulte Nordhult, H., Donggo. In *Ethnic Groups of Insular Southeast Asia*, vol. 1. (ed.) F. Le Bar (New Haven: Human Relations Area Files Press, 1972).

Sharum bin Yub, *Keris dan Senjata-Senajata Pendek* (Kuala Lumpur, 1967).

Skeat, W.W., *Malay Magic - Being an Introduction to the Folklore and Popular Religion of the Malay Peninsula* (London: Macmillan, 1900) (New York, Dover, 1967).

Skinner, C., (ed. & trans.), Entji' Amin *Sja'ir Perang Mengkasar*. Verhandelingen van het Koninklijk Instituut voor Taal-, Land- en Volkenkunde 40 (The Hague: Martinus Nijhoff, 1963).

Smedal, O.H., *Order and Difference: An Ethnographic Study of Orang Lom of Bangka, West Indonesia* (Oslo: Oslo Occasional Papers in Social Anthropology 19, 1989).

Solyom, B. & Solyom, G., *The World of the Javanese Kris* (Hawaii: East West Centre, 1978).

Sturtevant, W.C., *Guide to Collecting of Ethographic Specimens*. Smithsonian Information Leaflet 503. (Washington: Smithsonian Institution Press, 1977).

Stutterheim, W.F., *Studies in Indonesian Archaeology* (The Hague: Martinus Nihjoff, 1956) (trans. Koninklijk Instituut voor Taal-, Land- en Volkenkunde).

Syamsuddin, H., The coming of Islam and the role of the Malays as middlemen in Bima. In *Papers of the Dutch Indonesian Historical Conference* (eds.) G. Schulte & H. Sutherland (Leiden & Jakarta: Bureau of Indonesian Studies, 1980).

Swallow, D.A., Production and control in the Indian garment export industry. In *From Craft to Industry: the Ethnography of Proto-Industrial Craft Production* (ed.) E.N. Goody (Cambridge: Cambridge University Press, 1982).

Taylor, P.M. & Aragon, L.V., *Beyond the Java Sea: Art of Indonesia's Outer Islands* (Washington D.C.: National Museum of Natural History, Smithsonian Institution, 1991).

Teljeur, D., *The Symbolic System of the Giman of South Halmahera*. Verhandelingen van het Koninklijk Instituut voor Taal-, Land- en Volkenkunde 142 (The Hague: Martinus Nijhoff, 1990).

Tooker, D.E., Identity systems of highland Burma: 'belief', Akhazan and a critique of interiorized notions of ethno-religious identity. *Man* (1992) 27: 4, 799-820.

Tylor, E.B., *Anthropology Volume 1* (London: Watts & Co, 1946) (1881).

Valeri, V., Afterward. In *Priests and Programmers: Technologies of Power in the Engineered Landscape of Bali*. J.S. Lansing (Princeton, New Jersey: Princeton University Press, 1991).

Van Bekkum, W., *Manggaraische Kunst* (Leiden, 1946).

Van der Hoop, A.N.J. Th. à Th., *Indonesische Siermotieven, Ragam-*

Ragam Perhiasan Indonesia, Indonesian Ornamental Design (Bandung: Koninklijk Bataviaasch Genootschap van Kunsten en Wetenschappen, 1949).

Van der Kraan,A., *Lombok: Conquest, Colonization and Underdevelopment, 1870-1940* (Singapore: Heinemann Educational Books (Asia), 1980).

Van Hekkeren, H.R., *The Stone Age of Indonesia* (1972). Verhandelingen van het Koniklijk Instituut voor Taal-, Land- en Volkenkunde (1957).

Van Wouden, F.A.E., Social groups and double descent in Kodi, West Sumba (1956). In *Structural Anthropology in the Netherlands: A Reader*, (ed) P.E. de Josselin de Jong (The Hague: Martinus Nijhoff, 1977).

Van Wouden, F.A.E., *Types of Social Structure in Eastern Indonesia* (The Hague: Martinus Nijhoff, 1968).

Von Heine-Geldern, R., Urheimat dan früheste wanderungen der Austronesier. *Anthropos* (1932) 27, 543-619.Waddy, C.,*The Muslim Mind* (London: Longman, 1976).

Von Heine-Geldern, R., L'art prébouddhique de la Chine et de l'Asie Sud-est et son influence en Oceanie. *Revue des Arts Asiatiques* (1937) 11, 177-206.

Wagner, F.A., *Indonesia: The Art of an Island Group* (London: Methuen, 1959).

Wallman, S., (ed.), *Social Anthropology of Work*. ASA Monographs (London: Academic Press, 1979).

Wallman, S.,The boundaries of race - processes of ethnicity in England *Man* (1979) 13, 200-17.

Waterson, R., *The Living House: An Anthropology of Architecture in South-East Asia* (Singapore: Oxford University Press, 1991).

Wilkinson, R.J., Cooper, A.E. & Mohd. Ali Bin Mohamed, *An Abridged Malay-English English-Malay Dictionary* (London: Macmillan Co. Ltd, 1963).

Woodward, M.R., *Islam in Java: Normative Piety and Mysticism in the Sultanate of Yogyakarta* (Tuscon: University of Arizona Press, 1989).

Zollinger, H., Verslag van eene reis naar Bima en Soembawa en naar eenige plaatsen op Celebes, Saleier, en Flores. *Verhandelingen van het Bataviaasche Genootschap van Kunsten en Wetenschappen* (1850) 23.

Zollinger, H., Bima and Sumbawa. *Journal of the Indian Archipelago and Eastern Asia* (new series) (1856) 1, 233-65.

Index

adat, 42, 53, 54, 63, 75, 76, 101, 171
abangan, 6
Ahmed, A., 14
Amin, A., 25, 78, 79, 85, 149
Arabs, 4, 32, 51, 61, 63, 70, 137, 147, 179
Austronesian, 16-17, 28-9, 59, 60, 68, 84, 89, 125, 167-8

bagan, 27, 46
Bagus, I. Gusti, 159
Bajau, 12, 60, 159
Bali, 8, 15, 24, 33, 39, 64, 94, 111, 112, 124, 136, 161, 162, 164, 181, 188, 192
Bangka Island, 12
Barth, F., 10
Batavia, 147
Bateson, G. & Mead, M., 181
Bhima, 1, 22, 59
Bilāl, 13
Bima,
 basketry & pottery in: 102-4
 carpentry in: 144-6, 148, 152, 198
 geography of: 1, 21-8, 73-4
 history of: 1, 2, 28-37
 housebuilding & houses in: 95, 101, 136-44, 146-50, 152-5, 171
 Islam in: 2, 19, 38-43, 49-56, 63-5, 75-8
 krismaking in: 181-92
 languages in: 17, 29, 43, 59-61, 168
 material culture of: 18-19, 29, 62, 89-95, 181-92
 people of: 1, 19-20, 58-72
 position of women in: 83-4, 86, 90-1, 94-8, 101, 134, 171-2
 shipbuilding & ships in: 45-8
 Sultanate of: 1, 2, 32-4, 36, 44, 53, 65-6, 68, 70, 71, 74-6, 78, 79, 82, 83, 85, 86, 106, 107, 110, 112, 113, 115, 116, 148, 156, 157, 165, 173, 178
 Sultan of: 2, 32-7, 39, 42, 43, 52, 58, 66, 71, 73-83, 86, 87, 111, 112, 114, 120, 143, 145, 154, 156, 157, 170, 178, 184, 187, 190
 social organisation in: 18, 59-62, 65-72, 75-88, 150-2
 trade in: 3, 30, 33, 39-40, 48-9, 96-7
 weaving & cloth in: 62, 89-91, 95, 120-35, 171, 186-92,
Bima Bay, 1, 23, 31, 35, 41, 45, 46, 47, 60
Bird, B., 61
Bo, 32, 43
Brewer, J.D., 17, 18, 99, 101, 141
brocade, 2, 44, 126, 134-5
Bugis, 45, 62, 67, 69, 70, 90, 91, 98, 101, 105, 109, 121, 126, 130, 139, 159, 173, 184, 190
buffalo, 26, 27, 152-3
bumi 44, 74, 79, 81, 83, 148, 149, 173
Bupati, 36
Burma, 13

Chambert-Loir, H., 29, 30
China - cultural links with Indonesia, 112, 124, 144, 145, 168, 169, 179
Chinese, 57, 61, 68-71, 74, 137
circumcision, 55
Cooper, R., 164
Couvreur, A., 79
Crawfurd, J., 5

Dalton, B., 160, 162
dari, 44, 81, 84-5, 113, 144, 148

dieng, 40
Diponegoro, 27
doa, 54-5, 113, 150
dogs, 24, 28, 53
Dompu, 17, 21, 22, 30, 35, 64
Don-son, 29-30, 154
Dou Donggo, 18, 60, 62, 64, 65, 67, 68, 117, 172, 174
Dou Mbojo, 1, 2, 59, 66, 173
Dou Wawo, 60, 62, 66
Dutch scholarship, 15, 16, 17, 18, 91-2, 175
Dutch School, 15
Dutch, trade & politics, 33-5, 48-9, 147
Dayak, 12, 19

Eastern Sumbawa, 18-20, 26, 28, 30, 31, 34, 40, 48, 51, 59, 65, 67, 111, 125, 133, 158, 178
(see also Sumbawa)
Eidheim, H., 10
Elbert, J., 84, 128

Field of Anthropological Study, 16, 17, 18, 168, 170, 171, 175
Flores, 1, 17, 25, 33, 34, 64, 104, 111, 115, 122, 157, 158, 161
Furnivall, J.S., 57, 69, 70

Gardner, G.B., 107, 110
Geertz, C., 4, 5, 6, 39, 58
gelarang, 40, 75
Goethals, P., 18, 85, 140
Graburn, N., 164
'Groote Oost', 17, 19, 170, 174, 175

Hadith, 132
hajj, 14, 51, 54, 76, 88
Held, G.J., 18, 170
Henley, P. 185
Heringa, H., 121
Hindu-Buddhism, 7, 8, 14, 38, 39, 56, 82, 83, 147, 169

Hobsbawm, E & Ranger, T., 63, 77
Hodgson, M., 6
hukum, 42, 75

idolatry, prohibitions on, 5, 12, 117, 131-2, 154
India - cultural links: 3, 14-15, 17, 74, 81, 121, 130, 132, 168, 170, 184,
Islamic influence of: 4, 5, 6, 8, 39
Indonesia Handbook, 160, 162, 166
Islam in Java, 6, 7, 14

Jager Gerlins, J.H., 92, 171
Japan, 144, 145
Japanese, 35, 36, 49, 163
Jasper, J.E. & Mas Pringadie, 102
Java - connections with Bima: 1, 3, 23, 25-6, 30-1, 36, 39, 43, 48, 52, 83, 88, 91, 108, 110, 111, 112, 113, 119, 121, 122, 124, 130, 132, 136, 144, 145, 147, 156, 168, 169, 172, 173, 176, 179, 185, 188
Islam in: 5-8, 14-15, 39, 50, 170, 176
Josselin de Jong, de P.E., 4, 15, 16, 17, 91, 92, 168, 171, 175, 176
Just, P., 18, 35, 37, 172, 174

Ka'aba, 14
Kalimantan [Borneo], 13, 19, 29, 108, 175, 188, 190
Komodo, 22, 24, 47, 157-61, 166
Koran [Qur'an], 7, 13, 41, 51, 52, 54, 93, 142
kris, 2, 31, 40, 64, 66, 83, 87, 105-19, 171-2

Leach, E., 13
Leiden School, 15, 16
Levi-Strauss, C., 16, 175
Lom, 12
Lombok, 8, 17, 22, 24, 25, 50, 61, 95, 135, 136, 188

Mahabharata, 1, 22, 59

Majapahit, 8, 30, 31, 39, 48, 56, 112, 113, 168, 172, 173

Makasars, 2, 33, 38, 39, 40, 41, 45, 63, 67, 69, 70, 82, 83, 90, 102, 105, 111, 121, 126, 129, 139, 173, 174

Makassar, 8, 19, 27, 31, 32, 33, 34, 38, 50, 109, 111, 112, 170, 172, 179

Malays, 2, 3, 19, 34, 40-5, 60, 63, 66, 67, 68, 74, 76, 85, 98, 107, 109, 110, 112, 121, 131, 168, 172, 173, 174, 188

Marschall, W., 175, 176

Mauss, M. & Durkheim, E., 15

Maxwell, R., 130, 135

Mbojo, 17, 21, 22

Mecca, 51, 76, 78, 88, 155

Middle East, 4, 6

Miller, D., 11

Myanmar (see Burma)

naga, 1, 12, 42, 63, 83, 153

Nagarakertagama, 8, 30, 48, 173

Nas, P.J.M., 80

ncuhi, 31, 82, 172

Netherlands East Indies, 35, 49, 64, 66, 80, 157 (see also VOC)

Noorduyn, 32

Nusa Tenggara, 2, 22, 23, 25, 29, 161, 173

Ouwens, P.A., 157

Pancasila, 3, 51, 71, 88

patola, 121, 131, 132

pinisi, 45-6

Pires, T., 23, 48

Pitt Rivers Museum, 180, 181, 188, 189, 190, 191

Polynesian languages, 17, 29

Portuguese, 21, 48, 147

priyayi, 6

Qur'an (see Koran)

Raffles, 5, 25, 145

Religion of Java, The, 4

Renfrew, C., 176

rimpi, 53, 62, 97, 164

Sapé, 22, 26, 30, 46, 58, 60, 61, 67, 69, 161, 165

Sando, 55, 56

santri, 5, 6, 7

sara, 42

Sasaks, 17, 59

Shari'ah, 3, 6

sirih, 36, 42

Smedal, O., 12

Snouck Hurgronje, C., 4

songket, sungkit (see brocade)

Sturtevant, W., 180, 181, 182, 192

Sufism, 7, 50

Sulawesi, 8, 24, 25, 27, 29, 31, 33, 39, 41, 45, 68, 70, 75, 82, 98, 101, 107, 112, 124, 129, 130, 153, 168, 173, 175, 176, 188

Sultan Abdul Kahir, 1, 32, 36, 38, 39

Sumatra, 109, 111, 130, 188

Sumba, 1, 17, 34, 79, 100, 104

Sumbawa, 1, 8, 17, 19, 21, 24, 26, 33, 34, 35, 38, 40, 59, 68, 69, 70, 82, 83, 97, 122, 123, 129, 130, 138, 157, 158, 161, 162, 168, 176 (see also Eastern Sumbawa)

Sunni, 49, 63

Swallow, D., 184

Talu, A.D., 78, 149

Tambora, 25, 34, 49, 53, 168

Tau Semawa, 17, 18, 64

Timor, 17, 30, 35, 64, 78, 82, 104

Tourism, 22, 51, 61, 69, 72, 154, 156-7, 179

   development of: 159-62

   in Bima: 162-6

Toynbee, A., 14

Tureli, 77, 78

Tylor, E.B., 180

uma, 101, 137, 138, 139, 141, 142,
    143, 144, 171
UNESCO, 9

Valeri, V., 15
VOC, 26, 33, 34, 48, 49 (see also
    Netherlands East Indies)

Waterson, R., 12
Wood, R., 162
Woodward, M., 6, 7, 8, 14, 39
Wouden, van. F.A.E., 15, 17, 80, 170,
    174, 175

Yogyakarta, 5, 7, 156, 164

zakat, 52, 84
Zollinger, H., 25, 34, 43, 133